Financial Decisions in Emerging Markets

Financial Decisions in Emerging Markets

Jaime Sabal

New York   Oxford
OXFORD UNIVERSITY PRESS
2002

Oxford University Press

Oxford New York
Athens Auckland Bangkok Bogotá Buenos Aires Cape Town
Chennai Dar es Salaam Delhi Florence Hong Kong Istanbul Karachi
Kolkata Kuala Lumpur Madrid Melbourne Mexico City Mumbai Nairobi
Paris São Paulo Singapore Taipei Tokyo Toronto Warsaw

and associated companies in
Berlin Ibadan

Published by Oxford University Press, Inc.
198 Madison Avenue, New York, New York 10016
http://www.oup-usa.org

Oxford is a registered trademark of Oxford University Press

Library of Congress Cataloging-in-Publication Data

Sabal, Jaime.
  Financial decisions in emerging markets / by Jaime Sabal.
    p. cm.
  Includes bibliographical references and index.
  ISBN 0-19-514459-7 (alk. paper)
    1. Corporations—Developing countries—Finance 2. Investments, Foreign—Developing
  countries. 3. Capital market—Developing countries. I. Title.

HG4285 .S23 2001
658.15'09172'4—dc21

                                                              2001039094

Printing number: 9 8 7 6 5 4 3 2 1

Printed in the United States of America
on acid-free paper

I dedicate this book to my father, Arturo S. Sabal (1900–78)

Contents

Foreword

From the vantage point of New York or London, emerging markets come and go. Periods of rapid growth and attractive lending and investing opportunities are followed with depressing regularity by economic and financial crises as developing countries are hammered by external events and contagion or problems of their own making. Periodic debt restructurings and financial failure seem to accompany extraordinarily volatile local stock markets, making lender and investor commitments hazardous and requiring high risk premia. And with well over half of developing countries more or less permanently on the IMF's client list, some of these problems seem to have become chronic. All the while businesses have continued to operate in these environments, often profitably, while foreign direct investment flows have continued unabated, contrary to capital flows, via lending, bond issues, and portfolio equity. Direct investors seem to have confidence that the underlying comparative advantages of developing economies will ultimately prevail in the global system.

Corporate finance in emerging markets is different. Financial markets are often narrow and illiquid. Information and transparency may be limited, and transaction costs can be high. The legal and accounting infrastructures are often suspect or poorly enforced. Markets for corporate debt instruments may be absent entirely, crowded out by public borrowing, which often influences bank lending as well. All the while, exchange rates may be highly volatile or currency markets may be subject to exchange controls, even as the local inflation rate is often high and variable. Little wonder that financial management in emerging markets frequently poses an uncommon challenge—the training ground for some of the best financial managers in the world.

Jaime Sabal has done a superb job of applying modern constructs of corporate finance to the emerging market setting. When classic assumptions about efficient markets simply do not apply, financial managers must display extraordinary adaptability and improvisation. The author begins this volume with a cogent application of corporate finance concepts to the emerging markets context, and then looks at the issues from the perspective of the investor, also examining capital allocation decisions within the firm and financing to maximize a firm's value to shareholders under difficult conditions.

This book will appeal to practitioners, development experts, as well as students of finance interested in emerging markets—in the latter case perhaps using a standard textbook complemented by the present volume's perspective on "what's different?" In this context, the book should be welcomed by scholars and practitioners alike.

Ingo Walter
New York University

xi

Preface

For centuries, investors have explored business opportunities outside their countries of origin. Because of the accelerated global integration that the world has witnessed in recent years, however, international trade has grown exponentially. During 1980–97 global foreign direct investment (FDI) grew at an average rate of about 13% a year, reaching U.S. \$430–\$440 billion (i.e., \$430–440 $\times$ 10^9) in 1997. The total FDI stock by 1998 is estimated to be U.S. \$3500 trillion (i.e., \$3500 $\times$ 10^{12}).

As recipients of direct investments from developed nations, emerging countries have benefited enormously from this process. The developing countries' share of these flows jumped from 26% in 1980 to 37% in 1997. In addition, emerging countries have been direct investors in the more advanced nations. Their participation as investors in the developed world went from 3% in 1980 to 14% in 1997 (Mallampally & Sauvant 1999). Emerging countries, on a purchasing parity basis, now total 44% of the world's economy, and in the past decade emerging nations were responsible for two-thirds of the world's economic growth.

Every sound investment decision demands the application of modern financial theory. However, the theories that are advanced are set in the context of developed countries and do not capture the intricacies of operating in the developing world.

Despite the importance of investment flows to developing countries today, very little has been done to adapt financial principles to the special realities of these countries. This book has been written with the objective of filling this surprising lacuna.

ORIENTATION OF THE BOOK AND TARGET AUDIENCE

Financial theory is based on the assumption of efficient markets. Although this proposition rarely holds true, the assumption is relatively valid in the case of large companies and investors in the developed world. However, the concept of efficient markets does not hold in the case of individuals and firms investing in emerging markets.

This work reviews financial theory, with a focus on investment and financing decisions, as it relates to investors in emerging markets, a neglected but nevertheless significant constituent of the investment community. The objective is to juxtapose the assumptions of financial theory against the realities prevailing in emerging countries and to propose more relevant approaches for investment analysis in these nations. This publication does not pretend to compete with the numerous texts available on corporate finance. Instead, it is a practical complement for those interested in emerging markets.

We did not want to curtail the diffusion of these thoughts. For this reason some hypotheses and ideas are proposed with little or no empirical justification. It is our wish for this work to stimulate the academic community to initiate more research about these topics.

The target audience is students and professors of business schools (both in developing and developed countries) who are interested in emerging markets. Investment bankers, financial managers, and small investors seeking a more formal (i.e., theoretical) understanding of developing country finance can also benefit from this book.

Readers must be proficient in basic algebra and comfortable with tabular and graphical representations of analysis. In addition, knowledge of statistics and financial economics is highly desirable. However, where necessary, the book trades off theoretical verbiage for simplicity in expression. The terminology has been simplified to facilitate its comprehension by a wide audience.

Certain sections (printed in italics), intended specifically for students with quantitative inclinations, can be excluded from the perusal of readers who do not possess a quantitative orientation without compromising on the overall treatment of the subject.

STRUCTURE OF THE BOOK

The book has five sections: an introductory chapter, three main sections, and a concluding chapter. Each chapter begins with a brief description of the material covered and provides an extract of the main conclusions in the end. Additionally, the key ideas of each of the three main sections are summarized. Chapters 1 through 12 end with a set of questions; answers appear at the end of the book. Finally, throughout the text a number of real-life cases illustrate many important ideas.

To maintain the fluidity of the exposition, several chapters and sections that provide an overview of well-known financial principles are included. Readers can easily identify these by skimming through the introductory and concluding sections of each chapter. Hence, the reader who is proficient in financial theory can skip this material.

A brief description of the five sections follows.

Financial Theory in Emerging Markets (Chapter 1)

The meaning, usefulness, and limitations of financial theory are explained with a focus on emerging markets. We contrast emerging with developed countries, and inefficient with efficient markets, drawing attention to the gaps between market realities and the standard assumptions on which financial models are based.

The Investor and the Firm (Chapters 2 to 5)

The relationship between investment and consumption decisions is examined. The net present value (NPV) rule is introduced and questioned for the standard case (in developing countries), where investors face significant frictions in financial markets. The sources of value for investments in real and financial assets in emerging countries are explored. Portfolio theory is reviewed and applied for investors who do not hold well-diversified portfolios. An approach based on statistical confidence intervals is offered as a practical alternative to utility theory under uncertainty. The marginal effect of investments in real and financial assets on risk and expected return of existent portfolios is also assessed. The opportunity cost of a controlling stake in a company is cited as an example. (Chapters 3 and 4 are essentially a review of standard financial theory.)

Firm and Investment (Chapters 6 to 9)

Attention is focused on companies with a diversified shareholder base, where investment decisions no longer rest on the situation of individual shareholders. The capital asset pricing model (CAPM) and some of its variants and alternative models are introduced. It is concluded that for all its limitations, the CAPM is the only practical solution available to us. We criticize the traditional approach to treating country risk and propose a modified CAPM for investment evaluation in developing countries. Special problems related to the projection of cash flows in emerging markets are explored. This section concludes by examining the potential usefulness of real options in lieu of the considerable role that uncertainty plays in emerging markets. This last topic is handled without getting into major theoretical complexities. (Chapter 6 and part of Chapter 9 are basically a review of standard financial theory.)

Financing and Investment (Chapters 10 to 12)

This section of the book deals with the funding side of the investment problem. Capital structure theory is reviewed and issues pertaining to emerging markets are raised. A practical approach is suggested for determining and monitoring leverage in emerging markets. The section ends with suggestions on how to add value from the financing side, including flexible financing schemes and the process of accessing the capital markets and opening up the shareholder base. (Chapter 10 serves as a review of capital structure theory.)

Concluding Remarks (Chapter 13)

This chapter offers a summary of the key conclusions and insights derived from the preceding twelve chapters.

ACKNOWLEDGMENTS

I would like to thank all those who helped me reexamine the teachings of financial theory in the context of the realities of the developing world.

First and foremost, I thank my students at the Instituto de Estudios Superiores de Administración (IESA) in Caracas, Venezuela, who helped me redefine several ideas and concepts by asking intelligent questions and engaging in active discussions.

During the years that I spent in the consulting industry at Keisai Asociados, I was spurred to rethink the practical implications of financial theory. This was made possible by the stimulating association I had with my colleagues. In particular, I wish to emphasize the contributions of Neil Reines, Alexeis Perera, and especially Daniel Kern, my former partner in the firm. And no less significant is the role that my clients have played in shaping my understanding of financial theory in the practical realm of business.

The support of my friends from the Instituto Venezolano de Ejecutivos de Finanzas has been invaluable. The essays we wrote together benefited from their experience as financial managers in a range of companies. I am especially indebted to Fernando Aguerrevere and Juan A. Lovera, who revised several chapters and provided pertinent feedback.

The insight of other contributors also helped to enhance the quality of this work. I must mention David Babbel, Aaron Cohen, Antonio Osorio, Ramanjit Uppal, Elio Valladares, and the reviewers. From this last group, the suggestions of Michael Berkowitz and Paul Donnelly were particularly valuable.

Ingo Walter, director of the Salomon Center (Leonard N. Stern School of Business, New York University), deserves special gratitude for his help on specific aspects of the book. Further, his generosity in providing me with working facilities during my sabbatical (a good part of which was spent working on this book) at the prestigious Salomon Center will not be forgotten. I have also profited from my interaction with several prominent professors from the Stern School, in particular Aswath Damodaran, Edward Altman, Richard Levich, Roy Smith, and Edwin Elton. My sabbatical colleagues, Alvaro Cuervo and Ana Isabel Fernández, provided me with some very useful observations.

Mary Jaffier, Ann Rusolo, Lourdes Tanglao, and Robyn Vanterpool—administrative staff at the Salomon Center—provided me with significant support during my endeavor. I thank them all deeply.

For improvements in the language and style of this book I wish to thank Anita Balchandani. Finally, I am indebted to my wife, Estela, and my children, Karen, Erika, Alejandro, and Jaime, for the many hours and days that I took away from them during my work on this text.

Each chapter in this book begins with a relevant quotation, most of which have been collected over the period of a decade. Unfortunately, the names of several of the authors have been misplaced. I owe them an apology on two counts—first for not giving them the acknowledgment that is due to them, and second for the possibility of having misquoted them as a result of errors in translation.

For all remaining errors in this book, I claim full responsibility. Readers' comments and suggestions will be greatly valued. I can be contacted via e-mail (jsabal@iesa.edu.ve) or through my (Spanish) web page (www.iesa.edu.ve/Corporativo/profesores/Jaime_Sabal/).

Financial Decisions in Emerging Markets

CHAPTER 1

FINANCIAL THEORY
IN EMERGING MARKETS

"There is no more dangerous economist than the purely theoretical one, with neither practical experience nor an intuitive knowledge of the real world, seeking precision in an uncertain world."

—SIR AUSTEN ROBERTSON

1.1 FINANCIAL THEORY: WHAT DOES IT OFFER?

Financial theory focuses on **investment decisions.** Based upon investor behavior, financial theory has developed frameworks to mirror the way people invest their money. Its attention is not just centered on individual investors, but also on the firm[1] as an investment vehicle. Further, a key challenge it faces is to constantly validate the extent to which the principles of financial theory reflect business realities.

Financial theory is a relatively new branch of economics. It began to evolve in the 1950s when Markowitz discovered the relationship between risk and return in an investment portfolio (Markowitz 1952). This body of theoretical knowledge then developed very rapidly until its maturity two decades later, with the famous model of option pricing by Black and Scholes (Black 1973).[2]

Running the risk of underestimating many important advances, we can affirm that four key concepts form the basis for financial theory:

Net Present Value. This principle permits comparisons between projects with different risk levels and with different incomes and disbursements over a period of time.

Risk (or Portfolio) Theory. Portfolio theory gives us an approach to assess the risk associated with investment decisions.

Option Theory. Through option theory we are able to value purchasing and selling rights as well as to quantify the flexibility of investment and financing arrangements.

Capital Structure. This term refers to the impact of financing on investment decisions.

---

[1] The terms *firm, company,* and *organization* are used interchangeably.

[2] The true cornerstone of modern financial theory is the Fisher separation theorem, which establishes the conditions for the validity of the present value rule (Fisher 1930).

This book covers these four key concepts, with an emphasis on emerging markets. Where necessary, the terminology is simplified to facilitate comprehension by a wide audience.

Financial theory has met with much success. It is widely accepted and applied in both the academic and investment worlds. A number of financial theoreticians have also been awarded the Nobel Prize in economics. Despite numerous achievements, however, there still exists room for improvement, as we will elucidate during the course of this book.

1.2 THE LIMITATIONS OF FINANCIAL THEORY

Newton's laws of motion, the theory of relativity, and the theory of quantum mechanics are all models of physical sciences that attempt to explain natural phenomena in a precise manner. While these and other physical models can be fairly reliable, they have some limitations. Models are simplified expressions of a very complex and intricate reality. They do not capture all the intricacies of the real world, and to that extent, they are inadequate. It is very rare to be able to fully comprehend all the causes of particular events as well as their interrelationships.

These limitations are compounded when we consider models within the realm of the social sciences (e.g., economics and financial theory). Human behavior is at the core of the social sciences and is characterized by the interplay of a large number of variables related to one another in an intricate manner. Besides, these relationships are not only very complex but also unstable over time. Therefore, it is not surprising that we do not know much about the behavior of human groups. Further, as opposed to models in physics, the models in financial theory tend to be unreliable and incomplete.

If this is the case, why do we bother with financial models? While each model in itself is incomplete, the more models we study, the clearer these relationships become. Once we have grasped several models, we can begin visualizing economic relationships, as they exist in reality. This can be likened to the understanding that we are able to develop from the drawings of a house. Drawings are two-dimensional sectional representations of reality, and a single drawing alone is an unreliable proxy of the real structure. But once we have several drawings together, we are able to envision the three-dimensional configuration as it really is.

It is certainly an ambitious task to try to understand complex investment decisions, but it is better to subject them to the rigors of a modeling exercise than to rely purely on intuition.

Quantification presents the biggest danger in financial modeling. By their very nature, numbers convey a sense of precision and often make analysts believe that their analyses have the stamp of unquestionable veracity. This is, however, far from the truth. Numerical results are useful inputs, but in no way should they be the only criteria for investment decisions.

The closer the assumptions sustaining a model approximate reality, the more reliable will its numerical outcome be, and the greater the validity that can be accorded it. However, since the assumptions that support financial models correspond only partially to facts, their results must be treated with caution.

1.2.1 Behavioral Finance

For some time now, financial economists have been aware of the limitations of financial theory and have known that these limitations stem largely from the complexities of human behavior. A relatively new field, **behavioral finance,** is therefore being developed to explore the true behavior and actions of investors and their effect on financial models.

To illustrate the point, we provide some examples of how the findings of behavioral finance are shaking the bases of financial theory.

Some Findings Financial theory assumes that as soon as investors receive information, they are able to process it in a "rational" way and to incorporate it into asset prices. However, it has been found that this process often takes time and can be performed in several ways. Therefore, it is not perfectly clear when and/or how prices will react to a new piece of information.

Frequently, the true reasons behind a price change are difficult to ascertain. Assume that the price of *XYX*'s stock has increased. Can the rise be attributed to the identification of good investment opportunities, an improvement in the company's image, the promotion of a senior executive, or a combination of these causes?

Information processing is unclear and takes time for the following reasons:

a. *Economic Volatility and Interconnections Among Phenomena.* As soon as we understand the causes behind an event and their interactions, new causes may arise, others may disappear, and the rest may acquire a different set of interrelationships.

b. *The Particular Conditions Affecting Each Situation.* In economics, history rarely repeats itself. Owing to the intrinsic variability and complexity of the economic environment, it is very unusual (if not impossible) to find ourselves in a situation identical to one we experienced before. Experience in economics is less valuable than in other disciplines, and often does not yield as many lessons as we might believe.

c. *The Uncertain Period of Time Required for Causes to Translate into Effects.* Some causes have an immediate impact, while others may take years to manifest their effects. Frequently, we are not able to assess the effect of a cause and the time period in which it will take place.

d. *Differences in the Availability and Interpretation of Information.* Each person has access to different information and tends to process and interpret it according to the individual's unique perspective.

It has also been found that the form in which a postulate is extended can have a significant effect on decision making. In a well-known experiment, two apparently different situations were each presented to the same group of people. In reality, the situations were identical, except they had been stated differently. In both cases, the group made very different decisions (Tversky & Kanneman 1986).

One of the main findings of behavioral finance is that economic agents do not behave rationally, at least as financial theory defines rationality. Hence, a fundamental premise of financial economics is questioned. There is some consensus among experts over several investor decision rules that do not comply with the principle of rationality. In particular, Olsen (1998) lists four areas of divergence.

a. *Shifting Preferences.* Investor preferences tend to change over time depending on the situation being faced. Often, preferences take shape during the process of decision making. An individual staking money in a casino can be very averse to risk when it pertains to his or her personal investments. We also find that the attitude of an investor in relation to a particular project can change over time, even in the absence of new information to justify this.

b. *Shifting Information Processing.* Investors are not machines that can always process information in a predetermined fashion. The manner in which information is handled depends on the type of decision and the environment in which it is presented. The key determining factors in the decision-making process are the perceived complexity of the problem, the reversibility of the decision, the amount of time available to take the decision, the framing of the problem, and the emotional state of the investor. In addition, people tend to look for satisfying[3] solutions and rarely seek optimal ones.

c. *Shifting Interpretations of Information and Perceptions of Risk.* Investors tend to have short memories and to accord greater weight to the most recent piece of information. Further, they tend to ascribe greater importance to unfavorable information and are more averse to losses than to risk. Aversion to losses generally increases as the value of the assets invested in decreases.

d. *Group Pressure. Investors usually desire to be part of a group.* Hence, some decisions are made on the basis of how they will be accepted by other people. This behavior is rooted in the intrinsic insecurity of human beings. An extreme form of this behavior called "herd" conduct occurs when individuals increasingly join a trend for no apparent reason.

It appears that financial models should give consideration not only to relevant information, but also to the environment in which decisions are made. In conclusion, the fundamental bases of financial models are questionable, and this casts a doubt on the relevance and veracity of financial theory.

1.3 EMERGING COUNTRIES

The utility of financial models is restricted because of their failure to deal effectively with human complexities. But this is not their only deficiency. Financial economists

---

[3]*Satisfying* refers to the process of resolving a problem as satisfactorily as possible, given the various constraints on choices. This is an alternative to seeking a maximizing or optimizing solution. For additional information, see Simon (1959).

conceived these models with the realities of developed countries in mind. This significantly limits the application of financial theory to developing countries, where economic and social environments are very different from what we witness in the developed world.

It is imperative that we revise the fundamentals of financial theory in the light of the realities that exist in emerging countries. But let us first examine the characteristics of emerging countries and determine how they differ from developed ones.[4]

1.3.1 Key Characteristics

Broadly speaking, emerging countries are those that share some of the following attributes:

- A significant percentage of the population either is illiterate or has a very low level of education.
- The per capita gross national product is significantly lower than levels experienced in the developed world.
- The distribution of wealth tends to be uneven. A small minority controls a majority of the assets, while the rest of the population lives in poverty.
- The economic and political conditions tend to be unstable.

Dividing the world into two groups of nations—the developed and the developing—is simplistic. Saudi Arabia has a high per capita income, Uruguay has a highly educated population, and Costa Rica is a stable democracy. And yet, all of them are classified as developing countries.

The case of a number of countries that have recently liberated themselves from communism is an interesting one. Poland, Hungary, and the Czech Republic, to name a few, were all advanced nations not so long ago. Yet, after the fall of communism, their actual backwardness was revealed, and most analysts reclassified them as developing countries.

In short, we cannot categorize a country within the ranks of the developing world by strictly applying the key attributes just listed. It can only be said that emerging countries tend to display some or all of these characteristics in some measure. In contrast, developed countries do not share these characteristics.[5]

1.3.2 What Works Differently in Emerging Countries?

A detailed understanding of the general attributes of emerging countries is not necessary for our purposes. Instead, we must identify the differences in the workings of

---

[4]The expressions *emerging country, developing country,* and *less developed country* are used interchangeably.

[5]The differences in the nature and extent of development among countries can be explained largely by cultural and historical factors. Historians and economists have intensely debated this topic. For a detailed analysis of this subject, refer to Landes (1998).

TABLE 1.1 Corruption Perceptions Index (CPI)

Rank	Country	Score*
1	Denmark	10.0
7	Singapore	9.1
13	United Kingdom	8.6
18	United States	7.5
19	Chile	6.9
28	Taiwan	5.6
32	Malaysia	5.1
39	Czech Republic	4.6
40	Peru	4.5
44	Poland	4.2
45	Brazil	4.1
50	South Korea	3.8
54	Philippines	3.6
54	Turkey	3.6
58	China	3.4
58	Mexico	3.4
63	Egypt	3.3
71	Argentina	3.0
72	Colombia	2.9
72	India	2.9
75	Venezuela	2.6
82	Russia	2.4
87	Pakistan	2.2
93	Tanzania	1.9
96	Indonesia	1.7
98	Nigeria	1.6

*The higher the score, the less corruption prone a country is.

Source: © 1999 by Transparency International Website
www.transparency.org.

markets and institutions and contrast these with the assumptions behind financial theory. Six key differences are discussed next.

a. *Information Is Scarce and Unevenly Distributed.* A common assumption in financial theory is that all economic agents share the same information. This is untrue in any market, particularly in the context of emerging countries, where information is scarce, tends to be concentrated in the hands of a few investors, and flows slowly to the marketplace. Neither is there much transparency in the environment of an emerging country, making it difficult to determine whether a particular piece of data is accurate and reliable. These information inefficiencies often distort investment decisions.

b. *Underdeveloped Institutions.* Frequently, the legal and regulatory frameworks in emerging countries are poorly defined, inadequate, and full of contradictions. Further, judicial authorities tend to act in an erratic fashion and are occasionally corrupt. Therefore, contracts entered into in these countries can be unreliable.

Transparency International (www.transparency.org) publishes two important references on corruption: the Corruption Perceptions Index (CPI) is an indicator of corrupted countries and the Bribe Payers Propensity Index (BPI) is an indicator of corrupting countries. Tables 1.1 and 1.2 show the values of these indexes for a number of nations.[6]

c. *Importance of Monopolies, Cartels, and Groups.* A few companies that generally use all possible means to preserve their privileges control many product and service markets. Hence, prices tend to be higher than in more competitive environments. Another common characteristic is the supremacy of family-owned or group-controlled companies. For example, Chinese families are preeminent in the business environments of such Asian countries as Singapore and Malaysia. The dominance of the South Korean economy by a few centralized business groups, the so-called chaebol, is probably the best example of the second.

d. *Underdeveloped Financial Markets.* Financial markets in emerging countries tend to be modest in size, plagued by high operational costs, and, often, not very competitive.

TABLE 1.2 Bribe Payers' Index (BPI)

Rank	Country	Score*
1	Sweden	8.3
7	United Kingdom	7.2
9	United States	6.2
12	Spain	5.3
13	France	5.2
14	Japan	5.1
15	Malaysia	3.9
16	Italy	3.7
17	Taiwan	3.5
18	South Korea	3.4
19	China	3.1

*The higher the score, the less prone to bribe paying a country is.

Source: © 1999 by Transparency International Website www.transparency.org.

---

[6]U.S. law punishes bribers in emerging countries, a trend that is likely to spread throughout other nations. This will surely help diminish international corruption opportunities in the long run.

TABLE 1.3 Net Private Capital Inflows, Early 1990s

Country	Time Lapse	Cumulative Inflow (%)/GDP*	Maximum Annual Inflow (%)
Argentina	1991–94	9.7	3.8
Brazil	1992–95	9.4	4.8
Chile	1989–95	25.8	8.6
Colombia	1992–95	16.2	6.2
Hungary	1993–95	41.5	18.4
India	1992–95	6.4	2.7
Indonesia	1990–95	8.3	3.6
Malaysia	1989–95	45.8	23.2
Mexico	1989–94	27.1	8.5
Morocco	1990–95	18.3	5
Pakistan	1992–95	13	4.9
Peru	1990–95	30.4	10.8
Philippines	1989–95	23.1	7.9
Poland	1992–95	22.3	12
South Korea	1991–95	9.3	3.5
Sri Lanka	1991–95	22.6	8.2
Thailand	1988–95	51.5	12.3
Tunisia	1992–95	17.6	7.1
Turkey	1992–93	5.7	4.1
Venezuela	1992–93	5.4	3.3

* GDP at end of episode.

Source: The International Bank for Reconstruction and Development (1997).

As a result, there is a considerable gap between the remuneration received on savings and the cost of taking loans. This places a restraint on financial flows and creates particularly acute financing barriers for smaller companies and investors.

Another important outcome of financial underdevelopment is the exacerbated sensitivity to international capital flows. Occasionally, these countries' economies receive disproportionate inflows and outflows of foreign capital. The significance of such episodes in a selected group of nations can be observed as shown in Tables 1.3 and 1.4. A relatively minor (by global standards) inflow or outflow can have enormous impact on local liquidity, security prices, and interest and exchange rates. The end result is high volatility for local investments.

e. *Contagion.* The enormous weight of foreign capital flows in emerging capital markets also means that inflows/outflows in one place can be related to inflows/outflows in other places. The tendency of most international investment funds to look at emerging countries on a regional basis is probably one of the main causes behind this occurrence. When the economic situation in one particular country deteriorates, foreign capital leaves rapidly, not only from the affected market but also from the region as a whole, without much consideration to what is really going on in each country. This

TABLE 1.4 Large Reversals in Net Private Capital Flows*

Country	Time Lapse	% GDP
Argentina	1982–83	20
Argentina	1993–94	4
Chile	1981–83	7
Chile	1990–91	8
Malaysia	1993–94	10
Mexico	1981–83	12
Mexico	1993–95	6
Turkey	1993–94	10
Venezuela	1988–89	5
Venezuela	1992–94	9

* Short-term and long-term international flows.

Source: From Private Capital Flows to Developing Countries by World Bank, © 1997 by The International Bank for Reconstruction and Development/The World Bank. Used by permission of Oxford University Press.

phenomenon is known as **contagion.** Contagion can take place not just when economies underperform but also when performance is particularly favorable.

Occasionally contagion can spread between regions. The Asian crisis, which started with the Thai devaluation of 1997, forced other countries of the region to devalue as well. But things did not stop there; soon the crisis also affected Latin America.[7]

The country risk[8] graph for a selected group of emerging nations shown in Figure 1.1 reveals considerable similarity in bond yield patterns in seven countries. This might be an indication of contagion.

f. *Government Policies Are Not Conducive to Economic Growth.* Many emerging country governments initiate populist and interventionist policies that are not attractive to investors, hence impede economic growth. This causes investments to become riskier and the price mechanism to get distorted.

---

[7]There is evidence that some important international funds are beginning to abandon the "regional" approach and starting to pay more attention to countries.

[8]Country risk is a gauge of the risks of investing in a particular country. It is measured, as shown in Figure 1.1, by the difference in yields between long-term sovereign bonds issued by the corresponding emerging country and their U.S. Treasury counterparts. The larger the difference, the lower the relative prices of emerging market bonds. This pattern can be a signal of capital outflows. The concept of country risk is covered in detail in Chapter 7: A Modified CAPM for Emerging Countries.

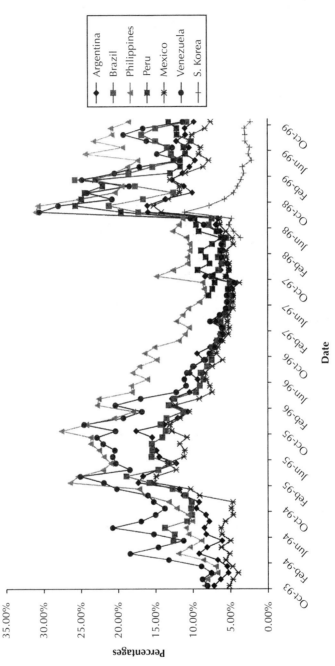

Figure 1.1 Country risk. *Source:* © Reuters 2000.

In essence all these characteristics imply that, as opposed to the more advanced nations, markets in the developing world fail to solve many allocation problems, and the economies of such countries end up with considerable inefficiencies.

Again we must recall that not every emerging nation displays these characteristics to the same measure. What is interesting is that they all share one or more of them to some degree, something that does not take place in the developed world.

1.3.3 What Is Changing in Emerging Countries?

Although government policies not favorable for economic growth proliferate in emerging countries, it is also true that many developing nations are starting to take important steps to adapt their economies to the impact of international capital flows and globalization to make their countries more attractive to foreign investors. The areas for action are basically three: macroeconomic policies, banking system reform, and capital market reform (The International Bank for Reconstruction and Development 1997).

Macroeconomic Policies Three main approaches to address the volatility caused by foreign capital inflows and outflows are being implemented:

Managing the Net Inflows of Foreign Exchange. The main policies deployed toward this end are of controls on capital inflows, liberalization of capital outflows, trade liberalization, limits on official borrowing, and management of the exchange rate.

Reducing the Impact of Reserve Fluctuations on Monetary Aggregates. Governments intervene in the foreign exchange market to stabilize the monetary aggregates. They also manage reserve requirements in the banking system to deal with the multiplier effect.[9]

Reducing the Impact of Capital Flows on Aggregate Demand. In addition to monetary policy, many countries have tightened fiscal policy to alleviate the impact of capital flows on aggregate demand in their economies.

Banking System Reform A sound banking system is key to ensuring macroeconomic and financial stability in a more integrated environment. This is especially true in developing countries, where banks play a dominant role in financial intermediation. The measures being put into practice include the following:

- Modernization of banking laws and regulations
- Strengthening bank supervisory agencies
- Improvements on credit risk controls of bank portfolios
- Increasing the capitalization of banks
- Implementation of better mechanisms to deal with banking crises promptly and effectively

---

[9]The *multiplier effect* is the expansion of bank deposits and the money supply that is tied to the ratio of reserves required by the monetary authorities (Santomero & Babbel 1997).

Capital Market Reform A growing proportion of flows to developing countries is being channeled through investment portfolios. This has caused a significant increase in activity in the nations' stock markets. Unluckily, most of these markets are still in their early stages of development, and to prepare them to better compete with their more advanced counterparts, changes must be introduced. Changes are focused on three areas.

Infrastructure. Clearance, settlement, registry, and payment system procedures as well as risk controls are being improved in numerous emerging stock markets.

Property Rights. The legal and regulatory frameworks are being upgraded to allow for fair treatment for all shareholders, as well as shareholder participation on important corporate decisions. Also measures are being taken to eradicate unethical practices.

The Regulatory Framework. International best practices are being adopted on disclosure and accounting procedures.

The institutional and market flaws described earlier make financial theory more questionable in the developing world than in the more advanced countries. The challenge here is to improve the applicability of financial theory in emerging markets. And this is precisely the objective of chapters that follow—to focus attention on the limitations of financial theory in the context of emerging markets, and to reduce these through practical suggestions for both students and practitioners.

1.4 CONCLUSIONS

- Financial theory deals with investment decisions and is based on four fundamental concepts: net present value, portfolio (risk) theory, option theory, and the theory of capital structure.
- Financial theory uses models as tools to mirror the decision processes of investors.
- Financial models are based on assumptions. The more these assumptions reflect reality, the greater will be the validity of the model, and vice versa.
- Behavioral finance has identified conducts that are inconsistent with many assumptions of financial theory. These include the variability of investors' preferences, the differences in the way investors process information, and the influence of group pressure on investment decisions. Thus, financial models reflect market realities only partially.
- Business environments in developing countries are quite different from those prevailing in developed ones. This makes the disparity between financial models and reality even more pronounced in developing countries.
- In comparison to developed countries, emerging markets are characterized by a mix of one or more of the following features: lower educational and income levels, uneven income distribution, and economic and political instability.

- The main factors that make financial models less valid in emerging countries are scarce and unevenly distributed information, underdeveloped institutions and capital markets, and government policies that restrict economic growth.

- Many developing nations are starting to take important steps to adapt their economies to the impact of international capital flows and globalization.

- Financial model results, especially in the context of developing countries, must be interpreted cautiously.

- The challenge faced by both theoreticians and practitioners is to find ways in which to apply the principles of financial theory in emerging markets in a realistic manner.

QUESTIONS AND PROBLEMS

1. The social sciences deal with many variables, which are interrelated in a very complex way. This reduces considerably the practical value of financial models. What, then, is the usefulness of these models? Is it not better to stay with concepts and ideas and avoid any attempts of quantification?

2. The behavioral sciences have taught us that economic agents frequently do not act rationally. How does this affect financial models?

3. Political instability is a typical characteristic of emerging markets. Democratic governments have ruled Mexico since the beginning of the twentieth century. Is this a good enough reason to exclude Mexico from the group of developing nations?

4. Brazil's is one of the largest financial systems in the world, even larger than those of a number of advanced nations of the European Union. Does this mean that modern financial theory is more relevant in Brazil than in many developed countries?

PART 1

THE INVESTOR
AND THE FIRM

Chapter 2: Consumption, Investments, and Value
The relationship between consumption and investment, the net present value rule, the sources of value for investments in emerging countries.

Chapter 3: The Impact of Risk
Interrelations between the risk–return characteristics of investment opportunities and the investor's attitude to risk.

Chapter 4: The Benefits of Diversification
A theoretical approach to selecting the optimal investment portfolio.

Chapter 5: Personal Investments
A practical approach to selecting the optimal investment portfolio.

CHAPTER 2

CONSUMPTION, INVESTMENTS, AND VALUE

On the troubles of development: "At first sight it looks like a problem of uneven distribution of wealth. But a closer scrutiny reveals a problem of inequality of opportunities. Perhaps it is really a difference in value systems."

We begin this chapter by establishing the relationship between consumption and investment. Further, we will discuss the conditions under which the net present value (*NPV*) rule can be applied as well as its limitations. The differences between the particular characteristics of firms and investments in developing and developed countries will be highlighted. The chapter also offers some practical conclusions with respect to investing in emerging markets. The chapter on valuation in emerging markets (Chapter 8) will later complement these ideas.

2.1 CONSUMPTION AND INVESTMENT: A COMPLEX RELATIONSHIP

We are said to engage in consumption when we exchange money for something that gives us satisfaction. For example, we buy food to relieve hunger, a ticket to the movies to distract us for a while, or a gallon of gasoline for the car to spare us from walking to our destination. The term "consumption" is used in a broad sense and includes acts such as endowments made to one's offspring or to a charitable trust.

An investment, on the other hand, refers to an exchange of money[1] for a higher income expected in the future. When we buy shares or deposit money in a bank, we are investing because, after a while, we expect to get more money. The word "expect" must be emphasized, since we do not always end up with more; if events do not materialize as originally envisioned, we may lose money. A wide interpretation to the term "investment" would include items such as college tuition, as this can be regarded as an investment in education, made with the expectation of deriving a larger income upon the completion of studies.

---

[1] Acts of consumption or investments do not necessarily entail monetary transactions. They can be performed in exchange for goods or services.

17

Investing, however, does not serve any purpose by itself. Its final objective is to consume whatever is invested plus the associated profits in the future. In other words, investment decisions are really (deferred) consumption decisions. Since consumption gives us satisfaction, investing requires giving up this satisfaction. A potential investor will not be willing to invest if expected profits do not compensate for the loss of satisfaction from consuming less. In this manner, investment and consumption are intertwined.

The difference between investment and consumption is not always straightforward. For example, the act of purchasing a house could be classified as an act of both consumption and investment. Take the case of a cash purchase of a house for $100,000.[2] Assuming an annual interest rate of 10%, there are two effects arising from this transaction. On the one hand, we relinquish the interest on our money, which amounts to $10,000 per year in this case. On the other hand, the rent payment is reduced to zero. This saving in rent corresponds to the consumption component of this transaction. The difference between the rent and the interest given up is the investment component. If the rent of a similar house were $7000, it would be the equivalent of consuming $7000 and investing $3000 annually ($10,000 − $7000) in real estate. As in the case of any other investment, presumably we will engage in it if we expect the value of the house in the future to have increased enough to make its purchase attractive now.

The satisfaction from consumption activities varies at different points in time. This introduces another dimension in the relationship between consumption and investment activities. People vary in their time preferences. Some might enjoy consuming more now than a year from now, for example, while others might enjoy consumption more after the end of their productive years.

We invest to consume more in the future. Thus, it is important to be able to exchange the outcome of our investment for goods and services that will be consumed in the future. Therefore, the type of investment made is also related to consumption habits. This point is illustrated through the following example.

Imagine an investor with all his investments in an emerging country E. This investor consumes only in developed country D. Say E's government imposes exchange controls that prevent people from exchanging local currency for D's currency. Thus even though the investments were highly profitable, our investor made a bad deal because he will not be able to consume the outcome of his investments.

This is an extreme situation, but even if there were no restrictions on the purchase of currency D, there would still be some risks involved. Depending on the price of currency D in terms of currency E (**the exchange rate**), the consumption basket to be acquired by the investor will differ. If currency D's price is too high (i.e., E's currency is undervalued), relatively less currency D will be bought and the consumption basket will be smaller. However, if currency E is overvalued, the consumption basket will be larger. Therefore, this risk can either benefit or harm the investor.[3]

---

[2] We ignore tax considerations in this example.

[3] For a more elaborate discussion of exchange risk, refer to Chapter 8: Valuation in Emerging Markets.

TABLE 2.1

		Scenario	
	Bad	Most Likely	Good
A	$10	$20	$30
B	-$10	$25	$40

Investment decisions become even more complicated when risk considerations are factored in. For example, how does one choose between two attractive investment projects with different risk levels? Should both be accepted? How much should be consumed and how much should be invested? These dilemmas are illustrated in the following example.

Suppose investment opportunities A and B both require an initial investment outlay of $10. Table 2.1 shows the results, a year later, for three different scenarios: bad, most likely, and good. Although B is more attractive in the two most favorable scenarios, it produces a loss in the worst case. Which investment decision is better? Or would it be better still to consume the $10 instead of investing it?

To summarize, investment decisions are complex and depend on answers to a number of questions:

- What is the satisfaction we derive from consuming in the present vs consuming in the future?
- How do we rate the attractiveness of investment opportunities?
- How do investment opportunities interact with consumption habits?
- How do we identify the risk associated with investment opportunities?

2.2 THE FISHER SEPARATION PRINCIPLE

It was mentioned that most financial problems are approached through models that are based on simplifying assumptions. One such basic model of financial theory is the separation principle of Irving Fisher (1930), which defines the following rule for consumption, saving, and investment decisions:

1. All projects with a return larger than the market interest rate must be accepted. The net present value (NPV)[4] of total investment is maximized at the point at which the market interest rate equals the return of the marginal project. NPV maximization implies maximization of the investor's wealth.
2. Consumption and savings levels are determined at the point at which the market interest rate equals the value to the consumer of the ratio between consuming now and consuming later.

---

[4]For a review of the concept of present value, refer to Appendix 2A.

The market interest rate is the only link between these two decisions. Since this rate is an observable parameter, it can be concluded that the investment decision (i.e., wealth maximization) is always the same and has nothing to do with an investor's preferences, whereas the consumption and savings decisions are personal and rest on the preferences of each individual. Everyone will agree on the optimal investment level, but there will likely be considerable disagreement on how much to save and consume. However, saving and consumption decisions are taken by every individual through the financial market, without affecting the investment decision on which all consent.[5]

The Fisher separation principle simplifies investment decisions by ignoring individual preferences and focusing on wealth maximization. This is particularly helpful when one is dealing with firms, since managers will not have to consult with individual stockholders about their preferences before accepting a project. Only decisions that maximize the value of the firm (and shareholder wealth) are accepted.

For the separation principle to hold, however, the following four conditions must be fulfilled:

1. There is a total absence of risk.
2. All investors must agree on the investment opportunity set.
3. All investors must have unrestricted access to the financial market.
4. The lending and borrowing interest rates must be equal and the same for all investors.

Let us momentarily forget about the first condition, since it will be discussed in Part II. Although it is unrealistic, the second condition is required for all investors to agree on the optimal investment level. However, it does not seem to be an important limitation when one is dealing with a few investors (as in the case of most emerging market companies). When this is the case, it is most likely that investors will negotiate and compromise on the characteristics of investment opportunities. And even if they do not manage to reach a consensus, the opinion of one or more investors (or managers) generally predominates because of their leadership or authority.

The third and fourth conditions are worrisome (although we will later see how investors get around them in practice). Therefore, let us observe what occurs with the *NPV* rule when these two conditions impede the separation of consumption and investment.

2.2.1 When Present Value Fails

In the absence of unrestricted access to financial markets, the separation principle does not hold: consumption and investment are not separable, and the investment decision maximizing *NPV* is not necessarily the best. This is because the *NPV* rule does not

---

[5]The interested reader can expand on the Fisher separation principle by referring to a text on corporate finance such as Brealey and Myers (1996) or Ross, Westerfield, and Jaffe (1999). A more advanced exposition appears in Copeland and Weston (1988).

TABLE 2.2

Time (T)	Cash Flows*		Present Values*	
	C_A	C_B	$PV_A(10\%)$	$PV_B(10\%)$
0	−1000	−1000	−1000	−1000
1	0	+3000	0	+2727.3
2	0	+3000	0	+2479.3
3	+30,000	+3000	+22,539.4	+2253.9
Totals	+29,000	+8000	+21,539.4	+6460.5

*Amounts are given in thousands of dollars.

allow for investor's preferences. Under *NPV* a project with no positive cash flows during a long period of time (hence not permitting consumption during that period) is preferable to another with a smaller *NPV*, but more evenly distributed cash flows. An investor facing barriers in the financial markets might not agree with this view. Let us illustrate with an example.

Observe the annual cash flows and present values for projects *A* and *B* given a 10% yearly discount rate, as shown in Table 2.2. The *NPV* of *A* is +$21.5 million, much larger than the *NPV* of *B*, which amounts to just +$6.5 million. According to the *NPV* rule, *A* is preferable to *B*. *A* does not produce positive cash flows during the first two years, but the *NPV* rule supposes that the investor, having unrestricted access to the financial market, can always borrow for consumption needs during that period. Thus, the only decision criterion is the impact of the project on his wealth (which is given by its *NPV*). If the investor does not have the option of borrowing, however, *B* might be a better decision.

2.3 CONSUMPTION AND INVESTMENT IN PRACTICE

The four necessary conditions that ensure the validity of the separation principle are negated in reality. The condition specifying the absence of risk will be lifted later, and the requirement that investors agree on the investment opportunity set is not regarded as very important. Nevertheless, the conditions that investors have unrestricted and equal access to financial markets and that the lending and borrowing rates be the same do not hold true in practice, particularly in the context of the underdeveloped financial markets of emerging countries.

This does not imply that investors take their consumption and investment decisions simultaneously. What usually happens is that investors tend to create two separate (imaginary) sets of funds: one for consumption and the other for investment purposes. The first one is generally invested in highly liquid assets such as bank accounts or monetary funds. The investment fund is managed independently, with the objective of (presumably) maximizing wealth.

Therefore, from a practical point of view, it is acceptable to assume that investors take their consumption and investment decisions separately—not because the separation principle holds, but because the interaction between consumption and investment is so complex that investors elect to simplify their approach to this problem. It is useful to recall that behavioral finance teaches us that investors tend to look for satisfying decisions and not necessarily for optimal ones (See Chapter 1: Financial Theory in Emerging Markets.) This is a good example of that finding.

In consequence, even though it is not always the optimal strategy, we will accept the assumption **of separation between consumption and investment** for the rest of this book.

In addition, we learned in Chapter 1 that wealth maximization is seldom the only variable that investors take into account when analyzing investments. Nonetheless, it is reasonable to assume that it is the most important criterion for most investors. Thus, from here on, we will also accept the assumption of **wealth maximization as the unique decision criterion for investment decisions.**[6]

Net present value will be our decision rule for investment analysis. But what makes *NPV* positive or negative? We will now move our discussion toward this topic.

2.4 REAL AND FINANCIAL INVESTMENTS

To begin with, we must distinguish between two basic categories of investments: real and financial investments. Real investments correspond to projects and include tangible assets such as buildings, plant and equipment, and working capital, as well as expenditures on items such as technical know-how, research and development, and training. Additionally, the acquisition of a firm is also considered to be a real project. Financial investments, on the other hand, are bound to the capital markets and comprise primarily bank deposits, and securities issued by financial institutions and private and governmental entities.

What is the difference between these types of investment?

Real investments are funds used directly for the acquisition of productive (i.e., real) assets, whereas financial investments are funds received by financial institutions, government organizations, and companies that are then channeled into the purchase of assets and business-related expenses. A good share of these assets ends up as real investment.

Let us discuss the main characteristics of real and financial investments from the perspective of both developed and developing economies.

2.4.1 Financial Investments

We will examine the market for financial investments and the working of the price mechanism in both developed and emerging economies.

---

[6]Another implication of the invalidity of the Fisher separation principle is that the application of the *NPV* rule by firms is incorrect. In practice, however, it is applied, but under certain specific conditions. This is further referred to in Part II.

Financial Investments in Developed Markets In a developed economy investors are able to buy and sell a large variety of shares, bonds, and other financial instruments with considerable ease. In addition, this is done in an environment of abundant financial information that is both timely and accurate.

A constant flow of information provides the basis for investors to adjust their expectations on the future returns on the securities under consideration. If the returns on a particular security are expected to increase, investors will be willing to either purchase it at a higher price or sell it at a higher price. Likewise, those who think that returns will decrease will adjust their buying and selling prices downward. Each investor compares the market price with the price that is reasonable according to his expectations. If the market price is high, the decision will be either to sell the instrument[7] or not to purchase it. If the market price of the security is low, the decision will be either to purchase it or not to sell it.

Thus, the price mechanism ensures that prices of financial assets reflect the average expectations of investors with considerable accuracy. Information flows are quick and complete, making it very difficult for everyone to benefit from privileged information. If the price of a security deviates excessively from average expectations, investors rapidly engage in buying or selling it, and a new equilibrium price that is better aligned with average expectations is arrived at.

We can conclude then that **developed financial markets tend to be efficient. Moreover, in such markets excessive returns are rare and the *NPV*s of investments in securities tend to be zero.**

Financial Investments in Emerging Countries Financial market conditions are not the same in the less-developed countries. These nations are not as wealthy as their developed counterparts and are characterized by low levels of savings and investments. Consequently, these financial markets are underdeveloped and small in relation to the size of the respective national economies and tend to be dominated by banks. It is for these reasons that financial resources that make their way to the stock exchange are modest.

In addition, the distribution of income in emerging economies is generally unequal and, as a consequence, financial resources not only are scarce but also are localized within a small investor base. Further, financial information is usually incomplete, not available in timely fashion, inaccurate, and concentrated among the few who control the bulk of wealth.

The outcome of this situation is that these financial markets have few participants with privileged information managing significant amounts of capital (at least relative to the size of the market). This setting offers numerous opportunities to obtain extraordinary returns by buying or selling securities at attractive prices. In addition, the possibility of moving large amounts of capital into and out of the market at short notice allows the profitable manipulation of prices.[8]

As mentioned in Chapter 1, globalization is causing emerging financial markets to become increasingly sensitive to portfolio decisions of major international investment

---

[7]We will use the terms *financial instrument, security,* and *financial asset* interchangeably.

[8]Price manipulation and purchase of financial instruments on the basis of privileged information are being increasingly monitored and penalized by the authorities in many emerging countries.

funds (Froot, O'Connell, & Seasholes, 1999). Consequently, it is usual for significant gaps to open up between the market price and the equilibrium price of many financial instruments. This presents investors with the ability to identify the best timing to buy or sell these securities to earn extraordinary returns. In short, in contrast to the developed world, **financial markets in emerging countries tend to be inefficient, and financial investments often yield excess returns and positive NPVs.**

2.4.2 Real Investments

In contrast to financial investments, real investments are less widely accessible. Only a few investors have the chance to install a cement plant or a refinery, or to establish a supermarket chain.

To identify an attractive real investment opportunity, an investor (whether it is an individual or a firm) or an entrepreneur needs to experience certain special conditions that place him at an advantage over others. These particular conditions, arising from some specific knowledge, special organizational abilities, or any other relevant advantage or capability, potentially grant the investor extraordinary returns on selected investments. This, however, is not the case with financial securities, since it is not necessary, for instance, to be knowledgeable about automobiles to buy shares of an automotive company, or to be an expert on steel to hold shares of a steel mill.

Any investor or promoter who displays these special characteristics is said to possess a **competitive advantage** for that particular business. Attractive real investment opportunities require that the investor or entrepreneur possess relative competitive advantages that are sustainable for long periods of time. This is clearly not the case with financial investments.

It is precisely the need to hold competitive advantages that keeps most investors away from real investments. In other words, these advantages create **entry barriers** for others. The presence of these entry barriers impedes the prices of real investments to equilibrate with expectations of returns. Therefore, we can conclude that **real investments can lead to excess returns, hence to positive NPVs.**

This conclusion is consistent with the Fisher model. Recall how investors undertook real investments up to the point at which the lending rate started to be more attractive. This decision rule was equivalent to accepting all real investments that increase wealth and thus yield a positive NPV.

We recognize that the source of competitive advantage rests in the special abilities of the investor or promoter. However, the abilities that are critical to success in developed countries are not identical to those that are crucial in emerging countries.

Real Investments in Developed Countries In developed economies there are two main sources of special abilities: the possession of strategic assets and the presence of special contractual structures (Kay 1995).[9]

---

[9]This is a brief summary of the salient ideas of one of several interesting approaches to the extensive topic of competitive advantages. The interested reader may refer to the original source (Kay 1995). Other useful references are Porter (1980), Mahoney and Pandian (1992), Nelson and Winter (1982), and Prahalad and Hamel (1990).

Strategic assets (e.g., exclusive rights to develop an oil field, a building lot in a preferential area, a well-known brand name) are held by a small number of individuals or firms. Strategic assets are also created from regulations limiting free entry or competition in specific markets. This applies in the case of patents, water and electricity monopolies, restrictions for telephone companies to participate in the cable business, and so on. Possession of strategic assets translates into entry barriers for potential competitors, and therefore, is a potential source of extraordinary returns for their holders.

Special contractual structures refer to the network of formal and informal contracts that support the activities of the investor. **Formal contracts** are explicit written documents, (e.g., contracts with suppliers and clients, agreements for professional services).

Informal contracts are implicit and not expressed in writing. They originate from long-term interactions among people. These interactions gradually create obligations that tend to be less precise than those arising from formal contracts. For example, reputation, teamwork, cooperation with other groups in the same market, leadership styles, and norms for promotion within an organization all imply an obligation to behave in a certain way.

Formal contracts are easy to imitate relative to informal contracts. This is why the creation of competitive advantages is mainly achieved through the conception of informal contracts. The key to producing and maintaining profitable sources of differentiation relative to competitors rests precisely in the skill to anticipate contractual relations worthy of cultivation, and to ensure that they are not easily replicable.

Firm and Management Competitive advantages have much to do with the inception and development of the firm. The firm can be understood as the center of a network of explicit and implicit contracts among all interested parties—suppliers, customers, employees, shareholders, creditors, or competitors. A contractual network with several interlinkages is quite difficult to maintain at a personal level, since this would oblige it to rest on just one individual and to be subordinate to whatever happens in his or her personal life. This is a critical reason for the selection of **the firm, and not the individual, to be the main vehicle for conducting real investment opportunities in most cases.**

Businesses in developed countries face intense competitive pressures that have been increasing rapidly. This is primarily due to the growing integration of international trade, that is, the **globalization** of business activities. Fierce competition is a powerful incentive to make all possible efforts to cultivate and reinforce competitive advantages, since failure in these crucial areas can erode a firm's competitive position, and in the extreme, even cause its disappearance. Growing business complexity and the considerable managerial effort required to keep pace with attempts at competitive differentiation is pushing such firms to focus their resources and activities in a restricted set of business niches. This is referred to as **specialization.**

Another outcome of broadening competition and globalization is the need to undertake increasingly larger capital investments that require the agglomeration of greater financial resources with a view to keeping unitary costs and quality at competitive levels and achieving **economies of scale.** The need to achieve scale economies not only justifies the existence of the firm as a preferred vehicle of investment, but also leads to the incorporation of a larger number of shareholders.

What used to be **closed** shareholder structures, with just a few managing owners, are now becoming **open**[10] shareholding structures, with a larger and increasingly anonymous and diffuse shareholder base. Behind this process, the vital links between real investments and financial markets and securities are clear. Firms can easily grow and open up their ownership structures because the financial system is always prepared to channel society's savings towards the more productive uses.

In many larger companies this process has evolved until dominant shareholders no longer exist and the company's administration rests in the hands of experienced managers. These managers do not hold significant stock in the company, and their compensation is determined primarily by their professional services.

Separation between shareholders and management leads to the much-researched **agency problem,** which did not exist before. It is natural to expect that, as human beings, managers have their own objectives, which are not necessarily be in consonance with the goals of the shareholders. As a consequence, investment decisions start being affected by the interests of managers. A greater degree of separation between managers and shareholders causes investment decisions to be biased in favor of the interests of managers as opposed to those of the shareholders.[11]

Real Investments in Emerging Countries The concept of competitive advantage specific to a particular line of business does not become invalid in the context of developing markets. However, emerging market investors, promoters, and firms usually need to develop additional competitive advantages specific to their cultural and political environment. Henceforth we will refer to these as **environmental competitive advantages,** to emphasize that markets in these countries are relatively inefficient, and financial institutions and the regulatory and legal frameworks are neither well developed nor reliable (see Chapter 1: Financial Theory in Emerging Markets).

In most developing countries it is possible to be surprised by changes in laws or regulations, by arbitrary decisions of public officials, or by a seemingly capricious interpretation of some law or norm. Stability and consistency in decisions and policies affecting the business climate are rare. In many instances, even the judiciary is open to questioning. The obvious effect of such conditions is that firms must operate in an atmosphere of considerable uncertainty.

Investors and firms usually attempt to avoid unpleasant surprises by ascribing priority to informal contracts over formal ones. This applies, in particular, to nurturing long-term ties with counterparts having a reputation for honesty and respect for their commitments. It also applies to the job market, to relationships with distributors, clients, suppliers, financial institutions, and with any other local party with an interest in the firm.

---

[10]Trading of a company's shares in the stock market does not guarantee an open shareholding base, since the firm might still be controlled by a small number of stockholders.

[11]The term *agency problems* encompasses all the incentive problems in and around the firm. It includes managers and shareholders as well as suppliers, creditors, customers, employees, and so on. Agency problems appear in all possible combinations among all parties with an interest in the firm.

It was explained before how nascent financial markets could disproportionately benefit those with sufficient capital and access to information. However, it is not merely the financial markets that are inefficient in these countries. The markets for labor and goods and services are also characterized by inefficiencies.

A pronounced scarcity of technical and managerial personnel impedes the normal execution of business affairs, and is possibly the most damaging failure of the labor market. The main problem in the markets for goods and services is the presence of monopolies and cartels that obstruct fair competition and distort the price mechanism.

In sum, undeveloped markets and institutions inhibit the flow of information and resources, obstructing their efficient allocation in emerging nations.

Diversified Conglomerates General inefficiencies cause certain business strategies that seem disadvantageous in developed countries to make much more sense in a developing country context. **Diversified conglomerates** may be the most obvious example. These are business groups involved in a wide range of unrelated businesses. It is not uncommon to find conglomerates operating in areas as diverse as automobile assembly, banking, airlines, and television. A case in point is the presence of these conglomerates in the banking sector, which enables them to take advantage of scarce financial resources and lend funds to other group companies. This arrangement is likely to cause trouble. Without adequate supervision from the banking authorities, the group can be tempted to benefit from this funding in an incorrect or even illegal manner.

Diversified conglomerates might be justified in emerging countries as an effective route to acquiring competitive advantages relative to the environment—advantages that are often more important than those specific to the business. Some ways by which diversified conglomerates can develop environmental advantages are (Khanna & Palepu 1997) as follows:

- Firms with links to the banking sector can insulate themselves from the uncertainty associated with obtaining bank financing. This is due not only to their eventual incorporation into a banking institution, but also because the mere weight that conglomerates usually have in local economies always places them in an advantageous position vis-à-vis regular customers of the bank.

- Stronger negotiating power with clients and suppliers is important when certain markets are dominated by monopolies or cartels.

- The superior career opportunities and higher levels of job security that these diversified groups offer attracts the best human resource talent.

- Having a large diversified organization also helps to leverage relations with governmental agencies. This is an important consideration given the institutional weakness and possible arbitrariness, of such agencies, as well as the likelihood of unfavorable decisions to the group from them.

- A diversified group is also in a better position to cultivate stronger implicit and explicit contractual relations with all parties associated with the group activities. This is important in situations in which the judiciary is not entirely reliable, as is often the case in developing countries.

TABLE 2.3

Firm	Country
Aracruz Celulosa	Brazil
Cemex	Mexico
Gazprom	Russia
Hutchinson Whampoa	China (Hong Kong)
Koor Industries	Israel
Korea Electric & Power	South Korea
Korea Telecom	South Korea
Matav	Hungary
Singapore Airlines	Singapore
Soquimix	Chile
Telmex	Mexico

Closed Firms Closed shareholding structures in emerging countries are another case in point. With a few exceptions, emerging country firms are small in scale and possess a closed shareholding structure relative to their counterparts in the more developed world. Among the exceptions are the sample of well-known emerging country firms shown in Table 2.3. These companies not only are significant players in the international business community, but also their shareholding structures are open enough for their stock to show acceptable levels of liquidity.

However, closed shareholding structures are the general rule. They have the advantage of ameliorating the agency problem because shareholders and managers ordinarily work together whenever important investment decisions are being considered. Yet, a closed shareholding structure can also be disadvantageous. Growth is restricted in closed firms, since equity financing is constrained to the extent that the existing shareholders can fund it.

This explains why financing in the initial stages of development is primarily done through bank loans (hence the importance of being close to one or more banks). Nevertheless, in many cases, after a certain point, closed companies must open up their shareholder base to amass enough reserves to compete with their peers in the more industrialized countries (see Chapter 12: Financing and Value). Despite this, even today only a modest number of firms in the developing world have truly open shareholding structures and are professionally managed, as opposed to being run by a small group of stockholders or dominant families.[12]

We have highlighted the ubiquity of closed firms in emerging countries. However, we must not forget that a majority of firms in the developed world are also closed, as is clearly corroborated by the large number of small businesses (bakeries, barbershops,

---

[12] In practice it is possible to achieve significant economies of scale without opening up the shareholding base as much: countries like Japan, South Korea, and Germany have frequently chosen the route that combines financial and industrial groups.

restaurants, dry cleaners, etc.) found everywhere in these countries. The difference, however, is with respect not to numbers but to proportions. A relatively higher proportion of firms in the developed world have open shareholding structures, and this is due to the effects of a strong competitive environment combined with easier access to both debt and equity capital.

Diversification Costs So far we have not accounted for risk considerations as a key variable associated with investment decisions (see Chapter 4: The Benefits of Diversification). In the chapters that follow we will relax this assumption. This will show us how important it is for investors to diversify their investment portfolios when risk is factored in. When diversification at the personal level is costly (as is so often the case in emerging countries), diversification by the firm in nonrelated areas may be advisable. This is another possible justification for the existence of diversified conglomerates.

2.5 INVESTMENTS IN EMERGING MARKETS: CONCLUDING REMARKS

How does the foregoing discussion affect investment decisions in emerging markets?

a. *Excess Returns in Financial Investments.* We know that in the presence of adequate capital and access to information sources, it is possible to earn excess returns in emerging financial markets.

b. *Advantages for Conglomerates.* Diversified conglomerates can often overcome institutional and market failures that occur in emerging markets. The result is that many investment opportunities that might not be attractive for investors with competitive advantages at the business level may be lucrative for a local conglomerate with competitive advantages at the environmental level.[13]

In addition, the conglomerate form facilitates the gathering of financial resources for growth, hence can help delay the crisis that usually accompanies the need to open up the shareholding base (see Chapter 12: Financing and Value). This is one reason for the great number of important companies that retain closed shareholding structures in the developing world.

c. *Closed Firms.* Investment decisions can be directly affected in closed firms. Recall that the existence of inefficiencies in the financial market was one fundamental cause for the failure of the Fisher separation theorem. When one or more shareholders face barriers to borrowing, we may find that some of them will prefer lower investment and higher dividends, while others will choose higher investment and lower dividends (see Chapter 12).

---

[13]One route to capitalizing on specific business advantages and environmental advantages at the same time is to form joint ventures between local conglomerates and specialized companies, a practice often seen in developing countries.

Differential borrowing access can certainly engender stockholder clashes that could, in extreme cases, threaten the survival of the firm. Only when a closed company possesses strong leadership can these problems be overcome, though not without frustrating certain shareholders.

2.5.1 NPV and Competitive Advantages

The projection of cash flows is a must for investment analysis. This requires setting up a series of premises about the future, both of the general economic environment and of specific aspects of the project under study. It is only natural for these assumptions and the resulting *NPV* to be uncertain, especially in highly volatile emerging countries. Furthermore, it is not uncommon for the projections to be manipulated by parties interested in either improving or worsening the investment results.

Consequently, it is important to contrast the premises and projections with a qualitative analysis on the lines described earlier. Here the objective is to assess the extent to which competitive advantages are present or not, and whether this in turn will lead to a positive (or negative) *NPV* for the project.

Thus far we have ignored risk. Nevertheless, one key success factor in emerging countries is the ability to invest and manage in highly uncertain environments, a topic we will cover (see Chapter 9: The Value of Flexibility). In the coming chapters we will introduce this crucial variable and learn how to deal with uncertainty in investment decisions.

2.6 CONCLUSIONS

- We invest with the purpose of consuming more in the future. Investment decisions are consumption decisions spread over a period of time.

- The separation of consumption and investment decisions is described in the Fisher separation principle. This principle allows investment decision making through the maximization of the net present value of cash flows, independent of investor's preferences.

- The Fisher separation principle (hence the separation of consumption from investment and the validity of the *NPV* rule) requires all investors to agree on the investment opportunity set and to have the same unrestricted access to the financial market. Additionally, the lending and borrowing interest rates must be identical.

- When consumption and investment are not separable, the *NPV* rule does not necessarily result in the preferred investment decision for the investor. This is because investments are intertwined with consumption preferences over a period of time.

- In practice, individuals usually make their investment and consumption decisions independently by the imaginary separation of their resources into two funds: one for each purpose. For this reason we will assume the separation between consumption and investment.

- Although wealth maximization might not be the only consideration when investment decisions are being made, it is possibly the most important objective. Therefore, from

now on, we will suppose wealth maximization to be the only criterion behind investment decision making.

- Real investments are those in productive assets (tangible or intangible), while financial investments are those made in financial markets.

- It is very difficult to obtain excess returns in financial markets in developed countries.
However, this is not the case in emerging markets where, given enough capital and the
right information, it is quite possible to get positive *NPV*s from financial investments.

- Competitive advantages at the business level are the source of positive *NPV*s in the
case of real investments. Nevertheless, competitive advantages at the environmental
level assume great importance in emerging countries.

- One key competitive advantage in developing countries is the ability to identify and
manage business opportunities in highly uncertain environments (see Chapter 9: The
Value of Flexibility).

- Diversified conglomerates are a vehicle for the development of competitive advantages at the environmental level in emerging markets. Therefore, investing through
these conglomerates can be beneficial.

- Closed companies, ubiquitous in emerging markets, give birth to potential conflicts
among shareholders when they face barriers to borrowing.

- The uncertainty associated with financial projections, especially in emerging markets, makes it imperative to reconfirm the assumptions behind the projections with a
strategic analysis with a view to verifying whether a firm possesses any competitive
advantages.

QUESTIONS AND PROBLEMS

1. How are consumption and investment decisions related?

2. Is it always better to consume today rather than tomorrow, and tomorrow rather than
the day after?

3. An investor undertakes an investment in Russia in rubles (the local currency). How
is the investor affected if the ruble ends up devaluing more rapidly than originally
expected with respect to the U.S. dollar?

4. Suppose investment opportunities A and B both require an initial investment outlay
of $50. A year later, the results for three different scenarios: bad, most likely and
good, are as shown in Table P2.4. Which investment decision is better?

TABLE P2.4

	Scenario		
	Bad	Most Likely	Good
A	$0	$100	$140
B	$10	$125	$120

TABLE P2.5

Year	Cash Flows		Present Values	
T	C_A	C_B	PV_A (12%)	PV_B (12%)
0	−700	−700	−700	−700
1	0	+2000	0	+1785.7
2	X	+6000	?	+4783.2
Totals	?	+7300	?	+5868.9

5. Why, according to the Fisher separation principle, are investment decisions independent of how conservative or willing to take risks the investor is?

6. The yearly cash flows and present values of investment opportunities A and B for a 12% yearly discount rate are as shown in Table P2.5. What is the range of **X** for A to be chosen over B? Analyze the following cases:
   (a) The investor has unrestricted access to the financial markets.
   (b) The investor has no access to financial markets.

7. The stock markets of emerging countries are equally accessible to all investors. Therefore, there is no reason for positive NPV investment opportunities to arise in these markets. Discuss.

8. Are environmental competitive advantages so important in emerging markets that real investments in nonrelated businesses are always justified?

9. In what way can the underdevelopment of financial systems in emerging markets impair the attainment of economies of scale in firms with few shareholders?

APPENDIX 2A

Net Present Value

2A.1 DEFINITIONS

A **cash flow** is a sum of money at a point in time. If it is positive it is an inflow; if it is negative, it qualifies as an outflow.

Present value (PV) is the amount of money today, which is equivalent to a stream of future cash flows discounted at a certain interest rate.

Net present value (NPV) is the difference between present value and the cash flow at time zero.

When we have only one time period, present value is given by:

$$PV = \frac{C_1}{1 + i}$$

where PV is present value, C_1 is the cash flow at time 1, and i is the interest rate.

When we have two periods, it is necessary to discount the time 2 cash flow to bring it to the end of the first period, and then add it to the time 1 cash flow and bring the total to time 0. The present value at time 1 of the cash flow at time 2 will be:

$$\frac{C_2}{1 + i}$$

Adding this result to the cash flow at the end of the first period and discounting, we obtain:

$$PV = \frac{C_1 + C_2/(1 + i)}{1 + i}$$

which is equivalent to:

$$PV = \frac{C_1}{1 + i} + \frac{C_2}{(1 + i)^2}$$

In general, for n periods, the present value will be:

$$PV = \sum_{1}^{n} \frac{C_1}{(1 + i)^1}$$

By subtracting the initial cash flow, the net present value NPV will be given by:

$$NPV = \sum_{0}^{n} \frac{C_1}{(1 + i)^1}$$

2A.2 An Example

Let us illustrate by this example. Given an interest rate of 10%, we will find the NPV of the following cash flow, as shown in Table 2A.1. To compute NPV, we rather add another column to the table, as shown in Table 2A.2. NPV at a 10% interest rate will be $+1149.6$.

TABLE 2A.1

Time T	Cash Flow C_t
0	-1000
1	$+1000$
2	$+1500$

TABLE 2A.2

T	C_t	PV (10%)
0	−1000	−1000
1	+1000	+909.09
2	+1500	+1239.7
Totals	+1500	+1149.6

This was an investment, since we had a negative cash flow at time zero, in exchange for positive cash flows from then on. Had it been a loan, the results would be identical but the signs would be reversed as shown in Table 2A.3. NPV is one of the most powerful concepts in finance because it allows us to compare different cash flow streams by converting them into equivalent cash flows at time zero.

We know whether an investment opportunity is attractive by looking at the sign of *NPV*. A positive sign means that the return is larger than the discount rate and that the investment must be accepted. When the sign is negative, the return is lower than the discount rate and the project must not be undertaken.[14]

Additivity of NPV

Another important advantage is that the *PV* of the sum of two independent investment opportunities equals the sum of the *PVs* of each one of them. This comes out directly from the *PV* formula. Say that we have investment opportunities $X(1)$ and $X(2)$ with their respective cash flows represented by $X_1(1), X_2(1), \ldots , X_n(1)$, and $X_1(2), X_2(2),$ . . ., $X_n(2)$ for periods 1 to n. Then,

TABLE 2A.3

T	C_t	PV (10%)
0	+1000	+1000
1	−1000	−909.09
2	−1500	−1239.7
Totals	−1500	−1149.6

---

[14] In the case of a loan, a positive *NPV* means a return lower than the discount rate, and a negative *NPV* a return higher than the discount rate. Notice that the *NPV* rule also works in this case. If *NPV* is negative the return (or cost of the loan) will be higher than the discount rate, hence will not be acceptable, and vice versa.

$$PV_{X(1)} = \frac{X_1(1)}{(1 + i)} + \frac{X_2(1)}{(1 + i)^2} + \cdots + \frac{X_n(1)}{(1 + i)^n}$$

$$PV_{X(2)} = \frac{X_1(2)}{(1 + i)} + \frac{X_2(2)}{(1 + i)^2} + \cdots + \frac{X_n(2)}{(1 + i)^n}$$

$$PV[X(1) + X(2)] = \frac{X_1(1) + X_1(2)}{(1 + i)} + \frac{X_2(1) + X_2(2)}{(1 + i)^2} + \cdots + \frac{X_n(1) + X_n(2)}{(1 + i)^n}$$

$$PV[X(1) + X(2)] = PV_{X(1)} + PV_{X(2)}$$

The same reasoning applies to *NPV*, since an investment in a group of projects must be equivalent to the sum of the investments in each of them.

Generalizing to n investment opportunities we have:

$$NPV\left[\sum_{i=1}^{n} X(i) \right] = \sum_{i=1}^{n} NPV_{X(i)}$$

CHAPTER 3

THE IMPACT OF RISK

"Economic progress can be defined as the ability to take risks.
Profits are the insurance premium for the risk of playing to the future."

—PETER DRUCKER

We will now discuss the role of risk in investment decisions with our focus on the personal investor who must decide on the best combination of assets, both real and financial, in which to invest. In this chapter, and in the next, we review portfolio theory. Readers familiar with this theory may proceed directly to Chapter 5 on personal investments.

We begin by visualizing the impact of risk on investment decisions, and on ways of using the concept of probability to handle investment analysis. Probability allows us to define a utility function to represent investor's preferences under uncertainty. Investment opportunities and the utility function are combined to illustrate, in principle, how investment decisions must be made under conditions of risk. Finally the advantages and disadvantages of the normal distribution as a probabilistic model for investment decisions are described.[1]

3.1 RISK AND INVESTMENT DECISIONS

Let us recall a former conclusion: although the Fisher conditions for the separation of consumption and investment decisions do not hold, in practice, investors find a way to separate them. For this reason, from now on we will ignore the consumption decision, focusing instead on optimizing the investment decision.

Up to now we have assumed returns from investments to be predictable; that is, there was no possibility for realized cash flows to differ from original projections. Under those circumstances, there was no doubt that the best decision was the one with the highest net present value.

In reality, however, we are never sure of investment returns. Our projections are merely estimates from which there could be both positive and negative deviations. In

---

[1]For a deeper treatment of this material, refer to a more advanced text such as Copeland and Weston (1988).

TABLE 3.1

Project				NPV ($)			
	Dismal	Very Low	Low	Fair	High	Very High	Excellent
A	40	60	80	100	120	140	160
B	0	40	80	120	160	200	240

other words, business opportunities are risky or uncertain[2] and investment decisions are not clear-cut. Let us illustrate with an example involving two investment opportunities with the *NPVs* for different scenarios as shown in Table 3.1.

Both projects described in Table 3.1 are attractive. But which one is better? The net present values associated with project A range from $40 to $160 and those for project B range from $0 to $240. Project B could lead to lower returns than project A, but in some cases, the returns could be higher. Therefore, the choice of project is not obvious and cannot be determined by merely comparing net present values.

Let us assign probabilities of three kinds—homogeneous, increasing, and decreasing—to each scenario,[3] as shown in Table 3.2. The expected net present values $E(NPV)$s, in dollars, and standard deviations for each project and scenario are as shown in Table 3.3.

Investors' preferences will be in the direction of lower dispersion over higher dispersion and higher $E(NPV)$s over lower $E(NPV)$s. Since the standard deviation is a measure of dispersion, the larger the standard deviation and the smaller the $E(NPV)$, the less attractive will a project be, and vice versa.

TABLE 3.2

				Scenario			
	Dismal	Very Low	Low	Fair	High	Very High	Excellent
NPV(A) ($)	40	60	80	100	120	140	160
NPV(B) ($)	0	40	80	120	160	200	240
Homogeneous	1/7	1/7	1/7	1/7	1/7	1/7	1/7
Increasing	1/28	2/28	3/28	4/28	5/28	6/28	7/28
Decreasing	7/28	6/28	5/28	4/28	3/28	2/28	1/28

---

[2]From now on we use the terms "risk" and "uncertainty" interchangeably. However, in a strict sense they are different concepts: uncertainty cannot be quantified, whereas risk can (Osuna 1997).

[3]Appendix 3A gives a review of the concepts of probability, expected value, and standard deviation.

TABLE 3.3

| | E(NPV) / Standard Deviation | | |
	Homogeneous	Increasing	Decreasing
A	100/40	120/34.6	80/34.6
B	120/80	160/69.3	80/69.3

Investors will be willing to accept a higher dispersion (i.e., standard deviation) if they are compensated with a larger $E(NPV)$. But how large must this compensation be? This would depend on how cautious the investors are. The more cautious they are, the larger the compensation [through a larger $E(NPV)$] they will demand for a given increase in standard deviation.

In the example of Table 3.3, project B shows a larger standard deviation than project A in all three probability distributions. Likewise, in all cases except one, the $E(NPV)$ of project B is larger than the $E(NPV)$ of project A. Only when the probability distribution is decreasing, will cautious investors prefer project A over project B, since both projects have the same $E(NPV)$, but project A has a smaller dispersion. In the other two cases, the best alternative is not clear. This would depend on the amount of compensation demanded for a larger standard deviation. In other words, it would depend on the degree of caution exhibited by individual investors.

3.2 THE UTILITY FUNCTION

Let us go back to our example and focus on projects A and B under the case of homogeneous probability distribution. For every investor, each NPV corresponds to a certain level of satisfaction. The measure of satisfaction for each level of NPV (or wealth) is called **utility.** The larger the NPV, the greater the utility, and vice versa.

The concept of utility under uncertainty is valid as long as the **axioms of cardinal utility** (Pratt 1964) hold. These axioms imply the following three assumptions about investor behavior:

Decision making is always rational.

Decision making requires all possible alternatives to be taken under consideration.

Everybody prefers more consumption to less.

Let us assume that the utility levels shown in Table 3.4 are associated with each net present value[4] for a specific investor.

---

[4]The absolute value of utility is not important; what is relevant is how utility varies with wealth. Utility levels are established from an initial arbitrary level associated with a certain wealth.

TABLE 3.4

				Scenario			
	Dismal	Very Low	Low	Fair	Good	Very High	Excellent
NPV(A)*	40	60	80	100	120	140	160
Utility(A)	10	30	48	62	70	74	76
NPV(B)*	0	40	80	120	160	200	240
Utility(B)	0	10	48	70	76	77	78
Probability	1/7	1/7	1/7	1/7	1/7	1/7	1/7

* Amounts are in dollars.

The objective must be to maximize satisfaction or utility, not merely wealth. Thus, the decision rule will be to choose the alternative with the **highest expected utility $E(U)$.**

The expected utility for our investor in project A, or $E(U_A)$, will be:

$$E(U_A) = \left(\frac{1}{7}\right)(10 + 30 + 48 + 62 + 70 + 74 + 76) = 53$$

and $E(U_B)$ will be:

$$E(U_B) = \left(\frac{1}{7}\right)(0 + 10 + 48 + 70 + 76 + 77 + 78) = 51$$

A is better than B because it has a larger expected utility. Observe that project A should be selected despite its lower $E(NPV)$. The reason is that the chosen utility function represents a cautious investor who prefers a lower $E(NPV)$ to a large dispersion.

3.2.1 The Attitude Toward Risk

How is cautiousness embedded in the utility function?

Focusing on project A for the homogeneous case, we see that it has an $E(NPV)$ of $100 (Table 3.3). Therefore, the utility of the expected value $U(E)$ is 62, which is higher than the expected value of utility $E(U)$ of 53. This is because the utility associated with a certain NPV of $100 (i.e., 62) should be larger than the weighted utility of a risky project with an $E(NPV)$ of $100. The investor who obtains a **certain** NPV of $100 instead of an **expected** NPV with the same value will always be more satisfied and experience higher utility. $U(E)$ is larger than $E(U)$ because every additional increment in NPV yields a smaller increase in utility. When this occurs, we say that the investor is **risk averse.**

Using wealth W instead of NPV, we can generalize that for every risk-averse investor:

$$U[E(W)] > E[U(W)]$$

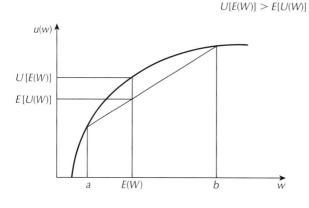

$U[E(W)] > E[U(W)]$ **Figure 3.1** Risk aversion.

This can be demonstrated graphically, as shown in Figure 3.1, where a and b represent two different levels of wealth (or *NPV*). Weighting them with their respective probabilities leads to an expected wealth $E(W)$ that corresponds to a certain utility of $U[E(W)]$ on the utility curve. Additionally, a and b also have their own utilities on the utility curve. Expected utility $E[U(W)]$ is obtained by weighting these utilities with their probabilities. When utility grows slower than wealth—in other words, when the utility curve is **concave**—we have a risk-averse investor, and it is shown that $U[E(W)]>E[U(W)]$.

When we are working with continuous probability distributions the former values are given by

$$E(W) = \int_{-\infty}^{+\infty} W f(W)dW$$

where $f(W)$ is the probability distribution of wealth

$$E[U(W)] = \int_{-\infty}^{+\infty} U(W)f(W)dW$$

where $U(W)$ is the utility function

Risk aversion depends on the shape of the utility curve: the more concave the curve, the higher the risk aversion. As the utility curve becomes increasingly concave, the compensation required to the investor in the form of incremental expected wealth is larger for a given increase in dispersion.

Although less common, it is also possible for an investor to display risk neutrality or risk propensity. An investor whose utility under a risky situation is greater than under

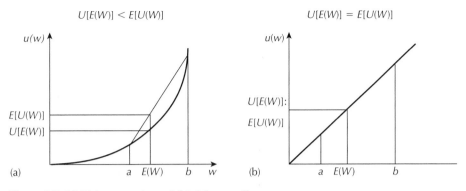

Figure 3.2 (a) Risk propensity and (b) risk neutrality.

a situation without uncertainty is said to be **risk propense.** In this case, the utility function is **convex** and it follows that[5]

$$U[E(W)] < E[U(W)]$$

An investor whose utility is the same in a risky situation as when there is no uncertainty is said to be **risk neutral.** Here the utility function is a straight line and it follows that

$$U[E(W)] = E[U(W)]$$

This can be demonstrated graphically, as shown in Figure 3.2.

In conditions of risk, the decision criterion is expected utility maximization. However, this requires the determination of the investor's utility function as well as the probability distribution of every investment opportunity. There are three problems with this procedure:

1. The assumptions behind the utility function under uncertainty (the axioms of cardinal utility) become questionable, especially in the context of developing countries.
2. Probability distributions of investment opportunities are difficult to find.
3. The determination of the utility function and the computation of expected utility may be cumbersome.

For now, we will not concern ourselves with problems 1 and 3, later on, however, we will propose a practical (though not theoretically robust) procedure, which obviates

---

[5]In real life we find risk propensity in games such as roulette, where expected net present value of wealth is always negative.

utility functions and simplifies computations considerably (see Chapter 5: Personal Investments).

We tackle the second problem by making a new assumption: that investment opportunities comply with the normal distribution.[6]

3.3 *NPV* AND RETURNS

NPV has been our yardstick for investment decisions. One of the main advantages of this method is that it takes into account both asset returns and the amount invested, as illustrated in Table 3.5, where projects *A* and *B* have the same return, but project *A*'s *NPV* is smaller because *B* involves a larger investment, while offering the same yield (20%).

NPV selects *B* over *A* precisely because it accounts not only for return, but also for the return obtained for each dollar invested. If the rate of return were used as the decision rule, projects *A* and *B* would be equally attractive. However, we know that this is not the case.

Despite the advantages of using *NPV,* for the remainder of Part I we will choose projects on the basis of their rate of return. Although this is not strictly correct, the rule is equivalent to *NPV* when there are no restrictions on the amounts invested. If in our example, *A* and *B* were not projects but financial instruments, say shares of firms *AAA* and *BBB,* we could purchase as many shares of each company as we wished, since generally financial markets do not impose limits on the amounts to invest in any asset. If we had $100,000 we could invest it in either stock and would obtain the same 20% return and the same *NPV* of $9090.9. Hence, both assets would be equivalent.

That is precisely the rationale behind our new assumption: that returns comply with the normal distribution and, based on the fact that this distribution can be specified with only two parameters (mean and standard deviation), **investments will be judged on the expected value and standard deviation of their returns.** *NPV* will not be used, since we suppose no limits for investing in any particular asset, as is common in financial markets. When we study the possibility of setting maximum or minimum limits on certain investments and give consideration to real investments, this restriction will be eliminated (see Chapter 5: Personal Investments).

TABLE 3.5

| Project | Time | | NPV (10%) | Return (%) |
	0	1		
A	−100	+120	$9.1	20
B	−1,000,000	+1,200,000	$90,909.1	20

---

[6]Appendix 3B offers a description of the normal probability distribution.

TABLE 3.6

Asset	E(R) (%)	σ (%)
A	5	2
B	8	4
C	10	7
D	15	6

Under the normal distribution, expected utility becomes a function of return R (instead of wealth W), and of the parameters of the distribution: mean (μ) and standard deviation (σ):

$$E(U) = \int_{-\infty}^{+\infty} U(R_i) \cdot f(R_i, \mu, \sigma) dR$$

Investment opportunities can be displayed in a graph with expected returns on the vertical axis and standard deviation on the horizontal axis. Let us assume the assets with their respective parameters as shown in Table 3.6.

This can be demonstrated graphically, as shown in Figure 3.3.

3.4 CHOOSING THE BEST INVESTMENT

We were able to represent investment opportunities by their expected return and standard deviation on a two-dimensional graph. Now the same must be done with the utility function. With both assets and utility function on the same diagram, the selection of the investment opportunity which maximizes expected utility is straight-forward.

Let us start by determining a measure of expected utility in the expected return–standard deviation space: the **indifference curves**.

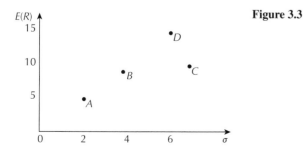

Figure 3.3

3.4.1 Indifference Curves

We assume that investors are risk averse (which is more reasonable than assuming risk propensity or risk neutrality). We found before that utility curves are concave for risk-averse investors, but these curves come from utility as a function of wealth and we need them as a function of the expected value and standard deviation of returns (see Figure 3.4).

Centering on an expected return $E(R)$, expected utility can be computed in its vicinity for different levels of dispersion. Note that for Dispersion 1 in Figure 3.4 we get $E[U(R)_1]$ and for Dispersion 2 we get $E[U(R)_2]$, and the second expected utility is larger than the first. This is logical for every expected return: the larger the dispersion, the lower expected utility must be for a risk-averse investor (i.e., for a concave utility function).

Focusing on Dispersion 2, if we want to obtain $E[U(R)_1]$ with this dispersion, expected return must diminish. This is another reasonable conclusion, given that we want to achieve the (lower) expected utility of a higher dispersion level for any dispersion, but this can happen only if the expected return is reduced.

Finally, let us get back to Dispersion 2 and ask what must be done to keep the same expected utility when dispersion is raised. Naturally, expected return will have to be increased as well, since this is the only way to keep the same utility when risk increases.

Recalling that the standard deviation is our measure of dispersion, we can draw the following conclusions:

- For the same expected return, the larger the standard deviation the lower the expected utility, and vice versa.
- For the same standard deviation, the larger the expected return the larger the expected utility, and vice versa.
- For the same expected utility, the larger the standard deviation the larger the expected return, and vice versa.

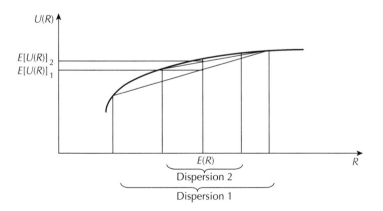

Figure 3.4 Utility and indifference curves for risk aversion.

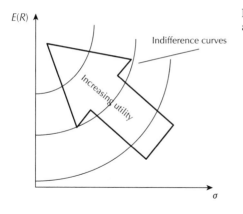

Figure 3.5 Indifference curves for risk aversion.

Now we can draw the family of so-called indifference curves in the expected return–standard deviation space. They are named indifference curves because on every point on a particular curve the investor attains the same expected utility hence is "indifferent."

To conform to the foregoing conclusions, such curves can have only the shape shown in Figure 3.5. Notice that the indifference curves of risk-averse investors are convex in a graph of expected return versus standard deviation.

A couple of comments must be made. As we move upward and to the left, utility curves of higher expected utility are reached. Also, the higher the investor's risk aversion, the larger will have to be the additional expected return for each increment of standard deviation to stay in the same indifference curve. Therefore, **the larger the risk aversion, the steeper the indifference curves, and vice versa.**

Now we place the investment opportunities and the indifference curves in the same graph and select the alternative that maximizes expected utility. Using the same assets we had before and for an arbitrary set of indifference curves, the preferred investment opportunity can be visualized as shown in Figure 3.6, where *B* is the

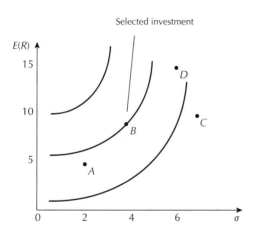

Figure 3.6 Utility maximization.

investment opportunity with the largest expected utility for the given family of indifference curves.

3.5 LIMITATIONS OF THE NORMAL DISTRIBUTION

Though the normal distribution greatly simplifies the investment decision process under uncertainty, it has two important limitations. The first limitation relates to the range of possible returns, and the second one to a failure in the selection process when real returns are not normally distributed.

3.5.1 Range of Returns

The range of possible values for the normal distribution extends from $-\infty$ to $+\infty$. Given that it is not possible to lose more than the total amount invested, returns below -100% are not feasible and all probabilities to the left of this point become unrealistic. Nevertheless, since cumulative probabilities below -100% tend to be small compared with the rest of the distribution, this does not seem to be a serious problem.

3.5.2 Nonnormal Returns

A more delicate problem is found when return distributions are not normal. Under such conditions, the optimization process can be erroneous. Imagine two assets with the returns and scenarios as shown in Table 3.7, where B's returns are either equal to A's or superior. Therefore, as long as the investor prefers a higher return, B will be chosen over A, irrespective of the utility function or the shape of the indifference curves.

Let us see what happens when these assets are compared on a risk–return graph. Assuming that all scenarios are equally likely (i.e., a homogeneous probability distribution), the parameters are as shown in Table 3.8.

This can be demonstrated graphically, as shown in Figure 3.7. Now the best alternative is not obvious. Depending on the individual's risk aversion, an investor could prefer either A or B. This is a clear failure, since we saw before that B will always be preferred over A, independent of the degree of risk aversion.

TABLE 3.7

| Asset | Returns (%) for Five Scenarios | | | | |
	Very Low	Low	Fair	High	Very High
A	0	2	4	6	8
B	0	4	8	12	16

TABLE 3.8

	A	B
$E(R)$	4	8
σ	3.16	6.32

This deficiency would not be relevant if returns were normal. Unfortunately, there is evidence that at least for stocks, return distributions are symmetrical but not normal. Instead they show "fat tails" and infinite variance (Fama 1965), as in Figure 3.8. Even if normality is discarded, it can be shown that mean–variance representation is acceptable as long as investors have **quadratic** utility functions. The general form of a quadratic utility function is:

$$U(W) = aW - bW^2$$

where, W is wealth, $U(W)$ is utility as a function of wealth, a and b are constants.

Unluckily, quadratic utility does not make much intuitive sense. For instance, it implies that an investor with total wealth of $1 million who sees that wealth decreasing by $250,000 (25% of the person's wealth) will lose more utility than the same person starting with a smaller wealth of, say $500,000 and losing $125,000 (25% as well). This does not seem reasonable, since we would expect that the greater the wealth, the smaller the loss in utility for the same proportional decrease in wealth.

In sum, the mean–variance representation is not correct if the real distribution of returns is not normal. In spite of this, we will accept the assumption that returns are normally distributed for two reasons: (1) the normal distribution is still an acceptable model for returns, and (2) the normal distribution considerably simplifies investment decision analysis.

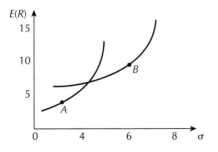

Figure 3.7 Failure of the normal distribution.

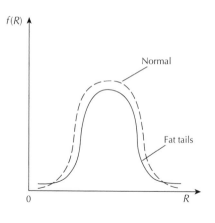

Figure 3.8 Symmetrical distribution with fat tails.

3.6 CONCLUSIONS

- We assume independence between consumption and investment decisions.
- Investment decisions under uncertainty depend on the likelihood of each possible *NPV*, on the alternatives being considered, and on the degree of caution exercised by the investor.
- A utility function under risk is defined. It depends on investor's wealth and compliance with the "axioms of cardinal utility."
- The concavity of the utility function is a measure of the degree of risk aversion. The greater the concavity, the larger the risk aversion, and vice versa.
- The decision rule for investment decisions under uncertainty is the maximization of the expected utility of the investor. There are three problems with this rule: (1) lack of realism of the axioms of cardinal utility, especially in developing countries; (2) the need to estimate the distribution of returns for every investment opportunity; and (3) the tendency to be cumbersome of the determination of the utility function and of expected utility. In this chapter we deal with the second concern, addressing the other two in later chapters.
- It is assumed that returns follow the normal distribution. One advantage of this distribution is that it can be defined with just two parameters: the mean and the standard deviation of returns.
- Return takes the place of *NPV* as the decision criterion for investment decisions. This, together with the normal distribution assumption, permits the characterization of every investment by its expected value and standard deviation of returns.
- Indifference curves on the mean–standard deviation space stem from the utility function. It is assumed that investors are risk averse, which implies that indifference curves are convex and that the higher the slope, the greater the risk aversion.
- The maximum expected utility choice is found by representing investment opportunities together with the indifference curves in a mean–standard deviation graph.

- The assumption of normality of returns creates some problems, and in certain instances can lead to mistakes.

QUESTIONS AND PROBLEMS

1. What must be the range of values of **X,** as shown in Table P3.1, so that a conservative investor always prefers *B* to *A*?

TABLE P3.1

	E(NPV)	σ
A	350	210
B	540	X

2. Under what conditions is expected *NPV* maximization equivalent to expected utility maximization?

3. Expected *NPV* maximization is equivalent to expected return maximization when the projects have the same life and the amounts invested are equal. Discuss.

4. In this chapter we have replaced the *NPV* rule for expected return maximization. Under what circumstances is this substitution valid?

5. Tell whether each of the following statements is true or false for risk-averse investors.
   (a) For the same expected return, the smaller the standard deviation the lower the expected utility.
   (b) For the same expected utility, the larger the standard deviation the larger the expected return.
   (c) The smaller the risk aversion, the steeper the indifference curves.

6. Why can the normal distribution lead to erroneous conclusions when one is selecting among risky investment opportunities?

7. Accepting the normal distribution as a reliable measure of the relationship between risk and return, what can a risk-averse investor conclude about the four investment opportunities shown in Table P3.7? Can any of them be discarded? Is any one clearly superior to the others?

TABLE P3.7

	A	B	C	D
E(R)	5	5	7	8
σ	3	6	3	6

APPENDIX 3A

Probability, Expected Value, and Standard Deviation

We begin with a look at the concept of probability and its effect on the attractiveness of investment projects.

3A.1 THE CONCEPT OF PROBABILITY

We live in a world characterized by uncertainty. We do not know what fate has in store for us, but we can hypothesize about different probable outcomes. Each such outcome is termed a scenario. Probability is the measure that allows us to assign a "weight" to each scenario. Let us say there are n scenarios that we call $X_1, X_2, X_3, \ldots, X_n$, and $P(X_i)$ is defined as the probability of scenario X_i.

Probabilities are ruled by the following axioms:

- The probability of a scenario or event is never negative and never larger than 1, that is,

$$O \leq P(X_i) \leq 1$$

- The probability that any one of the possible events or scenarios occurs is 1, that is,

$$\sum_{1}^{n} P(X_i) = 1$$

3A.2 PROBABILITY DISTRIBUTION

Given the foregoing axioms, it is possible to allocate probabilities to each scenario. The distribution of these probabilities across different scenarios leads us to a **probability distribution.** Probability distributions are **continuous** when they are assigned to infinite scenarios.

3A.3 EXPECTED VALUE

Expected value is an average of the values corresponding to each scenario weighted by their respective probabilities. When talking about expected *NPV* of project *A*, we will designate it as $E(NPV_A)$.

3A.4 STANDARD DEVIATION

The **standard deviation** σ is the most common measure of dispersion and is computed as the square root of the expected value of the squared differences between each value and the expected value. Mathematically,

$$\sigma = \sqrt{\sum_{1}^{n} P(X_i)[X_i - E(X_i)]^2}$$

Variance (σ^2) is defined as the square of the standard deviation.

The standard deviation and variance are always nonnegative because squared amounts are used to calculate them.

APPENDIX 3B

The Normal Distribution

The normal distribution is continuous and has the following characteristics:

- The distribution is symmetric around the mean.
- It ranges from $-\infty$ to $+\infty$
- It is defined by two parameters: mean μ and standard deviation σ (or variance).[7]
- The range between one standard deviation to the left and one standard deviation to the right of the mean comprises approximately 68% of possible events.
- The range between two standard deviations to the left and two standard deviations to the right of the mean includes approximately 95% of possible events.

The fact that the distribution can be defined with two parameters is key, since the only necessary information to calculate expected utility, in addition to the investor's utility function, is the expected value and standard deviation of returns. A normal distribution curve is as shown in Figure 3B.1.

---

[7]There are other distributions that require more than two parameters to be defined.

The normal distribution is given by the following formula:

$$f(y) = \frac{\exp[(y - m)^2/2s^2]}{s\sqrt{2\pi}}$$

where $f(y)$ is the probability distribution of "y," $s > 0$, $-\infty < m < +\infty$, and $-\infty < y < +\infty$.

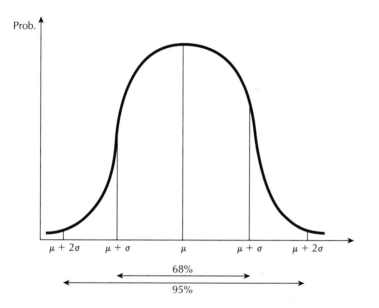

Figure 3B.1 The normal distribution.

CHAPTER 4

THE BENEFITS OF DIVERSIFICATION

> "To the extent that mathematical rules relate to reality, they are not true. To the extent that such rules are true, they do not relate to reality."
>
> —ALBERT EINSTEIN

In Chapter 3 we established that the maximization of expected utility is the basic rule that guides investment decisions. We also developed a procedure to select the best business opportunity from a range of available options. In this chapter we introduce portfolio theory by considering the possibility of taking advantage of the benefits of diversification by participating in more than one investment at the same time.[1] The reader who feels comfortable with this theory can proceed directly to Chapter 5: Personal Investments.

4.1 BUILDING INVESTMENT PORTFOLIOS

Let us consider the two assets with their corresponding returns under different scenarios as shown in Table 4.1. These returns are clearly related. An increase in X_1's return corresponds to an increase in X_2's return. Similarly, a decrease in X_1's returns corresponds to a decrease in X_2's returns. In this case, returns on one asset will give us information on what will happen with the other asset. This is because both assets are significantly **correlated.**

TABLE 4.1

Asset	Returns (%) for Five Scenarios (probability)				
	I (0.2)	II (0.2)	III (0.2)	IV (0.2)	V (0.2)
X_1	12	10	20	3	15
X_2	18	16	30	8	22

---

[1]We will not consider the possibility of bankruptcy or of the loss of the investment in one or more assets.

TABLE 4.2

Asset	μ	σ
X_1	12	6.28
X_2	18.8	8.07

The **covariance** is a measure of correlation. Computation of the covariance between X_1 and X_2 requires their means and standard deviations, as shown in Table 4.2. The covariance is computed as follows:

$$\text{Cov}(X_1,X_2) = 0.2 \, [(12 - 12)(18 - 18.8) + (10 - 12)(16 - 18.8) +$$
$$(20 - 12)(30 - 18.8) + (3 - 12)(8 - 18.8) + (15 - 12)(22 - 18.8)] = 40.4$$

The covariance is positive because these returns move in the same direction. If the returns had moved in opposite directions, the covariance would have been negative.

The **correlation coefficient** ρ is another measure of correlation. It can be shown that the correlation coefficient always ranges between a minimum of -1 and a maximum of $+1$. In our example, the correlation coefficient is

$$\rho_{12} = \frac{40.4}{(6.28)(8.07)} = 0.995$$

This value is very close to the upper limit of $+1$, meaning that there is a strong positive relationship between the returns on X_1 and X_2.

An **investment portfolio** is the set of assets that comprise an investment. For example, an investment of $100 in asset A, $200 in asset B, and $100 in asset C corresponds to a $400 investment portfolio with 25% in A, 50% in B, and 25% in C.

Say a percentage of w_1 of our money is invested in asset 1 and a proportion of w_2 in asset 2. This represents an investment portfolio P in assets 1 and 2. The expected value of this portfolio $E(P)$ is:

$$E(P) = w_1\mu_1 + w_2\mu_2$$

where μ_1 and μ_2 are the expected returns of assets 1 and 2, respectively.
Then σ_P^2, the variance of portfolio P, is given by:

$$\sigma_P^2 = w_1^2\sigma_1^2 + 2w_1w_2\sigma_{12} + w_2^2\sigma_2^2$$

where σ_{12} is the covariance and σ_1 and σ_2 are the standard deviations associated with the returns.

If in our example 50% of the money is invested in X_1 and 50% in X_2, the expected return and variance of the portfolio will be:

$$E(P) = (0.5)(12) + (0.5)(18.8) = 10.4$$

$$\sigma_P^2 = (0.5)^2(6.28)^2 + 2(0.5)(0.5)(40.4) + (0.5)^2(8.07)^2 = 46.34$$

In general, when there are n assets, the expected return and variance of a portfolio are computed as follows:

$$E(P) = \sum_{i=1}^{n} w_i \mu_i$$

$$\sigma_P^2 = \sum_{i=1}^{n} \sum_{j=1}^{n} w_i w_j \sigma_{ij}$$

In matrix form,

$$\mu_P = \mathbf{W}' \cdot \mu$$

$$\sigma_P^2 = \mathbf{W}' \cdot \mathbf{V} \cdot \mathbf{W}$$

where $\mathbf{W}$ is the vector of proportions invested in each asset, μ is the vector of expected returns, and $\mathbf{V}$ is the covariance matrix.

4.2 PORTFOLIO RISK AND RETURN

Imagine two assets with the returns as shown in Table 4.3, with corresponding parameters in Table 4.4. If all our money is invested in asset 1, the expected return is 9 and the standard deviation 8.03. If all our money is invested in 2, these values are 5.4 and 9.86, respectively. If half the money is invested in each asset, it seems the following values would be obtained,

$$\mu = \frac{9 + 5.4}{2} = 7.2$$

$$\sigma = \frac{8.03 + 9.86}{2} = 8.94$$

TABLE 4.3

	Returns (%) for Five Scenarios (probability)				
Asset	I (0.2)	II (0.2)	III (0.2)	IV (0.2)	V (0.2)
1	20	3	15	2	5
2	3	−5	20	10	−1

TABLE 4.4

Asset	μ	σ^2	σ	σ_{12}	ρ
1	9	64.5	8.03	23.4	+0.3
2	5.4	97.3	9.86		

Let us see if this result holds. Applying the formulas we saw before, we write

$$\mu = (0.5)(9) + (0.5)(5.4) = 7.2$$

$$\sigma^2 = (0.5)^2(64.5) + 2(0.5)(0.5)(23.4) + (0.5)^2(97.3) = 52.15$$

$$\sigma = 52.15 = 7.22$$

Therefore, the expected value is the weighted average of returns, but this is not so with the standard deviation. Further, we see that the covariance plays an important role in portfolio variance; that is, the lower the covariance, the lower the standard deviation and vice versa.[2]

4.2.1 The Effect of a Change in Correlation

The maximum standard deviation occurs when the correlation is $+1$. Let us assume for now that the correlation is $+1$. The covariance will be

$$\sigma_{12} = \rho_{12}\sigma_1\sigma_2 = +1(8.03)(9.86) = +79.22$$

And the standard deviation,

$$\sigma^2 = (0.5)^2(64.5) + 2(0.5)(0.5)(79.22) + (0.5)^2(97.3) = 80.06$$

$$\sigma = \sqrt{80.6} = 8.94$$

This is exactly **equal to the weighted average of the standard deviations.** When the correlation is $+1$, the standard deviation of a portfolio is equivalent to the weighted average of the standard deviations of its assets. If the correlation is less than $+1$, the standard deviation is smaller. The minimum standard deviation will take place when the correlation is -1.

The results obtained for different correlations in our portfolio are shown in Table 4.5. This can be demonstrated graphically, as shown in Figure 4.1. As the correlation decreases, so does the standard deviation, whereas the mean is not altered. When two

---

[2]An understanding of the concepts of covariance and correlation is necessary for a thorough comprehension of this chapter. A summary is offered in Appendix 4A.

TABLE 4.5

ρ	μ	σ
+1	7.2	8.94
+0.3	7.2	7.22
0	7.2	6.36
−1	7.2	0

assets that are less than perfectly correlated are combined, the total risk of the portfolio falls below the weighted risk of its assets. This is referred to as the benefit of **diversification**.[3]

4.2.2 The Effect of Changing the Proportions

In the preceding exercise half the money was always invested in each asset. We will now assume that the proportions invested in the two assets can vary. Going back to our example, and keeping the original correlation of +0.30, the mean and standard deviations can be found for different proportions invested in each asset, as shown in Table 4.6.

This can be demonstrated graphically, as shown in Figure 4.2.

4.2.3 Short Positions

So far, we have not considered negative investments in any asset. But such situations are possible.

When we deposit money in a bank we encounter a negative cash flow at the beginning, with the expectation of a positive cash flow in the future. However, when we take a loan, the situation is reversed.

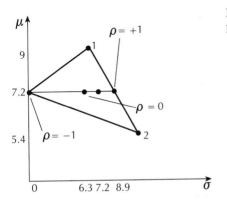

Figure 4.1 Portfolio risk and return: constant proportions and variable correlations.

---

[3]Notice that when the correlation is −1, the standard deviation is zero. This makes sense because if both assets have a perfect negative correlation it will always be possible to find a no-risk combination between them.

TABLE 4.6

Portfolios		Parameters	
w_1	w_2	μ	σ
0	1	5.4	9.86
0.2	0.8	6.12	8.50
0.4	0.6	6.84	7.52
0.6	0.4	7.56	7.07
0.8	0.2	8.28	7.26
1	0	9	8.03

Take the case of non-dividend-paying stock. A purchase of such stock leads to a negative cash flow to begin with. It also entails the expectation of selling at a higher price and realizing a positive cash flow sometime in the future. This makes the transaction similar to a bank deposit.

We could also use a stock to devise something that is similar to a bank loan. The share could be borrowed with a view to returning it at the end of a certain time period. Once it is in possession, the share could be sold, thus producing a positive cash flow (in the beginning). At the end of the time period the share would be bought from the stock market and given back to its owner, and thus the cash flow would become negative. As in the case of the bank loan, a positive cash flow is achieved at the beginning and a negative one at the end.

When an asset is sold with the intention of buying it back at a later date, it is said that a **short (or negative) position** has been taken on the asset. Short positions are common in advanced countries, but they are difficult to realize in most emerging countries because the financial markets are less developed. In the more general case, when an asset is purchased with the intention of selling it at a later date, it is said that a **long (or positive) position** has been taken on the asset.

When short positions are feasible the curve shown in Figure 4.2 is not truncated but extends to infinity, as in Figure 4.3.

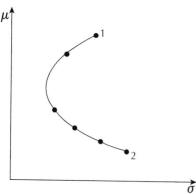

Figure 4.2 Portfolio risk and return: variable proportions and constant correlation.

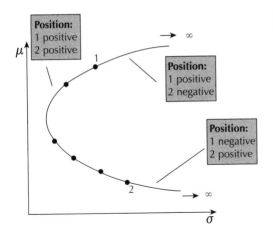

Figure 4.3 Portfolio risk and return with short positions.

Let us find the standard deviation as a function of the mean in our example for the case of a $1 portfolio, where $w is invested in asset 1 and $(1 − w) in asset 2:

$$\mu_P = w\mu_1 + (1 - w)\mu_2 = 9w + 5.4(1 - w)$$

$$\mu_P^2 = w^2\sigma_1^2 + 2w(1 - w)\sigma_{12} + (1 - w)^2\sigma_2^2$$
$$= 64.5w^2 + 46.8w(1 - w) + 97.3(1 - w)^2$$

Solving for σ_p

$$\sigma_P^2 = 8.87\,\mu_P^2 - 136.85\mu_P + 577.62$$

$$\sigma_P = \sqrt{8.87\mu_P^2 - 136.85\mu_P + 577.62}$$

It can be shown that the last equation corresponds to a hyperbola.

We have seen how the standard deviation and the correlation interact when the invested proportions are held constant. We have also seen how the means and standard deviations vary when the proportions are altered but the correlation is fixed. Finally, we learned what happens when short positions are attainable. A family of curves similar to that in Figure 4.3 can be drawn for different correlation levels between +1 and −1, as shown in Figure 4.4.

4.2.4 Portfolios with More than Two Assets

The number of possible portfolios grows considerably when more than two assets are available. But always, the point is to identify the most favorable combinations of assets—those with the highest expected returns and lowest standard deviations. For example, if we have two portfolios with a 10% expected return but one of them has a larger standard deviation, we must discard that portfolio and choose the less risky one.

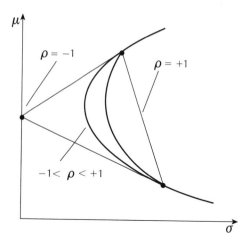

Figure 4.4 Family of curves.

Usually, the task of choosing the right portfolio is not easy, especially if the choice involves portfolios with several assets. However, in the case of portfolios with more than two assets, the set of optimal portfolios follows a curve that is similar to the one obtained with two assets. The difference between the two cases is that as more assets are included, the curve tends to open up, and it is possible to get larger expected returns for the same standard deviations (or smaller standard deviations for the same expected returns).[4] Note how the curves might change when more assets are included, as shown in Figure 4.5. Each of these curves is known as the **minimum variance frontier** for the corresponding group of attainable assets. Each point on the minimum variance frontier corresponds to the portfolio with the least variance for each expected return.[5]

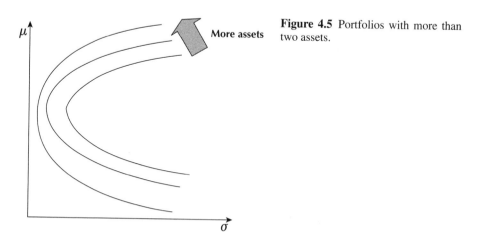

Figure 4.5 Portfolios with more than two assets.

---

[4]The curves do not open up if the risk–return characteristics of the newly included assets can be replicated with the existing assets.

[5]Although the risk–return relationship improves every time a new asset is added, this rate of increase tends to diminish. At a level of 20–30 assets, most of the benefits of diversification are already accomplished and adding new assets does not make much difference (Statman 1987).

Mathematically, the minimum variance frontier for "n" assets is computed by solving the following optimization problem:

$$Min \ \sigma_P^2$$

where

$$\sigma_P^2 = \sum_{i=1}^{n} \sum_{j=1}^{n} w_i w_j \sigma_{ij}$$

subject to

$$\sum_{1}^{n} w_i \mu_i = \mu_P$$

$$\sum_{1}^{n} w_i = 1$$

Refer to Appendix 4B for the solution.

It can be shown that the resulting function is also a hyperbola.

In this optimization problem it is assumed that there are no restrictions for investing in any asset. The more general case (i.e., when such restrictions are present) is treated in the next chapter.

The minimum variance frontier is important because it defines the set of best possible asset combinations.

4.2.5 Limits to Diversification

Up to now we assumed that all assets are tradable which allows us to optimize the minimum variance frontier by combining in portfolios any desired proportion of every possible asset. In reality everybody has **nonmarketable assets,** meaning assets the investor is not willing to trade with or cannot trade at all. For instance, it is not possible to sell the labor income for the rest of our lives in exchange for a lump sum, since slavery is outlawed. Some social compensations that are provided or regulated by governments cannot be sold either, such as social security, health benefits, or retirement plans. Similarly, many investors will not consider their own home as another asset that might eventually drop from their investment portfolio.

The presence of nonmarketable assets supposes minimum variance frontiers that are less optimal than otherwise. Nonmarketable assets will be discussed again in Chapter 6: The Classical Model.

4.3 FINDING THE OPTIMUM PORTFOLIO

By combining the minimum variance frontier with the indifference curves, we can solve the optimization problem for an individual investor. This can be visualized graphically as shown in Figure 4.6. The solution is evident. The optimum portfolio is the one that

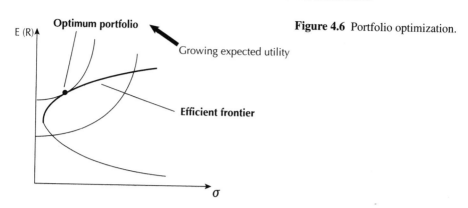

Figure 4.6 Portfolio optimization.

maximizes expected utility, and is represented by the contact point between the minimum variance frontier and the highest indifference curve.

The property of convexity of indifference curves guarantees that the optimum portfolio will always rest on the upper branch of the minimum variance frontier. This upper branch is the **efficient frontier,** and it corresponds to the set of portfolios with maximum expected return for each level of standard deviation.

The mathematical approach to this problem follows: Max E(U), where

$$E(U) = \int_{-\infty}^{+\infty} U(R_1) f(R_i, \mu, \sigma) dR$$

$U(R_1) = inventor's\ utility\ function$
$f(R_i, \mu, \sigma) = normal\ distribution\ of\ returns$

subject to

$$\sigma_P = g(\mu_P),\ representing\ the\ minimum\ variance\ frontier$$

At this point we conclude with the formal presentation of the portfolio optimization problem. However, this procedure has practical limitations because it involves the determination of the individual utility function of every investor. In the following chapter, we will visit an alternative methodology that is based on the probability distribution of returns. Although it is not as theoretically robust as the utility maximization approach, it is easier to apply in practice.

4.4 CONCLUSIONS

- A portfolio refers to the set of assets included in an investment.
- The expected return of a portfolio is the weighted average of the expected returns of the assets included.

- The standard deviation of the return of a portfolio is less than or equal to the weighted average of the standard deviations of the returns of its assets.
- The lower the correlation between assets, the farther away the standard deviation of a portfolio will be from the weighted average of the standard deviation of its assets, and vice versa.
- For any number of assets, it is possible to find all the portfolios with the minimum standard deviation for each level of expected return. This set of portfolios is termed the minimum variance frontier.
- The lower the correlation between assets, the closer the apex of the minimum variance frontier to the axis of expected returns, and vice versa.
- Portfolios with standard deviations as large as desired can be obtained when it is possible to take short positions.
- The more numerous the assets, the wider the minimum variance frontier tends to be, and the larger the maximum expected return for each level of standard deviation (or equivalently, the lower the minimum standard deviations for each level of expected return) generally is.
- The upper branch of the minimum variance frontier is the efficient frontier.
- The optimum portfolio for a particular investor can be determined by combining the efficient frontier with the indifference curves.

QUESTIONS AND PROBLEMS

1. A portfolio consisting of assets A and B is built with correlation 0.8. Are the following statements true or false?
   (a) The expected return of the portfolio equals the weighted average of the expected returns of assets A and B.
   (b) The standard deviation of the portfolio equals the weighted average of the standard deviations of assets A and B.
   (c) The larger the correlation between A and B, the larger the standard deviation of the portfolio.

2. Under what conditions does the standard deviation of a portfolio equal the weighted average of the standard deviation of its assets?

3. Under what conditions is it possible to build a no-risk portfolio by combining two assets with positive standard deviation?

4. Explain how a negative amount can be invested in a stock.

5. It is theoretically possible to build portfolios with expected returns as high as we wish whenever negative amounts can be invested without restrictions in any asset. Is this statement true?

6. Tell whether each of the following statements is true or false.
   (a) Each position on the minimum variance frontier represents a portfolio with the minimum possible variance for the corresponding level of expected return.

(b) On the minimum variance frontier it is possible to find portfolios with the same standard deviation and different expected returns.

(c) On the minimum variance frontier it is possible to find portfolios with the same expected return and different standard deviations.

7. For risk-averse investors all optimal portfolios rest on:

(a) the minimum variance frontier.

(b) the efficient frontier.

Are these statements true or false?

APPENDIX 4A

Covariance and Correlation

4A.1 COVARIANCE

The covariance between the returns of two assets X_1 and X_2, $Cov(X_1,X_2)$ is defined as follows:

$$Cov(X_1,X_2) = E[(X_1 - \mu_1)(X_2 - \mu_2)]$$

where μ_1 and μ_2 are the expected returns of X_1 and X_2, respectively.
Covariance is closely related to variance:

$$\sigma_X^2 = E(X - \mu_X)^2 = E[(X - \mu_X)(X - \mu_X)]$$

For this reason, covariance is also written as follows:

$$Cov(X,Y) = \sigma_{XY}$$

And the variance is sometimes expressed as a covariance:

$$Var(X) = Cov(X,X) = \sigma_{XX}$$

4A.1.1 The Covariance Matrix

When the number of assets is 3, the variance (σ_{11}, σ_{22}, σ_{33}) and the covariance (σ_{12}, σ_{13}, σ_{23}) between them is 3 in each case. If the number of assets increases to 4, the number of variances is also 4, while the number of covariances is 6. In general, when we consider "n" assets, we have n variances and $n(n - 1)/2$ covariances. The covariance matrix **V** represents the set of variances and covariances of a group of n assets as,

$$\mathbf{V} = \begin{vmatrix} \sigma_{11} & \sigma_{12} & \cdots & \sigma_{1n} \\ \sigma_{21} & \sigma_{22} & & \\ \vdots & & & \\ \sigma_{n1} & & \cdots & \sigma_{nn} \end{vmatrix}$$

The diagonal from the upper left to the lower right contains the variances, and the other values are the covariances. The covariances above and below the variance diagonal are identical since $\sigma_{ij} = \sigma_{ji}$.

4A.2 CORRELATION

The **correlation** ρ is another measure of the relationship between the returns of two assets. It is the covariance divided by the product of the standard deviations,

$$\rho_{12} = \frac{\text{Cov}(X_1, X_2)}{\sigma_1 \sigma_2} = \frac{\sigma_{12}}{\sigma_1 \sigma_2}$$

It can be shown that the correlation can never be less than -1 or more than $+1$. A positive correlation means that returns tend to move in the same direction. A negative correlation means that returns tend to move in opposite directions. A zero correlation implies that there is no relationship between the returns. The closer the correlation is to $+1$ or to -1, the closer the (positive or negative) relationship between the returns.

The covariance can take any positive or negative value, whereas the correlation is bounded between $+1$ and -1. This is why the correlation has a clearer meaning than the covariance. A correlation of $+1$ signifies a perfect positive relationship and a correlation of -1 a perfectly negative relationship, whereas the value of the covariance by itself conveys little information.

4A.3 THE CORRELATION MATRIX

As we saw in the case of the covariance, when we have "n" assets the correlation matrix **R** represents the corresponding set of correlations:

$$\mathbf{R} = \begin{vmatrix} \rho_{11} & \rho_{12} & \cdots & \rho_{1n} \\ \rho_{21} & \rho_{22} & & \\ \vdots & & & \\ \rho_{n1} & & \cdots & \rho_{nn} \end{vmatrix}$$

Here the upper left to lower right diagonal contains the correlation of every asset with itself, which is always $+1$.

The Minimum Variance Frontier for "n" Assets

The following variables and parameters are defined;

$\mathbf{V}$	covariance matrix
$\mathbf{e}$	unit vector
μ	vector of expected returns
$\mathbf{W}$	vector of invested proportions
$\mathbf{I}$	identity matrix
σ_P^2	portfolio variance
μ_W	expected return of portfolio $\mathbf{W}$

We know that

$$\sigma_P^2 = \mathbf{W'} \cdot \mathbf{V} \cdot \mathbf{W}$$
$$\frac{\partial \sigma_P^2}{\partial \mathbf{W}} = 2 \cdot \mathbf{V} \cdot \mathbf{W}$$

The problem is stated as follows:

$$Min\ \sigma_P^2 \quad \text{subject to} \quad \mu' \cdot \mathbf{W} = \mu_w$$
$$\mathbf{e'} \cdot \mathbf{W} = 1$$

or equivalently

$$\begin{vmatrix} \mu' \\ \mathbf{e'} \end{vmatrix} \cdot \mathbf{W} = \begin{vmatrix} \mu_w \\ 1 \end{vmatrix}$$

Let us define,

$$\lambda = \begin{vmatrix} \lambda_1 \\ \lambda_2 \end{vmatrix}$$

The Lagrange multiplier is

$$L = \mathbf{W'} \cdot \mathbf{V} \cdot \mathbf{W} - 2\lambda_1(\mu' \mathbf{W} - \mu_w) - 2\lambda_2(\mathbf{e'} \cdot \mathbf{W} - 1)$$

Deriving and equating to zero, we write

$$(\mathbf{V} \cdot \mathbf{W}) - (\lambda_1 \cdot \mu) - (\lambda_2 \cdot \mathbf{e}) = \mathbf{0} \rightarrow \mathbf{V} \cdot \mathbf{W} = |\mu \; \mathbf{e}| \cdot \lambda$$

Hence,

$$\mathbf{W} = \mathbf{V}^{-1} \cdot |\mu \; \mathbf{e}| \cdot \lambda$$

Premultiplying by $\begin{vmatrix} \mu' \\ \mathbf{e}' \end{vmatrix}$, we have

$$\begin{vmatrix} \mu' \\ \mathbf{e}' \end{vmatrix} \cdot \mathbf{W} = \begin{vmatrix} \mu' \\ \mathbf{e}' \end{vmatrix} \cdot \mathbf{V}^{-1} \cdot |\mu \quad \mathbf{e}| \cdot \lambda = \begin{vmatrix} \mu_W \\ 1 \end{vmatrix}$$

We define

$$\mathbf{A} \begin{vmatrix} \mu' \\ \mathbf{e}' \end{vmatrix} \cdot \mathbf{V}^{-1} \cdot |\mu \; \mathbf{e}| = \begin{vmatrix} a & b \\ b & c \end{vmatrix}$$

where

$$a = \mu' \cdot \mathbf{V}^{-1} \cdot \mu$$
$$b = \mathbf{e}' \cdot \mathbf{V}^{-1} \cdot \mu$$
$$c = \mathbf{e}' \cdot \mathbf{V}^{-1} \cdot \mathbf{e}$$

Then we have

$$\begin{vmatrix} \mu_W \\ 1 \end{vmatrix} = \mathbf{A} \cdot \lambda \rightarrow \lambda = \mathbf{A}^{-1} \cdot \begin{vmatrix} \mu_W \\ 1 \end{vmatrix}$$

where

$$\mathbf{A}^{-1} = \frac{1}{ac - b^2} \begin{vmatrix} c & -b \\ -b & a \end{vmatrix}$$

Therefore,

$$\mathbf{W} = \mathbf{V}^{-1} \cdot |\mu \; \mathbf{e}| \cdot \mathbf{A}^{-1} \cdot \begin{vmatrix} \mu_W \\ 1 \end{vmatrix}$$

which is the vector of weights of the portfolios on the minimum variance frontier.

CHAPTER 5

PERSONAL INVESTMENTS

"Information is a good in an uncertain world—it helps reduce uncertainty and identify new investment opportunities".

This chapter proposes a practical procedure for portfolio selection. This procedure will then be extended to allow for restrictions on certain investments and to permit the inclusion of real investments.

5.1 THE RELATIONSHIP BETWEEN PROBABILITY AND RETURN

Take the case of an investor who has a portfolio with the characteristics as shown in Table 5.1. Can the relationship between return and probability be utilized as a decision tool to aid portfolio selection in place of utility curves?

Suppose our investor wants to know the point x for a 5% probability of obtaining lower returns. The value of α (on the standardized normal distribution) for this probability is -1.65. The corresponding value for x will be[1]:

$$x = \mu - 1.65\sigma = 10 - (1.65)(5) = +1.75\%$$

This implies that there is a 5% probability of obtaining returns below $+1.75\%$ and a 95% probability of obtaining larger returns. The value of x serves as a measure of risk because it can be interpreted as a "minimum" return (given a 5% cutoff probability).

This is a practical (though not theoretically robust) method of portfolio selection that avoids the use of utility curves. An investor can select the desired combination of

TABLE 5.1

μ (%)	σ (%)
10	5

---

[1] An overview of the normal distribution and its relationship with the standardized normal distribution is offered in Appendix 5A.

returns on the basis of computed expected and minimum returns (using a selected cutoff probability) for a set of efficient portfolios.

In general, for any efficient portfolio (i.e., on the efficient frontier) with expected return μ and standard deviation σ, the cutoff point x for a given probability will be

$$x = \mu + \alpha\sigma$$

where α corresponds to the equivalent point on the standardized normal distribution for the given probability level.

5.2 PROBABILITIES, RETURNS, AND PORTFOLIO SELECTION

We have already examined how to choose portfolios based upon probabilities, returns, and the efficient frontier. We will now consider choices relating to asset selection when investment portfolios are being formed and offer some ideas about the estimation of the efficient frontier. An example of portfolio selection, when short positions are feasible and there are no restrictions in the proportions to be invested in any assets is shown. We will conclude with the more general case in which investment restrictions are present.

5.2.1 How Portfolios are Built in Practice

According to financial theory, a rational investor's portfolio should include many assets, both domestic and foreign, since this is the route to more favorable efficient frontiers (i.e., higher expected returns for each level of risk). However in practice, investment decisions do not reflect this rule: portfolios are neither as diversified nor as efficient as theory would suggest.

Instead, investors build portfolios according to layers of assets that are associated with particular goals and attitudes toward risk, and in which correlations between assets are overlooked. This trend is reinforced by the way many mutual fund companies inform their investors. For example, a Fidelity Investments brochure quoted by Statman (1999) describes how the risk of non-U.S. stocks appears in the portfolios of U.S. investors:

> Foreign investments involve risks that are in addition to those of US investments, including political and economic risks, as well as the risk of currency fluctuations. These risks may be magnified in emerging markets.

This statement clearly ignores the reduction in risk that can be achieved through diversification by including non-U.S. assets in a U.S. portfolio.

Even more, many investors are not familiar with the concept of the efficient frontier and only relatively more sophisticated investors apply the principles of portfolio theory. However, even members of this select group do not usually adhere strictly to these principles but instead base investment portfolio decisions on the following guidelines (Fisher & Statman 1997):

- Historical returns, variances, and correlations are not the only variables that are taken into consideration. Other factors such as the type of company, its image, and its competitiveness play an important role too. Although historical data are important, the key is to anticipate how risk and return will evolve in the future. Factors such as those suggested above help derive these expectations. This leads to a more comprehensive understanding of the choices.

- Many investors tend to accord greater weight to the variance of each asset than to its covariance with the rest of the portfolio. This is consistent with empirical studies that suggest that the variance of an asset is an important indicator of the return of the entire portfolio.

- Many investors are reluctant to accept efficient portfolios that are characterized by a strong concentration of a few assets. This appears to be a logical way for investors to guard against sudden unfavorable returns on particular assets (something that is ignored by the assumption of normality of returns).

- Investors tend to be cautious about statistical parameters on returns. This is justified because the composition of efficient portfolios is very sensitive to small alterations of the values of these parameters.

In reality, sophisticated investors treat the efficient frontier as the starting point in their decision-making process. Once the efficient frontier has been estimated, the investor makes adjustments in accordance with a particular investment strategy, individual expectations, additional information, and recommendations by financial specialists. Only then is the desired portfolio selected.

Additionally, upper and lower limits for both long and short positions in a number of assets are set up. The objective of identifying upper limits is to ameliorate the possible effect of unfavorable shocks. Restrictions on short positions make sense in emerging markets, where use of this financial strategy is restrained.

Lower limits are useful when we do not want drastic changes in an existing position. For instance, imagine a portfolio with a significant percentage in Latin American bonds and suppose that the region is in the midst of a financial crisis. A lower limit on this position might be advisable if we expect the prices of these securities to recover in the next few months.

Finally, we must not forget the role that financial derivatives (mainly futures and options) can play in managing portfolio risk. Although a comprehensive treatment of derivatives is beyond the scope of this book, we can say that these instruments make it possible to transfer part or all of the risk associated with certain asset prices (mostly for periods below one year) to other market participants.[2] Derivatives are usually a more cost-effective alternative to handling risk than the purchase or sale of assets.

In conclusion, portfolio selection is a complex and dynamic process, which depends on the economic conditions at every point in time in the different regions of the

---

[2]Chapter 9 (The Value of Flexibility) presents an introduction to option theory. For a general introduction to derivatives, the reader can refer to Brealey and Myers, (1996) or Ross, Westerfield, and Jaffe (1999). For a detailed exposition on the topic, Copeland and Weston (1988) and Hull (1997) are recommended.

world, the availability of information and its interpretation, as well as the investor's personal characteristics.[3]

Mutual Funds Mutual funds can be a cost-effective alternative means of achieving diversification in small portfolios. These funds consist of a large pool of resources invested in well-diversified financial assets with similar characteristics (referred to as an **asset class**), for instance: Southeast Asian stocks, high-grade European corporate bonds, or Latin American government debt.

Financial intermediaries such as commercial and investment banks manage mutual funds. These funds are ubiquitous in financial markets both in the developed world and in other markets. Small investors benefit from these funds because high diversification levels can be achieved within each asset class with a modest investment. Besides, the investor can rely on the financial expertise of the intermediary.

The Choice of the Investment Horizon In addition to selecting the asset classes, the investor must choose an investment horizon, that is, the time period for the investment. The investment strategy is expected to remain constant during this period.

The investment horizon depends on three factors:

1. The investor's expectations of changes in the capital markets
2. The actual movements in the capital markets
3. The investor's consumption and investment needs

If important events are expected in the markets or unexpected changes actually occur, the horizon must be shortened to permit more frequent adjustments to the investment strategy. Or if the investor is planning to retire or demands a higher cash income, the investment strategy and the time horizon will need to be revised.

Another key aspect is that the horizon has a close relationship with volatility. The longer the horizon, the lower will be the volatility. This is true for all asset classes, but the effect is more pronounced for the riskier securities. That is, the reduction in volatility due to a larger horizon is larger in shares than in bonds, and in emerging market instruments than in those from developed countries. This implies that the longer the horizon, the larger should be the weight of the riskier securities in the portfolio.

5.2.2 Determining the Efficient Frontier

Determining the efficient frontier, the first step in portfolio analysis, was relatively easy with only two assets because all portfolios were a simple combination of these two assets. All that was required was to vary the proportions invested in each asset and then to calculate the expected return and standard deviation of the corresponding portfolio.

The determination of the efficient frontier is more difficult when more than two assets are involved. This leads to a mathematical optimization problem that needs to be

---

[3]Portfolio management is a specialized topic and is not covered here. The interested reader can refer to Lederman and Klein (1994).

solved (see Appendix 4A). The situation is further complicated when there are restrictions on the proportions to be invested in certain assets. Fortunately, there are software programs in the marketplace that easily handle this problem for many assets.[4] These programs give us not only the expected returns and standard deviations of the efficient portfolios but their composition as well.

Parameter Estimation The first step in determining the efficient frontier is the computation of the corresponding asset parameters (i.e., expected returns, standard deviations, and correlation matrices). At first sight, this looks relatively simple. Historical returns for each asset must be collected and the parameters computed according to the procedure explained in Chapter 4.[5]

However, if the procedure stops at this point the results will almost always be quite imprecise. Thus, adjustments become necessary. Let us comment on this matter.

a. *The Future Is Not Necessarily Equal to the Past.* As mentioned before, investors realize that historical information alone is not sufficient. An exclusive reliance on it assumes that the historical efficient frontier is a good proxy for the future one. This is not a reasonable assumption, especially in the highly volatile environments of developing markets.

b. *The Parameters Must Be Consistent.* The relationship between expected risks and returns should make sense. The larger the expected return, the larger should the standard deviation be, and vice versa. Additionally, negative historical correlations must be viewed with suspicion: negative covariances are very rare in practice. We must be wary of all historical information that is not consistent.

As a point of reference: the historical (i.e., over decades) yearly return of the New York Stock Exchange stock index has been 8% above U.S. government Treasury bill yields. Therefore, at least in developed countries, the incremental return of stocks should be aligned with this historical result. On the other hand, the standard deviation of the same stock index has averaged 20% annually. These are both good reference points when one is estimating the volatility of assets (Hull 1997).

Historical yearly returns and standard deviations for different asset classes are as shown in Table 5.2 (Lederman & Klein 1994).

c. *Adjustments Are Almost Always Necessary.* If historical information is not a good proxy for the future, the expected returns and the correlation matrix must be adjusted according to expectations. As mentioned earlier, expectations are based on the recommendations provided by specialists (individuals and publications) and on the investor's intuition.

---

[4]The program used in this chapter is The Investment Portfolio, Version 1.0 (designed by Edwin J. Elton; Martin J. Gruber and Christopher R. Blake in association with Intellipro, Inc. Copyright © 1995 by John Wiley & Sons, Inc. Portions copyright © 1994 by Intellipro, Inc.) Prof. C. Harvey's web page offers a tool that draws the efficient frontier when there are no investment restrictions. See www.duke.edu/charvey/~camlinks.htm.

[5]A detailed exposition of this methodology can be found in statistics textbooks (e.g., Mendenhall, Scheaffer, & Wackerly 1981).

TABLE 5.2

Asset Class*	Return (%)	Standard Deviation (%)
Bonds		
Government, short term	6	1
Government, medium term	7	7
Government, long term	7.5	12
Corporate	7.5	11
Mortgage	10.5	10
Stocks		
Large corporations	14	20
Medium sized corporations	20	35
Real estate	7.5	14
European	15	23
Asian	16	30

* Asset classes are U.S. bonds and stocks unless otherwise indicated.

Source: "Global Asset Allocation," J. Lederman, R. Klein (Editors), © John Wiley & Sons. Translated with permission of John Wiley & Sons, Inc. All rights reserved.

An important point is that emerging country investors usually possess privileged information about their markets, and this information must be incorporated in the estimations.

d. *The Value of Parameters Can Shift Unexpectedly.* Parameter values can change abruptly and unexpectedly. The Asian financial crisis of 1997–98 is a case in point. Just after the crisis, the correlations between emerging and developed markets increased significantly.[6]

Although the parameters tend to be highly unstable, the growing interlinkage among different economies is contributing to a long-term trend in the direction of a gradual increase in correlations between all market returns.

e. *Sensitivity Analysis Is Always Advisable.* In practice, it is always beneficial to experiment with various efficient frontiers for different sets of parameters.[7]

In the following examples we assume a one-year time horizon and four classes of assets (each one of them is a specialized mutual fund), *X, Y, Z,* and *T.* However, the

---

[6]Beside, it has been found that the emerging market returns and the New York Stock Exchange Index (a popular proxy for the "market portfolio") have a dynamic relationship. Whenever the index has dropped dramatically (more than 10%), its correlation with emerging markets tends to increase (*The Economist* 1999a).

[7]A more formal way of estimating the parameters is through time series statistical methods. These methods are based on past trends as a springboard for predicting the future. However, this approach does not appear to be reliable for emerging countries, where the past frequently does not tell us much about the future and unpredictable shocks are always a possibility. Diebold (1998) offers an introductory approach to this methodology.

TABLE 5.3

Asset	μ (%)	σ (%)	Correlations			
			X	Y	Z	T
X	13.3	28.5	1	0.084	0.287	−0.107
Y	3.0	3.8	0.084	1	0.468	0.267
Z	6.2	11.5	0.287	0.468	1	−0.133
T	4.6	6.2	−0.107	0.267	−0.133	1

example could as easily include any number of assets or financial instruments. The corresponding parameters are shown in Table 5.3.

The first problem we face is the presence of a very large number of portfolios on the efficient frontier (since investment in each asset can vary by amounts as small as one cent). Thus, we have no choice but to begin working with a selected number of portfolios.

Imagine that the five portfolios shown in Table 5.4 are selected: A is the most conservative and E the most aggressive. Table 5.5 shows their respective compositions. Let us look at some practical cases based upon these results.

5.2.3 In the Absence of Any Restrictions

Assume that there are no restrictions at all to invest in any asset and that the investor wishes to invest $100,000 with a 5% cutoff probability. In other words, for each of the portfolios A, B, C, D, and E, we want to know the point for which there is a 5% probability of obtaining less favorable returns (and 95% probability of more favorable ones). We know that for 5% the corresponding value of α is 1.65. Then for portfolio A we have:

$$x_A = \mu_A - \alpha\sigma_A = 5.00 - (1.65)(4.6) = -2.59\%$$

Repeat the calculation for the other portfolios as shown in Table 5.6.

TABLE 5.4

Portfolio	μ (%)	σ (%)
A	5.00	4.6
B	6.00	5.9
C	7.00	7.2
D	8.00	8.8
E	9.00	10.4

TABLE 5.5

Portfolio	μ (%)	σ (%)	Composition (%)			
			X	Y	Z	T
A	5.00	4.6	+6.892	+26.490	+14.931	+51.687
B	6.00	5.9	+10.248	−7.603	+25.794	+71.561
C	7.00	7.2	+13.348	−39.096	+35.829	+89.920
D	8.00	8.8	+16.680	−72.947	+46.614	+109.653
E	9.00	10.4	+20.011	−106.789	+57.397	+129.381

A conservative investor would prefer portfolio A. For a 5% cutoff probability the "worst-case" scenario would be a loss of return of 7.59%, which translates into an income that is less than the expected income by $7590.

A much more aggressive investor is likely to prefer portfolio E, with a 9% expected return, 4% higher than the return on A. In exchange for this larger expected return, the investor will have to cope with a "worst-case" income loss (below the expected one) of $17,160. Each investor will select the most desirable portfolio depending on his or her aversion to risk.

If the investor was not able to decide over two portfolios, say B and C, one or more portfolios with intermediate expected returns and standard deviations would have to be determined, and the final portfolio would be chosen in a similar manner.

5.2.4 Restrictions on the Proportions Invested

Let us examine the situation in which there are restrictions on the proportions to be invested in some (or all) of the assets. First we will see what happens when short positions are not allowed. We will then generalize for the case in which there are other limits.

TABLE 5.6

Portfolio	μ (%)	σ (%)	x (%)*	$\mu-x$ (%)†	Value ($)‡
A	5.00	4.6	−2.590	+7.590	−7,590
B	6.00	5.9	−3.735	+9.735	−9,735
C	7.00	7.2	−4.880	+11.880	−11,880
D	8.00	8.8	−6.520	+14.520	−14,520
E	9.00	10.4	−8.160	+17.160	−17,160

* x represents the 5% point for each portfolio.
† $\mu-x$ shows the loss of return at each point.
‡ *Value* refers to the impact of this loss of return on the $100,000 invested.

---

[8]The same letters are used to designate the selected portfolios in the example discussed in connection with Tables 5.3–5.8. The corresponding portfolios have identical expected returns but not necessarily the same composition.

TABLE 5.7

Portfolio	μ (%)	σ (%)	x (%)	$\mu - x$ (%)	Value ($)
A	5.00	4.6	−2.59	+7.59	−7,590
B	6.00	6.0	−3.90	+9.90	−9,900
C	7.00	8.0	−6.20	+13.20	−13,200
D	8.00	11.0	−10.15	+18.15	−18,150
E	9.00	14.1	−14.26	+23.26	−23,260

When Short Positions are not Possible Table 5.7 shows what Table 5.6 would look like if short positions were not allowed.[8] For the same expected returns, the corresponding standard deviations are either equal to or greater than before, implying a less favorable efficient frontier. Naturally, the restriction on short positions must result in an efficient frontier that is lower than the one with no restrictions. Now both the conservative and the aggressive investors face possible lower expected returns. For instance, although A's expected return in the "worst-case" scenario is the same as before (−2.59%); the other portfolios show widening differences.[9]

Other Restrictions In addition to the impossibility of short positions, let us say also that no more than 25% of the portfolio can be invested in T and that at least 10% of the portfolio must be allocated to Y, as shown in Table 5.8. As was expected, the frontier becomes even less favorable with these new restrictions. The exercise can be repeated with as many restrictions as desired.

It bears repeating that the problem to be solved when there are restrictions on the proportions to be invested is more complex than the one confronted when no restrictions are present (see Appendix 4A). The optimization problem in the former case is one of quadratic programming with the following characteristics:

Min σ_P^2 where

$$\sigma_P^2 = \sum_{i=1}^{n} \sum_{j=1}^{n} w_i |w_j| \sigma_{ij}$$

subject to

$$\sum_{1}^{n} w_i |\mu_i| = \mu_P$$

$$a_i \leq w_i \leq b_i \text{ for each "}i\text{"}$$

---

[9]Both A portfolios have the same risk–return relationship. The reason is that in both cases the optimal portfolio requires long positions in every asset and the restriction on short positions is not a binding constraint. For all the other portfolios the situation is not the same: the optimal portfolios without restrictions demand short positions.

TABLE 5.8

Portfolio	μ (%)	σ (%)	x (%)	μ − x (%)	Value ($)
A	5.00	5.1	−3.410	+8.410	−8,410
B	6.00	7.0	−5.550	+11.550	−11,550
C	7.00	9.0	−7.850	+14.850	−14,850
D	8.00	11.5	−10.975	+18.975	−18,975
E	9.00	14.5	−14.925	+23.925	−23,925

5.3 BENEFITS AND COSTS OF A CONTROLLING STAKE

We have not factored in real investments into our analysis so far. However, many investors do have real investments, and they should be considered.[10]

The investor–entrepreneur holding a significant proportion of his portfolio in the stock of a single firm is a case in point. Companies with only one owner, those with just a few shareholders, and family-owned businesses could be included in this group. This type of investment introduces considerable rigidity in the portfolio because it is not possible to alter the investment position in the firm except by selling or purchasing shares. In most instances this implies considerable costs.

Let us go back to our example and assume that the investor has a total portfolio of $1 million of which $200,000 (20% of the portfolio) is invested in a wholly owned firm. The rest of the portfolio is invested in the same asset classes as before.

Our first problem entails the determination of the firm's parameters, that is, expected returns and standard deviation. However, these might not be too difficult to estimate because of the experience, knowledge, and the expectations of the entrepreneur. Let us assume that this is a relatively risky business with an expected return of 25% and standard deviation of 50%.

The main obstacle relates to the estimation of the firm's correlations with the other asset classes. The trial-and-error method of using different levels to assess the corresponding effect on the efficient frontier can be employed. However we might have a good starting point: the historical correlation of the returns of most emerging country businesses with securities traded in the developed world (the ones corresponding to our asset classes) has been quite small.

For instance, if the firm under analysis were a toy factory serving the local market, movements in the U.S. stock market or changes in the monetary policy of the European Central Bank should not significantly affect its profits. Our starting point might then be to assume zero correlation. Later we can see what occurs at higher levels of correlation.

---

[10]The assumption of return normality can be more problematic when one is considering real investment opportunities because bankruptcy considerations (see Chapter 3: The Impact of Risk) might cause the range of returns below −100% to be significant in many instances.

We can also run a regression of the firm's historical returns (or those of a closely related business) with the historical returns of each asset class. If the regression is given by

$$\tilde{R}_i = \hat{\alpha} + \hat{\beta}\ \tilde{x}_i + \tilde{e}_i$$

where $\tilde{x}_i$ are the historical returns of asset class i, $\tilde{e}_i$ is the error term, $\hat{\alpha}$ is the estimated return at the origin, $\hat{\beta}$ is the estimated regression coefficient, and $\hat{R}_i$ are the historical returns of the firm,
then,

$$\rho(R,x) = \frac{\hat{\beta}\ \sigma_x}{\sigma_R}$$

These correlations carry information about the past only. To the extent that the past is not a good proxy for the future, their value will serve more as a point of reference than as a reliable estimator.

Elaborating on the foregoing example, two different cases can be examined. First, we can examine the situation in which the investor is the sole owner of the firm. Second, we can look at a situation in which the investor controls the firm but does not fully own it.

5.3.1 Full Ownership of the Firm

Table 5.9 shows the corresponding parameters at a zero-correlation level. If short positions are not allowed and the entrepreneur holds the entire firm's shares, on the other hand, the results are as shown in Table 5.10. Table 5.11 allows us to assess the impact of the firm on the efficient frontier by comparing the results of Table 5.10 with the results of Table 5.7, obtained when there was no firm and short positions were not allowed.

Table 5.11 illustrates that the effect of the firm is significant. Without the firm, the most conservative portfolio (A) yielded a minimum loss of 2.59%. With the firm, its counterpart F can result in a negative result of 8.655%. However, this is compensated

TABLE 5.9

Asset	μ (%)	σ (%)	Correlations				
			X	Y	Z	T	Firm
X	13.3	28.5	1	0.084	0.287	−0.107	0.000
Y	3.0	3.8	0.084	1	0.468	0.267	0.000
Z	6.2	11.5	0.287	0.468	1	−0.133	0.000
T	4.6	6.2	−0.107	0.267	−0.133	1	0.000
Firm	25.00	50.00	0.000	0.000	0.000	0.000	1

TABLE 5.10

Portfolio	μ (%)	σ (%)	x (%)	$\mu - x$ (%)	Value ($)
F	9.00	10.7	−8.655	+17.655	−176,550
G	10.00	11.2	−8.480	+18.480	−184,800
H	11.00	12.5	−9.625	+20.625	−206,250
I	12.00	14.5	−11.925	+23.925	−239,250
J	13.00	17.1	−15.215	+28.215	−282,150

by a larger expected return of 9%, which is significantly higher than the original figure of 5%. This is due to the high expected return of the firm (25%).

Another way to analyze this result is by comparing portfolios with the same expected return. Take E and F, both with a 9% expected return. Without the firm, E results in a worst-case return of −14.26%. The equivalent figure with the firm is −8.665% for portfolio F. This is certainly a better outcome. Therefore, keeping the firm within the portfolio seems to be worthwhile.

Nonetheless, this is a premature conclusion. Recall that this result corresponds to certain levels of expected return and standard deviation, and to the best possible correlation (i.e., zero) for the firm. If these parameters had been less favorable, keeping the firm in the portfolio would have been a less attractive proposition. Also, depending on the transaction costs involved, selling the firm's shares (either partially or in full) could become the best strategy.[11] In addition, only one asset (the firm) representing 20% of the total investment makes the portfolio highly susceptible to any negative shock at the company.

5.3.2 Partial Ownership of the Firm

Imagine that the investor sells 40% of the company to a third party. Thus, the investment in the firm will be $120,000 (12% of the portfolio). Let us use Table 5.12 to compare this case with the situation we had before in which the investor remained the sole

TABLE 5.11

	Without the Firm				With the Firm		
Portfolio	μ (%)	σ (%)	x (%)	Portfolio	μ (%)	σ (%)	x (%)
A	5.00	4.6	−2.59	F	9.00	10.7	−8.655
B	6.00	6.0	−3.90	G	10.00	11.2	−8.480
C	7.00	8.0	−6.20	H	11.00	12.5	−9.625
D	8.00	11.0	−10.15	I	12.00	14.5	−11.925
E	9.00	14.1	−14.26	J	13.00	17.1	−15.215

---

[11]The effect of these transaction costs can be factored in by reducing the expected return of the firm's shares in the event that they are sold.

TABLE 5.12

	100% Firm				60% Firm		
Portfolio	μ (%)	σ (%)	X (%)	Portfolio	μ (%)	σ (%)	x (%)
F	9.00	10.7	−8.655	K	8.00	7.7	−4.705
G	10.00	11.2	−8.480	L	9.00	9.0	−5.850
H	11.00	12.5	−9.625	M	10.00	11.4	−8.810
I	12.00	14.5	−11.925	N	11.00	14.1	−12.265
J	13.00	17.1	−15.215	P	12.00	16.9	−15.885

owner of the firm. For simplicity, we assume no transaction costs associated with the sale of the firm's shares.

This new assumption has an important effect on the results. The most conservative portfolio yields a minimum return of −4.705%, about four percentage points lower than our previous result −8.665%. Comparing two portfolios with the same expected return—for instance, F and L,—the worst-case return is better when the firm's shares are sold. However, this result does not necessarily hold if we contrast portfolios with larger expected returns. For G and M, the minimum returns are practically identical. For H and N the results favor keeping full ownership of the firm.

In conclusion, the best strategy depends on the investor's risk aversion. If risk aversion is high, selling part of the company seems to be the best decision; but as risk aversion decreases, the most convenient strategy might be to maintain full ownership.[12] Of course, the preferred strategy will also be influenced by the transaction costs of selling the firm's shares.

Control and Expected Return A firm's expected return can change with the shareholding position of its dominant stockholders. On the one hand, when a company has a few stockholders, its administration tends to be more flexible, and this can result in higher levels of efficiency and profitability. As more stockholders are incorporated, an increasing number of formalities are introduced. These might lead to rigidities in the organization, higher expenses, and lower profitability. On the other hand, a closed shareholding structure could contribute to lower levels of discipline, but this might be corrected when new shareholders are incorporated, thus improving performance.

The results of our last example did not incorporate any change in expected return when the shareholder structure was altered. The analysis would have to be adjusted in the event that the 25% expected return might be affected. Increasing the number of asset classes, changing the ownership percentage in the firm, or modifying the values of the parameters can extend this exercise. In this manner, the different risk–return choices can be better visualized, allowing the investor to make a more informed portfolio decision.

---

[12]Risk management tools are also available to adjust portfolio risk. In addition, when capital is rationed, portfolio choice is not independent of the investment opportunities available and of the level of interest rates (see Chapter 11 Financing in Practice).

This is particularly important when the values of the parameters are open to question, as is often the case in the highly uncertain environments prevailing in emerging markets.

5.4 THE EVALUATION OF REAL INVESTMENTS

The methodology just described can also be utilized to assess the inclusion of real investments in a portfolio (e.g., a participation in a real estate development project). Nonetheless, evaluating real investments through portfolio analysis raises some difficulties.

5.4.1 The Presence of More than One Investor

When two or more investors contribute money to a real investment project, the impact of the new business in each investor's portfolio will be different. The higher the barriers (and the costs) to readjusting individual portfolios to each investor's preferences, the more likely is it for investors to differ in opinion about the attractiveness of the investment.

COUNTRY DIVERSIFICATION

Abu Dhabi Containers Limited, a container shipping firm valued at 1.5 billion dirhams ($409 million) was set up as the United Arab Emirates attempted to diversify its income sources. The new company, jointly owned by the Abu Dhabi Investments Company and NorAsia Shipping Company, will own ten express container ships.

Source: "New Shipping Firm Set Up in UAE," *Financial Times,* Nov. 22, 1999.

Comments   This is a typical case of a government taking decisions on behalf of its citizens in a country highly dependent on oil revenues. Several questions come up.

Does the UAE really have competitive advantages in the container business? If it does, how were they developed? If it does not, will NorAsia Shipping provide them? At what cost? In short, how certain is the UAE government that this investment decision will not yield a negative *NPV?*

There are at least two other ways for the UAE citizens to diversify their income sources:

(a) The government could hand out the shares of the oil business to the country's citizens, who could turn sell them in the open market, adjusting their individual portfolios as they wish. This option might not be viable, however, since it would require the authorities to lose managerial control of the business, something they might not be willing to do.

(b) The government could invest its excess cash in a diversified international portfolio on behalf of its citizens. If well managed, such a portfolio is unlikely to produce a negative *NPV* in the long run.

5.4.2 Adjusting for Lack of Liquidity

Real investments tend to be illiquid in comparison to financial investments. It is usually difficult to transform them into cash rapidly, at reasonable prices. For instance, it is difficult to sell an apartment or a going concern within a few days. At best, this could be achieved at a very low price. However, this is not the case with securities, which can generally be liquidated easily in the capital markets. When we include a real investment in a portfolio, we must recognize and account for this problem.

The impact of the lack of liquidity of real investments on portfolio return depends on the maturity of the investment in relation to the horizon of the investor. Imagine that the horizon is one year and that the real investment matures in two years. Upon reorganizing our portfolio at the end of one year, we might decide to liquidate the real investment totally or partially and sacrifice some or all of its value. Hence, the expected return of the investment must be adjusted to allow for this possible loss.

The situation is different if the real investment matures before the horizon. In this case the full value of the investment is recovered, but we cannot include the expected return of the real investment from its maturity up to the end of the horizon. Therefore, some kind of assumption must be made about the types of asset in which this money will be invested during that period of time.

5.4.3 From NPV to Return

Portfolio analysis requires the conversion of the expected *NPV*s of real investments into expected return equivalents, an exercise that is sometimes problematic. Whenever there is more than one change of sign in a cash flow, there can be more than one expected return equivalent. To illustrate, let us take the case of a two-year project with the cash flows shown in Table 5.13. The equivalent expected return r is computed in the following manner:

$$E(NPV) = -\$1000 + \frac{\$4000}{1 + r} - \frac{\$3800}{(1 + r)^2} = 0$$

The solution to this equation gives two values for r,

$$r = 144.7\% \quad \text{and} \quad r = 55.3\%$$

Which one should we choose?

TABLE 5.13

	Time		
	0	1	2
Cash flow ($)	−1000	+4000	−3800

Fortunately, this is not a very relevant problem in practice. Cash flows seldom have more than one change of sign, and even in these instances, only one realistic solution for r usually exists.[13]

5.4.4 Real Investments in a Personal Firm

The impact on the investor's portfolio of real investments or disinvestments in a firm in which the investor is a significant shareholder is another aspect to consider.

These real investments or disinvestments alter the risk–return characteristics of the firm as well as its correlation with other assets. Hence, their impact on the investor's portfolio must be evaluated and a possible readjustment considered. The scope of the readjustment depends on the associated costs. The costs are likely to be negligible if the readjustment can be fully accomplished by buying or selling securities in capital markets. However, the costs could be considerable if the readjustment demands changes in the investor's shareholding in the firm.

Another aspect relates to the evaluation of the impact of the loans that the firm might have taken. The solution is simple—loans must be included as additional financial instruments, but in a short position.[14]

The relevance of these analyses depends on the size of the new investments (or disinvestments) in relation to the total assets of the firm, and on the percentage of shares that the investor holds. The larger the investment (or disinvestment) in relation to the firm's assets and the more significant the investor's shareholding, the more justified will these analyses be.

5.4.5 NPV and Portfolio Analysis

In Part II we will see that the traditional method of evaluating real investments is by computing their *E(NPV)* at a discount rate that is consistent with project risk. This approach ignores the special characteristics of investors. The validity of this methodology relies on the assumption that investors are well diversified, which is not necessarily the case in emerging markets. When the investor is not well diversified and the project being evaluated comprises a significant proportion of his portfolio, the analysis discussed in this chapter must be employed to assess the project's impact on the investor's portfolio.[15]

---

[13]The term "realistic solution" implies a real (nonimaginary) number. In the event that more than one realistic value exists, the problem can be resolved by separating the cash flow into investment and loan components. The reader interested in this subject is referred to textbooks in corporate finance such as Brealey and Myers (1996) or Ross, Westerfield, and Jaffe (1999).

[14]Tax issues are another consideration. When one is evaluating a real investment, the tax impact on the portflio of both the investment itself and its financing must be factored in and planned for.

[15]In Chapter 6, The Classical Model, we shall introduce an equilibrium model for the expected return on investments when nonmarketable assets are present. This model can be useful for the estimation of the expected returns of new investment opportunities when investors are not well diversified, but it is not a practical substitute for portfolio analysis.

In conclusion, the more diversified the investor is, the more relevant will $E(NPV)$ be as a decision tool. Portfolio analysis is more appropriate when the investor is not well diversified. In practice, it is always advisable to perform both types of analysis, since this aids us in obtaining both pieces of information: the impact of the project on the investor's portfolio as well as its attractiveness to a well-diversified investor. Hence, a better-informed decision can be arrived at.

Two final comments follow.

Real investment valuation has certain special attributes in emerging markets. This topic will be covered in Part II (see Chapter 8, Valuation in Emerging Markets, and Chapter 9, The Value of Flexibility).

Additionally, the method that is proposed in this chapter is not a novel treatment of the subject. Banks, mutual funds, and institutional investors have used portfolio analysis extensively for a long time. However, its use has been restricted to a relatively limited number of specialists. The contribution of this book has been merely to simplify portfolio analysis and place it in the hands of individual investors, especially those evaluating both financial and real investments in emerging markets.

5.5 CONCLUSIONS

- The properties of the normal distribution are employed to replace the indifference curves with computation of minimum returns for a given probability level.
- Investors are not generally well diversified and their portfolios contain few assets, especially in emerging markets. Mutual funds are usually convenient vehicles to achieve a high degree of diversification.
- Investors define their investment horizon based on their market expectations and their consumption and investment needs.
- The determination of the efficient frontier and its corresponding portfolios requires the solution of relatively complex mathematical problems. Fortunately, there is adequate software available to help us get around this problem.
- Portfolio analysis is best suited to evaluating control stakes in firms as well as real investments when investors are not well diversified, which is typically the situation in emerging markets.
- When real investments are included in a portfolio, their expected returns must be adjusted to reflect their relative illiquidity. This adjustment depends on the relationship between the maturity period of the investment and the horizon of the investor.
- It is advisable to use the NPV method (to be covered in Part II) to complement portfolio analysis when evaluating real investments for undiversified investors

QUESTIONS AND PROBLEMS

1. The normal distribution does not allow for jumps in returns, but it is a fact that many assets are susceptible to shocks. How do investors seem to take this into consideration when building their portfolios?

TABLE P5.4

Portfolio	μ (%)	σ (%)	x (%)	$\mu - x$ (%)	Value ($)
A	10.00	5			
B	14.00	15			
C	20.00	19			

2. The longer the investment horizon, the lower the weight of riskier assets in a portfolio. Is this statement true?

3. Discuss the value and limitations of historical information as input for parameter estimation for the efficient frontier.

4. For a 5% cutoff probability:
   (a) Complete portfolios A, B, and C, as shown in Table P5.4 on the efficient frontier for the case of an investor investing $200,000.
   (b) In which of the portfolios in Table P5.4 does the investor have a 5% probability of losing money?
   (c) In which of the portfolios does the investor have a 10% probability of losing money? ($\alpha = 1.28$)

5. A real investment has a weight of 50% in a portfolio. What are the main issues to consider in deciding whether the investment must be kept intact, or partially (or totally) liquidated?

6. The impact of the relative lack of liquidity characterizing real investments on portfolio return is a function of each real investment's horizon in relation to the horizon of the investor. Discuss.

APPENDIX 5A

Probabilities on the Normal Distribution

On the normal distribution it is possible to determine the probability for a return to be below or above a certain cutoff level. Let us illustrate by way of a distribution with the characteristics as shown in Table 5A.1. Observe what happens for returns above and below 3% as shown in Figure 5A.1: the probability of a return below 3% is 8.1%, and the probability of a negative return is 2.3%. Since the area under the distribution curve must add up 1, the probability of returns above 3% and zero is 91.9 and 97.7%, respectively.

These probabilities are obtained from the **standardized normal distribution** with mean 0 and standard deviation 1. Given that the distribution is symmetric, the probability

TABLE 5A.1

μ (%)	σ (%)
10	5

of returns below and above zero is 50%. As values increase, the probability of obtaining **larger** values decreases. As values decrease, the probability of obtaining **lower** values decreases as well.

The formula to transform any point x on a normal distribution into its equivalent on the standardized distribution is

$$\alpha = \frac{x - \mu}{\sigma}$$

where μ and σ are the distribution parameters, x is the point whose equivalent we want to compute, and α is the equivalent on the standardized distribution.

In our example, for $x = 3$,

$$\alpha = \frac{3 - 10}{5} = -1.4$$

Because the standardized distribution is symmetrical the probability of values above, say, $+2$ has to be equal to the probability of values below -2. It is for this reason that in working with the standardized normal distribution, only its positive branch is taken into account.

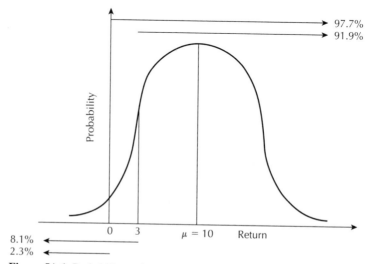

Figure 5A.1 Probability and return.

PART 1 SUMMARY:
THE INVESTOR AND THE FIRM

Investment decisions are essentially deferred consumption decisions. The interrelationship between consumption and investment is so complex that it is necessary to find a way to assess the two decisions separately.

Fisher established the conditions under which investment and consumption decisions can be made independently. These are:

- The absence of risk
- Free and unrestricted access to the financial markets and the absence of transaction costs
- A consensus among investors on the investment opportunity set

When these conditions are met, the net present value rule becomes valid for the valuation of investment opportunities.

Unfortunately, Fisher's conditions are not realistic. The first (absence of risk) and the second (equal access to financial markets) conditions are limiting. For instance, when the access to financial markets is restricted, investments that do not have the highest net present value may be preferable if their income stream is better bound to the investor's consumption needs.

Hence strictly speaking, investment and consumption decisions are not separable, and the net present value rule is not valid. However, a practical solution to overcome this problem is generally advanced. Most investors respond with the imaginary creation of two funds: one with liquid assets to finance consumption needs and the other for investment purposes, whose objective is presumably to maximize wealth.

Therefore, although the Fisher conditions do not hold at the personal level, in practice usually investment and consumption decisions are made separately. Based on this, we accept the assumption of separation between consumption and investment at the level of the individual investor. Companies avoid the separation problem by adopting the net present value rule. This topic will be covered in Part II.

The factors that determine whether an investment opportunity is or is not attractive vary between developed and developing countries. In the case of financial investments, the scant development of capital markets, the presence of few investors, and the scarcity of capital and information combine to make the possibility of extraordinary returns in emerging markets more feasible. With real investments, it is often necessary to possess competitive advantages related to the political and institutional climate ("environmental competitive advantages"). As a result, investors and promoters considered to possess competitive advantages for a particular business in a developed country could be at a disadvantage in a developing one. At the same time, investors and entrepreneurs from emerging markets who do not possess significant competitive advantages in the developed world for a certain line of business could be competitive in their own country. This apparent paradox could justify the existence of diversified conglomerates in developing countries.

Further, the ability to identify and manage investment opportunities in uncertain environments is a key success factor for doing business in developing countries too (see Chapter 9: The Value of Flexibility).

Another problem faced in investment analysis is that cash flow projections are always questionable, especially in highly volatile emerging countries. Therefore, to verify whether a positive net present value is justified, it is important to subject the assumptions behind these projections to a strategic assessment.

For investment evaluation at the personal level, we had to substitute expected net present value for expected return and to assume that returns follow a normal distribution. Although these assumptions have some shortcomings, they are justified in lieu of the considerable simplification they introduce to the analysis.

These simplifications facilitated the determination of expected returns and standard deviations for the best combinations of investment assets (i.e., the efficient frontier). Also, the utility functions and indifference curves were expressed in terms of risk and return. The superimposition of the indifference curves over the efficient frontier yielded the maximum expected utility for the investor, that is, the optimal portfolio.

The problem with this methodology is that we are obliged to work with the investor's utility curves, which are often difficult to estimate. To resolve this problem, we propose to replace the use of indifference curves with computation of minimum returns for a given level of probability. This is not a theoretically robust approach, but it has the advantage of being more practical.

Another important issue is that in real life, investors do not generally hold diversified portfolios. Instead they tend to concentrate their investments in relatively few assets. However, with the help of easily accessible computer software, it is possible to experiment with efficient frontiers defined by the incorporation of different investment asset sets. In this manner, the effect of the different sets on the risk–return relationship can be assessed. Not only can one alter the investment sets, but also one can vary the amount invested in each type of asset as well as the expected return, correlations, and so on. The high volatility prevailing in emerging markets justifies this kind of sensitivity analysis. Through this exercise, investors are able to better understand the implications of each investment strategy and to feel more comfortable with their portfolio decisions.

This procedure is not restricted to financial securities. It can also be utilized to include real investments (e.g., selling a personal firm totally or partially, evaluating a new venture) and to assess the potential impact of a controlling position in a firm on the risk–return characteristics of the portfolio.

Portfolio analysis is the right method for investment evaluation when the investor is not well diversified (the standard case in emerging markets). When the investor becomes increasingly diversified, the net present value rule starts having more relevance. However, even if the investor is not well diversified, it is always advisable to calculate the net present value of investment opportunities to complement the analysis.

PART 2

FIRM AND INVESTMENT

Chapter 6: The Classical Model

Description of CAPM, the classical asset pricing model, as the most widely used model to determine discount rates for investment evaluation at the firm level. Other models are also introduced.

Chapter 7: A Modified CAPM for Emerging Countries

Critique of existing approaches for investment valuation in emerging markets and proposal of a modified CAPM adapted to the conditions in these countries.

Chapter 8: Valuation in Emerging Markets

Various issues relating to investment valuation in emerging countries including the impact of inflation and exchange rates, subsidies, capital rationing, horizon and terminal value, adjustments to the calculation of NPV, and index-based valuation.

Chapter 9: The Value of Flexibility

The relevance of creating flexibility in emerging market–related investments and an approach for the quantification of flexibility.

CHAPTER 6

THE CLASSICAL MODEL

"Every theory is based on an analogy and sooner or later it loses validity because the analogy turns out to be false. However, a theory helps to solve the problems of its time."

—J. Bronowsky

Our analysis has focused on the point of view of the individual investor. We saw how he or she selects the most convenient investment portfolio according to the assets' risk–return characteristics, their interaction and the individual's risk aversion, taking into consideration possible investment restrictions as well. This analysis was also expanded to real assets.

Now we examine the investment decisions from the point of view of the firm.

We comment on real investments at the firm level and reintroduce Fisher's separation principle, this time under conditions of uncertainty. The capital market line is explained as a starting point for the capital asset pricing model (CAPM). The properties, advantages, and disadvantages of the CAPM with an emphasis on emerging markets are discussed. We finally introduce other models as alternatives to the CAPM.

This chapter reviews fundamental financial principles. The reader who feels comfortable with this material is advised to skip it.

6.1 REAL INVESTMENTS AND THE FIRM

In Chapter 2, "Consumption, Investments and Value," we saw how the firm is the best vehicle to undertake real investments. However, up to now real and financial investments have been intertwined, and our interest has been focused on the risk–return characteristics of the investor's portfolio. At no point were real investments analyzed with the firm as an investor. This makes sense in principle because the firm, by itself, is not important — its shareholders are, however, and the key consideration must always be the impact of every investment decision on their personal portfolios.

However in real life, as firms grow and shareholders increasingly delegate tasks to management, investment decisions gradually become the responsibility of the firm's administration. As operations become more complex, investment opportunities increase, and it is impractical to consult with shareholders on every investment decision, particularly when such investments do not involve large financial outlays.

On the other hand, the eventual participation of a shareholder in an investment decision is directly related to the proportion of that person's stake in the company, and the more fragmented the shareholder structure, the smaller will be the number of share-holders to consult.

Thus, the degree to which investment decisions are more justifiably delegated to management is inversely proportional to the size of the investment opportunity relative to the firm's total assets and directly proportional to the fragmentation of the ownership of the firm.

In practice, firms devise norms defining the size of the investment decisions on which stockholders are to be consulted. Although logical, this normative rule requires management to adopt some method for accepting or rejecting projects without taking shareholder preferences into consideration. And, this methodology will be acceptable as long as the investment in question is independent of the particular situation of the stockholders. We saw in Chapter 2, in the no-risk case, the conditions under which this kind of separation is valid. Now we will identify these conditions when there is uncertainty.

6.2 SEPARATION BETWEEN CONSUMPTION AND INVESTMENT UNDER UNCERTAINTY

In the absence of risk, when there are no barriers in the financial markets and investors agree on the investment opportunity set, firm value maximization implies the maximization of investors' wealth. This is known as the Fisher separation principle and justifies the *NPV* rule (see Chapter 2: Consumption, Investments and Value).

It can be shown that Fisher separation holds under certainty as well as uncertainty and that the maximization of firm's value (and of *NPV*) automatically implies the maximization of investor's expected utility as long as **markets are complete and perfectly competitive, and transaction costs are absent** (De Angelo 1981). But, what do these conditions mean?

6.2.1 Complete Markets

In complete markets cash flow patterns of all sorts can be traded under all conceivable conditions of risk.

To clarify, think of an investor who wishes to buy a financial instrument that pays $100 if the following conditions are satisfied by the year 2020: first, the orange harvest in Brazil must reach a certain percentage of total world production, and second, Latin America must become the main supplier of bananas to the European Union.

Although this example is an exaggeration, something similar is quite possible. Nowadays, it is perfectly feasible to devise bets of all kinds by combining financial instruments and/or making special agreements with banks or other financial institutions. If the investor is willing to pay the price, there is almost always someone willing to play. In practice, markets are more complete than is generally thought.

A more formal definition of complete markets can be obtained from a state contingent framework.

TABLE 6.1

States of Nature	Securities / Payoffs		
	A	B	C
Good	2	0	0
Fair	1	3	0
Bad	0	1	4

Under a state contingent framework the possible future values of securities are represented by their payoffs for each future state of nature. The investment opportunities available to an individual are given by the linear combinations of the set of available securities.

A market is complete when the number of linearly independent securities equals the number of possible future states of nature.

Let us illustrate with an example. Imagine three securities with the following payoffs for three possible states of nature, as shown in Table 6.1.

What must be the linear combination (w_A, w_B, w_C) of securities to obtain the payoffs shown in Table 6.2?

Solving a simple system of linear equations:

$$2w_A + 0w_B + 0w_c = 4$$

$$1w_A + 3w_B + 0w_C = 3$$

$$0w_A + 1w_B + 4w_C = 2$$

The solution is:

$$w_A = 2$$

$$w_B = \frac{1}{3}$$

$$w_C = \frac{5}{12}$$

TABLE 6.2

States of Nature	Payoffs
Good	4
Fair	3
Bad	2

> *Given that the three securities are linearly independent, it is always possible to combine them for any desired payoff structure. Therefore, this is a complete market.*
>
> *If for instance, security C were replaced by a linear combination of A and B, say the sum of the payoffs of A and B, there would be only two independent securities for three possible states of nature and the market would not be complete.*

6.2.2 Perfectly Competitive Markets

Take the case of the production and distribution of diamonds, which is controlled by a few players. This means that if the Russian company who is the leader in this business drastically reduces its inventories, diamond prices will most likely fall all over the world. This is an example of a noncompetitive market because the actions of one agent (in this case, the Russian company) have a significant impact on the other market participants.

In contrast, apple production is a competitive market because production is distributed between many growers. If the harvest of a particular participant is lower than expected, the international price of apples probably does not change significantly. And, the other producers of apples worldwide are not affected.

To summarize, in a perfectly competitive market, the actions of any single participant cannot significantly affect the economic well-being of other participants.

6.2.3 Absence of Transaction Costs

The absence of transaction costs implies that buying, selling, or acquiring information is not costly. As a consequence, all market participants can adjust their consumption and investment portfolios costlessly and always have the same information.

In complete markets all cash flow patterns are feasible, and everything new in the financial markets can be replicated as a combination of existing cash flows and/or financial instruments. Alternatively, in incomplete markets some investors' initiatives could impact the existing opportunity set for other economic agents. Under conditions of uncertainty, Fisher's separation principle requires complete markets to assure independence between the investment opportunity sets of individual investors and the decisions of individual firms.

Perfectly competitive markets are required for the decisions of any particular firm not to affect prices or quantities in the rest of the economy. The absence of transaction costs is necessary for agents to be able to adjust their investment and consumption decisions at no cost.

Significant transaction costs and/or changes in quantities, prices, or the set of investment and consumption opportunities would make the investor's utility maximization process dependent on other agents' actions. The conditions stated earlier are necessary to assure that the firm's investment and financing decisions affect only the wealth of investors, hence, guarantee the validity of the *NPV* rule. These are not very realistic assumptions, but they must be accepted if one is to proceed.

It was mentioned that delegation of investment decisions to managers is more justifiable when the investment is small in relation to total firm assets and when the investor does not own a significant portion of the firm's equity. From now on, we will assume that this is the case: that is, the investment is small relative to the firm's total assets and the investor holds an insignificant proportion of the firm.

To summarize, we will assume the validity of the Fisher separation principle under uncertainty, and that $E(NPV)$ **maximization is consistent with expected utility maximization for all investors.**

Let us focus on the firm and develop a method of optimizing investment decisions at the managerial level. For this, we need a model that will enable us to estimate expected return for any asset. This expected return corresponds to the rate at which cash flows will be discounted to compute $E(NPV)$ for an investment opportunity.

6.3 A NEW EFFICIENT FRONTIER: THE CAPITAL MARKET LINE

Imagine a financial instrument with no risk, one whose return is predictable and independent of any imponderable factors. In statistical terms this means zero standard deviation and zero covariance with any other asset.

This kind of instrument is feasible. Think of a U.S. Treasury bill with a 4% yearly interest rate payable in 6 months. If our investment horizon is also 6 months, the contractual 4% return cannot change, and the probability of default by the U.S. government is negligible.

Default is unlikely for two reasons: first, the U.S. government has a long-standing reputation as a reliable debtor, and second, even in the unlikely event of insolvency, the U.S. government could always honor its obligations by issuing new currency. Therefore, for our six-month horizon it can be said that this bond has zero standard deviation. An instrument such as this is known as a **risk-free** asset.[1]

There would be risk for a horizon longer than six months, since the T bill proceeds will have to be reinvested after the sixth month, and the reinvestment interest rate is unknown at the outset. If the horizon were less than six months, the T bill would have to be sold before maturity, and its price would depend on the interest rate prevailing at the time of sale. And since this rate is also unknown at the beginning, the final return would be uncertain in this case as well.

6.3.1 The Risk-Free Asset in Emerging Countries

Unlike the case in developed countries, in developing countries government compliance with its obligations is not assured. Although when bonds are issued in local currency, new currency could be issued if necessary to pay them, the situation is different when bonds are issued in a foreign currency. Furthermore, it is not unusual for default risk to be higher for the government than for some highly reputable local banks and private companies. Therefore, the least risky instruments are often those issued by strong local firms, not the government. In any case, as long as such instruments are issued in a foreign currency, none of them can be considered to be risk free.

Thus, it can be concluded that **as a general rule, risk-free assets in strong currencies do not exist in emerging countries.**

---

[1]Later in this chapter a more formal definition of a risk-free asset is offered.

In the next chapter (A Modified CAPM for Emerging Countries), we propose that investments be valued in a strong currency such as the U.S. dollar, the yen, or the Euro. Therefore, in our discussion about risk-free instruments in these countries we will refer to those issued in strong currencies and not in local currencies.

Any asset whose standard deviation of returns is zero can be combined with portfolios on the efficient frontier to get a new and more favorable efficient frontier. This new efficient frontier is defined by a straight line drawn from the risk-free return R_f to the portfolio with the highest possible expected return on the original efficient frontier, as shown in Figure 6.1. The portfolio with the highest expected return on the old efficient frontier (corresponding to the tangency point M in Figure 6.1) is named the **market portfolio** [with an expected return of $E(R_M)$]. The new straight-line efficient frontier is known as the **capital market line.**

When there is no risk-free asset, the efficient frontier is a curve. When a risk-free asset exists, the efficient frontier is a straight line. But we could find ourselves in an intermediate situation in which there is a "quasi"-risk-free portfolio with very low standard deviation. In this situation, the minimum variance portfolio (on the apex of the frontier) might be so close to the vertical axis (representing expected returns) that the efficient frontier, though still a curve, could be considered to be a straight line for all practical purposes.

6.3.2 The Market Portfolio and the Risk-Free Asset

The capital market line is the first step for the derivation of the capital asset pricing model (**CAPM**). Though we will talk about this model extensively at later, we will now introduce some concepts about the CAPM.

The CAPM will allow for investment valuation at the firm level without any consideration of investors' preferences. Since we are looking for a common model for all market participants, one of the key assumptions is that all investors consider the same set of assets and have the same risk–return expectations about these assets when forming their investment portfolios. This is the case of **homogeneous expectations.** Moreover, it must also be assumed that all investors have the **same investment horizon.**

Homogeneous expectations and a common investment horizon imply that all investors envision exactly the same risky-asset (original) efficient frontier and the same

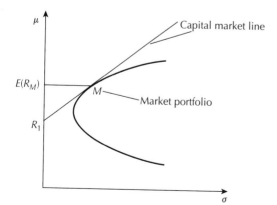

Figure 6.1 The capital market line.

risk-free asset. Therefore, they also share the same capital market line and market portfolio. Depending on the shape of his or her indifference curve, each investor's portfolio will be a simple combination of the risk-free asset and the market portfolio.

What the Market Portfolio Means Let us focus on the market portfolio, that is, on the portfolio of risky assets. At every point in time one or more investors must hold every risky asset. In addition, supply and demand determine the price of each asset. Therefore, every asset has a price and is owned by at least one investor.

To simplify, imagine a financial market with only two risky assets: 1000 shares A with a unit price of $100 and 3000 shares B with a unit price of $50. At any moment each of these shares has a price and is possessed by some investor.

According to the CAPM, all investors have the same portfolio of risky assets (the market portfolio). In our example, this means that every investor has the same proportion of A and B shares. Say that each investor has 1 A share for every 3 B shares. The risky-asset portfolio will comprise blocks of $250, as shown in Table 6.3.

Portfolios that are not a multiple of $250 demand fractional shares, and for the shares to be divisible, **transaction costs will have to be zero.** In addition, remember that supply and demand determine stock prices. If demand for A increases in relation to the demand for B, A's price will increase and B's price will decrease, and vice versa. But at any point in time it is assumed that the market is in equilibrium and that share prices are fixed.

We can compute the proportions of every asset in the risky-asset portfolio knowing only the number of shares of each type and their prices. We can consider a unique imaginary investor possessing all the risky assets and prepare, Table 6.4, which is quite similar to Table 6.3. In our example, the market portfolio comprises shares of A (40%) and B (60%),[2] which is the proportion, held by our imaginary investor.

The reason for the terms "market portfolio" and "capital market line" is clear now: both terms stem from the behavior of the financial market as a whole (under homogeneous expectations: no transaction costs and the same investment horizon for all investors). Under the capital market line (and the CAPM), the market portfolio is not restricted to a particular financial market but comprises all possible risky assets the world over.

TABLE 6.3

Share	Unitary Price ($)	Number of Shares	Amount ($)	Percentage (%)
A	100	1	100	40
B	50	3	150	60
Totals			250	100

---

[2]Irrespective of the shape of his utility function (as long as it is concave) or his level of wealth, every investor chooses the same risky-asset portfolio. When this occurs we have **portfolio separation.** It can be shown that portfolio separation holds for all risk-averse utility functions when the distribution of returns is normal, which is our case.

TABLE 6.4

Share	Unitary Price ($)	Number of Shares	Amount ($)	Percentage (%)
A	100	1000	100,000	40
B	50	3000	150,000	60
Totals			250,000	100

How to Determine the Risk-Free Rate The return of the risk-free asset is called the **risk-free rate** and depends on the supply and demand of the risk-free asset. The relatively more risk-averse investors optimize their portfolios somewhere between the risk-free asset and the market portfolio, and will distribute their holdings between these two assets by holding long positions in both. The relatively less risk-averse investors optimize their portfolios to the right of the market portfolio and will take a short position in the risk-free asset and a long one on the market portfolio.

Those wishing to take long positions in the risk-free asset will buy it. Those wishing to take short positions will sell. The interaction between its buyers and sellers will establish the price of the risk-free asset, hence the risk-free rate, at every point in time.

The capital market line is a straight line starting at the risk-free return, with a slope equal to the difference between $E(R_M)$ and R_f divided by σ_M. Its equation is given by

$$E(R_P) = R_f + \frac{E(R_M) - R_f}{\sigma_M} \sigma_P$$

where, p stands for any portfolio on the capital market line.

Two essential conditions are needed to guarantee a single market portfolio and capital market line: there must be a constant risk-free rate, and investors must be allowed to take short and long positions in the risk-free asset.

If (for practical purposes) U.S. Treasury bills are defined as the risk-free asset, investors will have to be able to take short positions in these bonds. If the risk-free asset consists of bank loans and deposits, investors will have to be able to take loans.

However the risk-free asset is defined, we will still run into problems, even if both short and long positions are feasible. Buying and selling T bills implies transaction costs. Hence, there will be a gap between short and long yields. On the other hand, banks' transaction costs ensure that there is always a difference between bank lending and borrowing rates. In conclusion, whatever the risk-free instrument, we will encounter two risk-free rates and two, instead of one, tangency points on the efficient frontier, one for each risk-free rate. In consequence, there would be several "market portfolios" between the tangency points.

The risk-free rate can be unique only if transaction costs do not exist.

6.3.3 The Risk–Free Asset Revisited

A more formal definition of a risk-free asset comes from Black (1972): a risk-free asset corresponds to a portfolio with zero correlation with the market portfolio.

Black shows that as long as short sales are not constrained, it is always possible to find the uncorrelated counterpart of any efficient portfolio on the minimum variance frontier. Since the market portfolio is on the efficient frontier, it follows that there will always be a portfolio that is not correlated with the market portfolio. Therefore, such a portfolio will represent the "risk- free asset."

We have found a simple relationship between standard deviation and expected return for any portfolio on the capital market line; each of these portfolios is a linear combination of the risk-free asset and the market portfolio. But for this, we have paid a high price, namely, the need to accept the following assumptions:

- Homogeneous expectations
- A common investment horizon
- No transaction costs

Undoubtedly these assumptions are unrealistic, both in developed and developing markets. We will come back to this point shortly (see Chapter 7: A Modified CAPM for Emerging Countries).

In addition, the capital market line gives us the expected rate of return of the risk-free asset, the market portfolio, or any combination between the two. It does not provide us with the expected rates of return of other assets, which is what we really need to assess specific investment opportunities. Therefore, up to this point we do not yet have a useful model in our hands. Fortunately, the CAPM will solve this last problem.

6.4 THE CAPM

Starting from the same assumptions as the capital market line, the CAPM gives us the expected return for **any asset or portfolio** as a function of a measure of risk called **beta** (β).

The equation for the CAPM is:

$$E(R_i) = R_f + \beta_i[E(R_M) - R_f]$$

where, $E(R_i)$ is the asset's expected return, R_f is the risk-free rate, $E(R_M)$ is the expected return of the market portfolio, and β_i is the measure of risk for asset i.

To find β_i, we write:

$$\beta_i = \frac{\text{Cov}(R_i, R_M)}{\text{Var}(R_M)} = \frac{\sigma_{iM}}{\sigma_{MM}}$$

6.4.1 The Meaning of Beta

Beta is the quotient resulting from dividing the covariance of asset i with the market portfolio by the variance of the market portfolio. When i is the risk-free asset, its covariance with the market portfolio is zero and so is its beta.

When i is the market portfolio, the quotient becomes

$$\beta_M = \frac{\sigma_{MM}}{\sigma_{MM}} = 1$$

implying that beta for the market portfolio is 1.

As the covariance of an asset with the market portfolio increases, so does its beta. The beta of an asset is 1 when the covariance equals the variance of the market portfolio. And beta is larger than 1 when the covariance is larger than the variance of the market portfolio.

This brings the correlation coefficient ρ_{iM} to our mind. The relationship between ρ_{iM} and beta is given by

$$\beta_i = \frac{\sigma_{iM}}{\sigma_{MM}} = \frac{\sigma_{iM}\, \sigma_i \sigma_M}{\sigma_i \sigma_M\, \sigma_{MM}} = \rho_{iM} \frac{\sigma_i}{\sigma_M}$$

Notice that for a beta value of 0, the correlation is 0 as well. For a beta value of 1, the correlation is also 1. But for betas between 0 and 1 or betas larger than 1, beta and ρ_{iM} are not necessarily equal.

The **risk premium** of an asset, i, is defined as the difference between its expected return and the risk-free rate:

$$E(R_i) - R_f$$

The risk premium for the market portfolio is known as the **market (risk) premium** and is given by

$$E(R_M) - R_f$$

Appendix 6A gives a proof of the CAPM.

6.4.2 Systematic and Nonsystematic Risk

The relationship between the CAPM and the capital market line is shown graphically in Figure 6.2, with the CAPM is at the left-hand side and the capital market line at the right. R_f is the risk-free rate with zero beta, and $E(R_M)$ is the expected return of the market portfolio with a beta of 1.

Let us focus on assets A and B. On the capital market line both have the same expected return, but B has a larger standard deviation. On the CAPM, both have the same expected return but the same beta. What does this mean? Does it make sense for two assets with different standard deviations (and different risk) to have the same expected return? How can any investor be satisfied with the same expected return for two assets with different associated risks?

A thorough understanding of this dilemma is crucial to understanding the CAPM. Indeed, B has a larger standard deviation but, according to the CAPM, the standard deviation does not have a direct relation to expected return. What is really important (and determines expected return) is beta as a measure of the asset's covariance with the market portfolio. In our example, A and B have the same covariance with the market portfolio and the same beta, hence the same expected return, despite their differing standard deviations.

Imagine the standard deviation of an asset as having two parts: one part that varies with the market portfolio and the other having no relation whatsoever to the market portfolio. In our example, the part that has a covariance with the market portfolio is equal for both assets but the other part is larger for B. Therefore, both assets have the same beta even though B has a larger standard deviation.

Remember that, in theory, the market portfolio is the most diversified portfolio of all containing all the risky assets. A change in the return of the market portfolio affects the return of every risky asset according to its beta. The larger the beta, the more sensitive the asset's return to changes in the return of the market portfolio, and vice versa.

It is impossible to construct a more diversified portfolio than the market portfolio. Thus, its risk is unavoidable and the effect of this risk on every risky asset will be unavoidable as well. This is precisely what beta quantifies, namely, the unavoidable portion of an asset's risk. And, since this portion of the asset's risk is unavoidable, investors will demand an appropriate level of expected return as compensation for taking it.

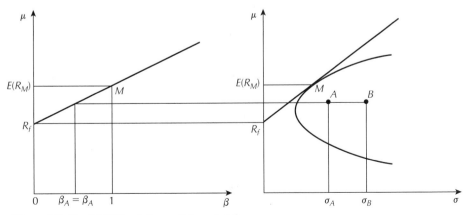

Figure 6.2 The CAPM and the capital market line.

The situation is different with the portion of risk unrelated to the market portfolio. This portion is totally unpredictable and has no relation to the return of any other asset. Consequently, we can expect it to neither increase nor decrease at the same time for every asset. Instead, given that all investors hold well-diversified portfolios, the favorable results of some assets tend to be offset by the unfavorable results of the others. On average this portion of risk is diversified away and tends to be negligible.

The intuition of the CAPM is that **investors will not demand any expected return for risks not covarying with the market portfolio, since these tend to disappear in well-diversified portfolios.**

The effect of portfolio diversification on portfolio variance can be better understood by the following argument.

Imagine a portfolio with the same amount invested in every one of N assets. The variance of this portfolio will be:

$$\sigma_P^2 = \sum_{i=1}^{N} \sum_{j=1}^{N} x_i x_j \sigma_{ij} = \sum_{i=1}^{N} \sum_{j=1}^{N} \frac{1}{N^2} \sigma_{ij}$$

If V^2 is the average variance and C is the average covariance, portfolio variance will be given by

$$\sigma_P^2 = \frac{1}{N^2} NV^2 + \frac{1}{N^2}(N^2 - N)C = \frac{1}{N}V^2 + (1 - 1/N)C$$

As N increases (and the portfolio becomes more diversified), the variance tends to have less importance and the covariance tends to have greater importance. In the limit, we have

$$\lim_{N \to \infty} \left[\frac{1}{N}V^2 + (1 - 1/N)C \right] = C$$

In other words, in the limit portfolio variance depends only on the covariance and is independent of the individual asset variances.

The portion of risk that covaries with the market portfolio is known as **systematic or nondiversifiable risk,** and the part that is independent of the market portfolio is called **nonsystematic or diversifiable risk.**

The systematic and nonsystematic portions of risk can be identified within the total variance of an asset. Let us express the CAPM as follows:

$$E(R_i) = R_f + \beta_i[E(R_M) - R_f] = R_f(1 - \beta_i) + \beta_i E(R_M)$$

We define a new variable,

$$\alpha_i = R_f(1 - \beta_i)$$

Thus,

$$E(R_i) = \alpha_i + \beta_i E(R_M)$$

This formula represents the risk–return relationship from an expectation point of view, that is, ex ante. Using historical information and preparing a linear regression, we can obtain the corresponding ex-post relationship:

$$\tilde{R}_i = \alpha_i + \beta_i \, \tilde{R}_M + \tilde{e}_i$$

where $\tilde{e}_i$ is the error term.
The following condition is true in the case of a linear regression,

$$\sigma(R_M, \, \tilde{e}_i) = 0$$

Therefore,

$$\sigma_i^2 = \beta_i^2 \sigma_M^2 + \sigma_{e_i}^2$$

$$1 = \left(\frac{\beta_i \sigma_M}{\sigma_i}\right)^2 + \left(\frac{\sigma_{e_i}}{\sigma_i}\right)^2 = \left(\frac{\sigma_{iM} \sigma_M}{\sigma_M^2 \sigma_i}\right)^2 + \left(\frac{\sigma_{e_i}}{\sigma_i}\right)^2$$

$$1 = \rho_{iM}^2 + \left(\frac{\sigma_{e_i}}{\sigma_i}\right)^2$$

where the squared correlation term represents the portion of the variance that covaries with the market portfolio (the systematic risk) and the other term is the nonsystematic risk.

6.4.3 The Additivity Property of Beta

As is the case with present values, an important property of the CAPM is that the beta of a portfolio is the weighted average of the betas of its assets. For example, if we have asset X with a β_X value of 0.5 and asset Y with a β_Y value of 0.8, the beta of a portfolio with these assets will be

$$\beta_P = a\beta_X + b\beta_Y$$

where a and b are the proportions invested in X and Y, respectively. If a is 30%, then the beta of the portfolio will be:

$$\beta_P = (0.30 \times 0.5) + (0.70 \times 0.8) = 0.71$$

For N assets, we write

$$\beta_P = \sum_{i=1}^{N} w_i \beta_i$$

where w_i is the proportion invested in asset i.

Let us prove additivity for the simple case of two assets beginning with the definition of beta:

$$\beta_P = \frac{E\{[aX + bY - aE(X) - bE(Y)][R_M - E(R_M)]\}}{\sigma^2(R_M)}$$

$$\beta_P = a\frac{E\{[X - E(X)][R_M - E(R_M)]\}}{\sigma^2(R_M)} + b\frac{E\{[Y - E(Y)][R_M - E(R_M)]\}}{\sigma^2(R_M)}$$

$$\beta_P = a\beta_X + b\beta_Y$$

6.4.4 The Assumptions of the CAPM

We will now verify the practical usefulness of the CAPM by examining its assumptions.

a. *Every Investor Is Risk Averse.* This is acceptable. Although it is true that in certain situations people can be risk loving (as in the case of gambling), the overwhelming majority are risk averse when investing their money.

b. *All Investors Maximize Expected Utility.* The expected utility maximization assumption is problematic because it requires that the axioms of cardinal utility hold. However, it has been shown that these axioms do not faithfully reflect the true behavior of investors (see Chapter 1: Financial Theory in Emerging Markets).

c. *All Investors Have the Same Horizon.* This is an unrealistic proposition.

d. *There Is a Risk-Free Asset.* This assumption is not unacceptable. After all, as mentioned earlier, it is always possible to acquire bonds issued by sound governments that do not possess a significant default risk. It could be said that this argument is not valid in emerging markets. However, as a consequence of globalization, emerging market investors have gained the same access to these instruments as their counterparts in the developed world.

e. *No Transaction Costs.* In reality, transaction costs are always important, particularly in emerging countries where financial markets are not sufficiently developed.

f. *Homogeneous Expectations.* In developing countries, where the scarcity and inaccuracy of financial information is widespread, it is unrealistic to hold homogeneous expectations.

TABLE 6.5

Assumption	Acceptability		
	Low	Medium	High
Risk aversion			√
Expected utility maximization		√	
Common horizon	√		
Risk-free asset			√
No transaction costs	√		
Homogeneous expectations	√		
Normal distribution		√	

g. *Returns Are Normally Distributed.* As we said in Chapter 3 (The Impact of Risk), the normal distribution assumption is not always reliable. Nonetheless, in comparison to the considerable simplification in the analysis that this assumption brings, the problem is minor.

Table 6.5 summarizes our point of view about the acceptability of these assumptions in the case of emerging markets. We can see that as a whole, the acceptability of these assumptions is poor. However, several studies about the CAPM have concluded that the relaxation of some assumptions does not invalidate the model. We mention the following for illustrative purposes:

- As we saw before, even if there is no zero variance asset, linearity between risk and returns holds in the CAPM as long as short positions are allowed and building a zero beta portfolio is feasible (Black 1972).
- Normal returns are not essential. As long as the distribution of returns is symmetrical and stable, the standard deviation can be substituted by other measures of dispersion without invalidating the CAPM (Fama 1965).
- The CAPM is valid with certain restrictions in the absence of homogeneous expectations as long as expected returns, variances and covariances are expressed as weighted averages of investors' expectations (Lintner 1969).

However, the assumptions still remain difficult to accept. This is precisely the main problem with the CAPM—although it offers a simple method for the determination of expected returns, its assumptions are divorced from reality.

6.4.5 Other Models

After the CAPM was developed, many other models were proposed. We briefly describe some of the more interesting.[3]

---

[3]Elton and Gruber (1995) and Copeland and Weston (1988) offer more detailed treatments of this topic.

The CAPM with Nonmarketable Assets In Chapter 4 (The Benefits of Diversification) it was mentioned that all investors have assets that are not marketable, either because individuals do not wish to trade them or because the assets cannot be traded at all. Income from future labor, social benefits, and owned homes were given as examples.

Mayers (1972) has shown that when investors are required to hold nonmarketable assets with risky rates of return, the CAPM takes the following form:

$$E(R_i) = R_f + \lambda[V_M \cdot \text{Cov}(R_i, R_M) + \text{Cov}(R_i, R_{ii})]$$

where

$$\lambda = \frac{E(R_M) - R_f}{V_M \sigma_M^2 + \text{Cov}(R_M, R_H)}$$

and V_M represents the market value of all marketable assets and R_H is the return on all nonmarketable assets.

This model implies the following:

1. When the nonmarketable assets are not risky and their covariances are zero, the equation collapses to the standard CAPM.
2. If $\text{Cov}(R_M, R_H)$ is positive, the expected return $E(R_i)$ might be lower or higher than its equivalent in the standard CAPM, depending on the value of the covariance between the asset and the nonmarketable assets $\text{Cov}(R_i, R_H)$.

This model could be useful for evaluating investments when diversification is costly and investors are required to hold nonmarketable assets, but it is not a valid alternative to portfolio analysis when the purpose is to assess the impact of specific assets in portfolios that are not well diversified (see Chapter 5: Personal Investments).

Multiperiod CAPM One of the assumptions of the CAPM is that all investors face the same single period horizon. The portfolio selected at any point in time is just a step in a series of lifetime portfolios. Actually, many investors make decisions taking into consideration their entire lives.

Several models have been proposed in a multiperiod context. We will concentrate on the consumption-oriented CAPM proposed by Breeden (1979). This model is based upon the following assumptions:

Investors maximize utility of lifetime consumption through a multiperiod utility function.

Investors have the same expectations on asset returns.

The population is fixed and lives forever.

There is only one consumption good.

The capital market allows investors a consumption pattern that cannot be improved by additional trades.

The CAPM under these conditions turns out to be:

$$E(R_{it}) = \alpha_i + \beta_i E(C_t)$$

where

$$\beta_i = \frac{\text{Cov}(R_{it}, C_t)}{\sigma^2(C_t)}$$

$E(R_{it})$ is the expected return of asset i in period t, α_i is an intercept term, $E(C_t)$ is expected consumption in period t.

The Arbitrage Pricing Model Proposed by Ross (1976), this model offers a different approach for asset pricing. All CAPM-inspired models require general equilibrium and assume that it is optimal for investors to choose investments on the basis of expected return and variance. Instead, the model based on arbitrage pricing theory (APT) derives asset prices by banning profit opportunities through arbitrage (i.e., taking advantage of possible price disequilibria among assets).

According to the model, asset returns are linearly related to a set of factors, as follows:

$$E(R_i) = R_f + \beta_{i1}f_1 + \beta_{i2}f_2 + \ldots + \beta_{in}f_n$$

where $E(R_i)$ is the expected return on asset i, R_f is the risk-free rate, f_n are factors affecting expected return β_{in} is the sensitivity to factor n.

In equilibrium, all portfolios built with the set of assets under consideration, using no wealth and having no risk, must earn no return on average. To form a portfolio with no wealth it is necessary to combine short positions with long positions so that the net amount invested is zero. If the weighted average of the beta components for each factor is zero as well, the portfolio will have no risk and hence no expected risk premium.

The APT has the following main advantages compared with the CAPM:

It is not restricted to any particular return distribution.

General equilibrium is not required, only a partial equilibrium among asset returns.

There is no need for a market portfolio.

The difficulty of identifying the factors is the main disadvantage of the APT. The APT requires the factors to be completely uncorrelated to each other and, so far it has been impossible to link the factors with observable uncorrelated variables such as the GNP or a stock index.[4]

---

[4]Chen, Roll, and Ross (1983) identified macroeconomic variables that provide valuable insight on the APT factors.

Multifactor Models Because they are required to be uncorrelated to each other, the APT factors are difficult to interpret, and it is hard to identify what are the observable variables behind them. Multifactor models address this problem by selecting the factors a priori from available data. However, a price must be paid for this: the factors tend to be correlated to each other, causing statistical problems ("collinearity") and affecting the reliability of the estimates. In addition, multifactor models are less robust, since they do not require any type of equilibrium among assets.

A particular multifactor model that deserves to be mentioned is the one developed by Fama and French (1996). Besides the market factor, this model includes two other factors: one represents the difference in returns between smaller and larger companies (the "size effect" empirically detected long ago), and the other is the ratio of a firm's accounting book value to its market value. This model is interesting because it seems to better explain asset returns. Yet, other studies lend renewed support to the CAPM, questioning the validity of the multifactorial approach (Kothari, Shanken, & Sloan 1995; Jagannathan & Wang 1996).

Regardless of these difficulties, multifactor models are being used by many analysts for the selection of securities and the management and the evaluation of portfolios.[5]

All these newer models are laudable. Unfortunately, their statistical limitations and conceptual complexity have curtailed their practical application in the business world. Therefore, in the absence of any other model that is clearly superior to the CAPM, we will focus on it throughout the rest of this book. In fact, despite its shortcomings, it remains the most popular model among financial analysts and business schools.

In the words of Jagannathan and Wang (1996):

> In spite of the lack of empirical support, the CAPM is still the preferred model for classroom use in MBA and other managerial finance courses . . . [it seems to] have the ability to come back to original shape after being blown to pieces or hammered out of shape.

However, we must exercise caution when applying the CAPM, and its results should never be accepted unquestioningly.

6.4.6 Advantages and Disadvantages of the CAPM

Let us now address the advantages and disadvantages of the CAPM.

Advantages

- The CAPM presents a positive relationship between risk and return, and this is intuitively sound.
- It takes the benefits of diversification into account.
- In the relatively more efficient markets of developed countries, it has been shown that the relationship between beta and return is linear, as predicted by the CAPM.

---

[5]Solnik (1996) offers a good review of multifactor models.

• The linear relationship between risk and return simplifies working with portfolios to a great extent. In the same way that the return of an investment portfolio is the weighted average of the returns of its components, the beta of a portfolio also corresponds to the weighted average of the asset's betas.

Disadvantages

• Most investors do not hold a combination of the risk-free asset and the market portfolio.

• Nobody knows what the "market portfolio" is. Most analysts use a well-diversified stock index as a proxy: for example, the Standard & Poor's 500 (S & P 500) in the United States or the Morgan Stanley Capital International (MSCI) Index worldwide. However, none of these indexes come close to the strict definition of the market portfolio according to the CAPM (comprising all possible risky assets available in the world).[6]

• The risky portfolios of investors are different from what could be termed a "market portfolio."

• Empirical studies have found that the probabilities of extreme asset returns (when returns are too high or too low) seem to be larger than those implied by the normal distribution (i.e., the distribution has "fat tails").

• Other studies have shown that other factors, particularly the standard deviation, can explain returns as well as the beta can.

• The CAPM yields unsatisfactory results for stocks of small or fast-growing companies (Cochrane 1999).

Recall the ex-post model associated with the CAPM,

$$\widetilde{R}_i = \alpha_i + \beta_i; \widetilde{R}_M + \tilde{e}_i$$

Although the empirical evidence points to the conclusion that the CAPM does not reflect the risk–return relationship accurately, this ex-post model seems to work quite well for shares. Parameters α_i and β_i of this model for many stocks can be found in several reports. The values for beta in these reports are often adjusted to correct for statistical errors of estimation. The values for beta serve as the starting point for discount rate determination (see Chapter 7: A Modified CAPM for Emerging Countries).

6.5 CONCLUSIONS

• In practice, firms undertake most real investments. Since many of these investments must be decided by management without consulting the shareholders, it is necessary

---

[6]Refer to Roll (1977) for a famous critique on this point.

to create a model for discount rate determination that is independent of shareholders' preferences.

- Severing the link between investment decisions at the firm level and investors' preferences requires revisiting the Fisher separation principle, but this time under conditions of uncertainty.

- It can be shown that the Fisher separation principle under uncertainty holds when markets are complete and perfectly competitive, and there are no transaction costs. These are unrealistic assumptions that we have no choice but to accept.

- The market portfolio contains all possible risky assets. The risk-free asset has zero standard deviation or, more formally, is a portfolio that is uncorrelated with the market portfolio.

- The capital market line gives the relationship between standard deviation and expected return for portfolios combining the risk-free asset and the market portfolio.

- The CAPM is based on the capital market line and allows for the estimation of expected return for any asset, which makes it a very useful model.

- The intuition behind the CAPM is the segmentation of asset risk into two components: systematic (nondiversifiable) and nonsystematic (diversifiable) risk. The first demands an expected return, while the second does not.

- The assumptions of the CAPM are divorced from reality. However, in the absence of another clearly superior model, it is still widely used.

- The CAPM is the most popular model in business schools and among analysts for the determination of the expected returns of real investments.

QUESTIONS AND PROBLEMS

1. Under what circumstances might it be reasonable for managers to make investment decisions without involving the shareholders?

2. Under uncertainty, Fisher separation holds when markets are complete and perfectly competitive and there are no transaction costs. Why are these conditions necessary?

3. A six-month T bill qualifies as a risk-free asset for an investor having a consumption basket of U.S. dollars with an investment horizon that is not longer than six months. Is this statement true?

4. Why may the less risky financial investments in some emerging countries be private company issues, not government securities?

5. The capital market line corresponds to the minimum variance frontier when there is a risk-free asset. Is this statement true?

6. The capital market line requires (a) the absence of transaction costs and (b) that all investors have the same investment horizon and expectations. What are the reasons for this?

7. Why is the CAPM the right model to use in estimating the discount rate for risky assets whereas the capital market line is not?

8. Is it possible for two assets that differ in variance to have the same expected return according to the CAPM?

9. According to the CAPM, investors do not demand any expected return from that part of asset risk not related to the market portfolio. Why is this so?

10. Asset A has a beta of 0.2 and asset B has a beta of 1.8. Find all combinations between A and B yielding a portfolio with a beta equal to the market portfolio.

APPENDIX 6A

Proof of the CAPM

Beginning with the capital market line, we form a portfolio between an asset i within the minimum variance frontier and the market portfolio, as shown in Figure 6A.1.

Let us invest w in i and $(1 - w)$ in the market portfolio M. The expected return and standard deviation of this portfolio are

$$E(R_P) = wE(R_i) + (1 - w)E(R_M)$$

$$\sigma_P = \sqrt{w^2\sigma_i^2 + (1 - w)^2\sigma_M^2 + 2w(1 - w)\sigma_{iM}}$$

Figure 6A.1

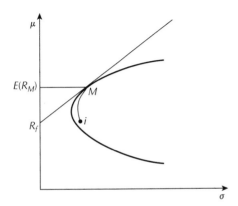

Varying *w*, we move along the minimum variance frontier defined by i and M. The slope of this frontier at any point is given by

$$\frac{\partial E(R_P)}{\partial \sigma_P} = \frac{\partial E(R_P)/\partial w}{\partial \sigma_P/\partial w}$$

Deriving,

$$\frac{\partial E(R_P)}{\partial w} = E(R_i) - E(R_M)$$

$$\frac{\partial \sigma_P}{\partial w} = \frac{1}{2\sigma_P}[2w\sigma_i^2 - 2(1 - w)\sigma_M^2 + 2\sigma_{iM}(1 - 2w)]$$

For *w* = 0, both frontiers must have the same slope, which is

$$\frac{E(R_M) - R_f}{\sigma_M}$$

Therefore,

$$\frac{\partial E(R_P)}{\partial \sigma_P}\bigg|_{w=0} = \frac{[E(R_i) - E(R_M)]\sigma_M}{\sigma_{iM} - \sigma_M^2} = \frac{E(R_M) - R_f}{\sigma_M}$$

and

$$E(R_i) - E(R_M) = \left(\frac{\sigma_{iM}}{\sigma_M^2} - 1\right)[E(R_M) - R_f]$$

$$E(R_i) - R_f = \beta_i[E(R_M) - R_f]$$

CHAPTER 7

A MODIFIED CAPM FOR EMERGING COUNTRIES

"There is nothing as practical as a good theory."

—KURT LEWIN

The CAPM was introduced in Chapter 6 as a basic tool for the determination of the expected return from real investments. Although it has a number of flaws, in the absence of a better model we will continue to use it. In this chapter we will try to adjust the CAPM to make it more suitable for investment analysis in emerging markets.

We begin by reviewing the main limitations of the CAPM in an emerging market context. The idea of country risk is introduced, and the traditional way of incorporating it in investment analysis is criticized. A modified CAPM for assessing investments in developing countries is proposed, and its advantages and disadvantages are discussed.

7.1 APPLICABILITY OF THE CAPM

Despite its limitations, the CAPM is the most popular model for discount rate determination in real investments in the financial community. Much of its popularity stems from its ease of applicability.

However, the CAPM is not as relevant in the developing world for the following reasons:

- Greater uncertainty causes investments in emerging markets to tend to be riskier than investments in developed markets. When one is applying the CAPM, this particular risk factor, referred to as "country risk," must be somehow quantified.

- The main indicator for what could be considered to be the "market portfolio" in emerging countries is the stock price index. But this index is rarely a good proxy of the real local business environment (more about this later).

- Local businesses are subject to strong foreign impacts in much greater measure than their counterparts in developed countries.

- To a far larger degree than in the developed world, the great majority of companies are controlled by family groups or a few shareholders. In general, such investors are not well diversified, since these businesses usually represent an important proportion of their portfolios (see Chapter 1: Financial Theory in Emerging Markets). The

CAPM ignores the impact of the project on investors' portfolios, but often this cannot be done in developing countries.

We do not envision a practical way out of this problem. We will, therefore, be aware that the more relevant this situation is, the less significant will be the results obtained through the CAPM (or a modified CAPM) and the *NPV* rule, and greater importance must be given to a portfolio analysis approach (see Chapter 5: Personal Investments).

In the rest of this chapter, we focus on how the CAPM can be applied in emerging markets while taking into consideration country risk and the problems associated with the market portfolio and foreign impacts.

7.2 WHAT COUNTRY RISK MEANS

According to the CAPM, the only relevant risk is given by beta: a measure of the covariance between the project's return and the return of the market portfolio. Hence, a telephone company, a restaurant, and a pin factory will each have different (relevant) risk.

Nonetheless, this rationale does not account for geography. The Libyan and the Swiss telephone companies are not comparable. It is true that both are in the same business and share a similar exposure to tariff regulation, costs of supplies, the uncertainties of technological advances and possible competition from other fast-growing sectors (e.g., cable television, the Internet). But investors know that Libya is riskier, if only because it is plagued with all the uncertainties of an emerging country (see Chapter 1: Financial Theory in Emerging Markets), whereas Switzerland is a developed and stable nation.

This is why investors frequently demand different returns from the same business depending on its location. This particular risk associated with the geographic location of the investment is known as **country risk.**

Reputation is the key for assessing country risk. Reputation is built upon a country's social peace and institutional behavior through time. A high degree of social stability and extended periods of institutional consistency and continuity earn a nation trustworthiness and low levels of country risk. Observe that country risk does not have as much to do with the quality of economic policies as with their stability and consistency.

7.2.1 How Country Risk Is Traditionally Quantified

Traditionally, country risk is quantified as the difference between the yield of what is considered a zero risk investment in a country of reference and its closest equivalent in the country under analysis. This incremental return is known as the **country risk premium.**

The adjusted (for country risk) discount rate is computed by adding the country risk premium to the discount rate that would correspond to an equivalent investment in the country of reference. This last rate comes from a model such as the CAPM. This adjustment amounts to an increase of the risk free rate in the CAPM. Hence, the larger the country risk premium, the higher the discount rate will be.

To compute the country risk premium, information is needed about two types of financial instrument:

1. A bond of negligible risk such as a U.S. Treasury bill.

2. A bond from the country under analysis. This bond must be a good proxy for the minimum possible level of risk in the country and have the following attributes:
   (a) Its maturity must closely match the project's horizon. This allows us to measure country risk as perceived by the financial community for the length of time of the investment.[1,2]
   (b) It must not have any options or special provisions that could affect the value of the bond, hence its yield.

Following this procedure and based upon the yield differences between sovereign bonds[3] and U.S. T bills, the country risk premiums for a group of countries were computed as shown in Table 7.1. These are the figures that had to be added to the risk-free rate in the United States to adjust the CAPM to the case of these nations in November 1999.

Some Comments Following, we comment on some important points related to the procedure just explained.

TABLE 7.1

Country	Country Risk Premium (%)*
Argentina	8.74
Brazil	10.23
Mexico	6.25
Peru	11.90
Philippines	19.57
Poland	2.93
South Korea	1.88

*November 1999. Horizon 30 years (except 10 years for South Korea).

Source: © Reuters 2000.

---

[1] If the probability of default is significant, for the purposes of yield estimation, the relevant bond's cash flows are not the contractual ones. Thus, they must be rescheduled according to the real expectations of payment.

[2] In strict terms the match must not be between the bond's and the project's maturities but between their durations. Duration, a kind of maturity weighted by the size of the cash flows, is a concept we will not discuss in this book. The interested reader can refer to Ross, Westerfield, and Jaffe (1999).

[3] A bond is "sovereign" if it issued by a government.

a. *Lack of Theoretical Justification.* The procedure became widely used in practice owing to its simplicity and intuitive appeal, but we must stress that there is no theoretical justification behind it.

b. *Changing the Country Risk Premium.* Some analysts alter the country risk premium throughout the life of the project as conditions change in the country. If they expect conditions to improve some time in the future, the premium is diminished starting at that particular time, and vice versa.

This is an erroneous practice. Table 7.1 was based on bonds with a maturity of 30 years (except for those of South Korea). These bonds' yields represent the expectations over the whole period. In other words, the financial community's expectations of country risk during that time span is already built into its price. We can think of the bond yields as reflecting an "average" of the country risk for the full life of the bond.

c. *When Reference Bonds Do Not Exist.* Estimating the country risk premium for countries that have no government debt trading in international financial markets is another matter. The way out of this problem is to rely on some country risk ranking. A few sources (such as *The Economist*) regularly publish risk rankings for most countries. These rankings are based on a number of economic indicators and opinions by individual observers. Let us illustrate how we can take advantage of these rankings.

Suppose country *ZUY* does not have foreign-traded government debt and is ranked at level 25. Say countries *FRS* and *TGK* do have foreign-traded government debt, and thus their country risk premiums are known. These two countries are ranked 23 and 29, respectively. This information is summarized in Table 7.2.

ZUY's country risk premium can be computed by interpolation in the following manner:

$$R_{country} = 7.40 + \frac{10.20 - 7.40}{29 - 23}(25 - 23) = 8.33\%$$

Rating Agencies Rating agencies offer an alternative way to assess a country's risk. Periodically they use a scale to classify long-term debts issued by emerging countries. The position in the scale depends on perceived default risk that is mirrored by a corresponding yield in the financial markets. The greater the risk, the larger the yield, and

TABLE 7.2

Country	Rank	Country Risk Premium (%)
FRS	23	7.40
ZUY	25	Unknown
TGK	29	10.20

TABLE 7.3

Standard & Poor's	Moody's
Low default risk	
AAA	Aaa
AA	Aa
A	A
BBB	Baa
Higher default risk	
BB	Ba
B	B
CCC - CC	Caa
C	Ca
In default	
DDD - D	C

vice versa. The differences between these yields and the return on a "risk-free" instrument (e.g., a U.S. T bill) can be interpreted as country risk premiums.

The scales used by Standard & Poor's and Moody's, the two best known rating agencies, are shown in Table 7.3. There are grades within each rating. Standard & Poor's adds a + or a − sign to point out that a particular issue is slightly less or more risky. For instance, BBB+ would be less risky than BBB−. Moody's uses numbers from 1 to 3 to signal less to more risk (e.g., ratings Aa1, Aa2, and Aa3 indicate increasing risks).

Standard & Poor's credit ratings are based on the following considerations (www.standardpoor.com):

Likelihood of payment, meaning capacity and willingness of the debtor to meet its financial commitments on an obligation according to the terms of the obligation.

Nature and provisions of the obligation.

Protection afforded by and relative position of the obligation in the event of bankruptcy, reorganization or other arrangements under laws affecting the creditor's rights.

We can observe Moody's long-term ratings (with their yields and implicit risk premiums) for the sovereign debt of a sample of countries as shown in Table 7.4.

Comparing these results with the ones obtained by subtracting U.S. T-bond returns from sovereign debt yields (see Table 7.1), we can see that the figures for the country risk premiums turn out significantly different, as shown in Table 7.5. The reason for these differences might be that rating agencies tend to take a long-term view of country bond perspectives and thus their classifications are relatively stable. Instead, bond yields are likely to be highly volatile and are affected by erratic international capital flows (see Chapter 1: Financial Theory in Emerging Markets).

TABLE 7.4

Country	Moody's Rating	Yield (%)	Country Risk Premium (%)
Argentina	Ba3	10.10	4.00
Bahrain	Ba1	8.60	2.50
Bolivia	B1	10.60	4.50
Brazil	B2	11.60	5.50
Bulgaria	B2	11.60	5.50
Canada	Aa2	6.75	0.65
Chile	Baa1	7.30	1.20
China	A3	7.05	0.95
Colombia	Baa3	7.55	1.45
Costa Rica	Ba1	8.60	2.50
Czech Republic	Baa1	7.30	1.20
Hungary	Baa2	7.40	1.30
India	Ba2	9.10	3.00
Indonesia	B3	12.60	6.50
Israel	A3	7.05	0.95
South Korea	Baa3	7.55	1.45
Kuwait	Baa1	7.30	1.20
Malaysia	Baa3	7.55	1.45
Mexico	Ba2	9.10	3.00
Morocco	Ba1	8.60	2.50
Pakistan	Caa1	13.60	7.50
Philippines	Ba1	8.60	2.50
Poland	Baa3	7.55	1.45
Romania	B3	12.60	6.50
Russia	B3	12.60	6.50
Saudi Arabia	Baa3	7.55	1.45
Singapore	Aa1	6.70	0.60
South Africa	Baa3	7.55	1.45
Taiwan	Aa3	6.80	0.70
Thailand	Ba1	8.60	2.50
Turkey	B1	10.60	4.50
United Arab Emirates	A2	7.00	0.90
United Kingdom	Aaa	6.10	0.00
United States of America	Aaa	6.10	0.00

Source: Reprinted with the permission of Professor Aswalth Damodaran © 1999. www.stern.nyu.edu/~adamodar/
New-Home-Page/home/htm, December 1999. All rights reserved.

7.2.2 Critique of the Traditional Approach to Country Risk

The approach to country risk just described has been widely adopted by most financial analysts, and for many years it has been practiced without questioning. Nonetheless, from our perspective it is flawed for at least three reasons.

TABLE 7.5

| Country | Procedure* | |
	Yield Difference (%)	Moody's (%)
Argentina	8.74	4.00
Brazil	10.23	5.50
Philippines	19.57	2.50
Mexico	6.25	3.00
Poland	2.93	1.45

*Final months of 1999.

Country Risk Is Not Totally Systematic and Is Unstable Adding the country risk premium to the risk-free rate, hence to the discount rate, implicitly assumes that country risk is fully systematic or nondiversifiable. However, evidence suggests that public stock returns in developing and developed countries are not highly correlated. To the extent that these returns are truly representative of the local economies, it seems that at least a good portion of country risk is diversifiable.

As a general rule: it is right to add the country risk premium to the discount rate only if country risk is fully systematic. If country risk is partly systematic, just a portion of it should be added to the discount rate. If country risk is fully nonsystematic, none of it should be added to the discount rate.

As shown in Table 7.6, empirical evidence points to the possibility that country risk may be diversifiable to a considerable extent. The second column contains the

TABLE 7.6

Country	Correlation*
Argentina	0.44
Brazil	0.43
Chile	0.57
Colombia	0.24
India	0.03
Malaysia	0.47
Mexico	0.44
South Korea	0.36
Taiwan	0.38
Turkey	0.09
United States	0.79
Venezuela	0.27

*Monthly data representing 4–10 years up to November 1999.

Sources: © Reuters 2000 and Morgan Stanley.

correlations between each country's stock index and the MSCI developed country index for a group of nations.

Emerging market stock indexes usually comprise a very limited number of selected companies and thus are very far from being truly representative of local business. Therefore, the above correlations of Table 7.6 must be interpreted cautiously, serving only as a point of reference, since they might be quite an imprecise proxy for the true correlations between each country's economy and the MSCI index. However, to the extent that these correlations may be representative, we can see how emerging countries do not tend to show important correlations with the developed world.

Nevertheless, a couple of comments must be made:

1. As the process of globalization integrates emerging countries with the developed world, we should expect these correlations to increase. Hence, the diversification effect of investing in the developing world will become less beneficial.
2. To complicate matters, the evidence from the emerging markets crisis that started in Thailand in 1997 seems to indicate that volatility and the systematic and nonsystematic components of country risk can change drastically. In consequence, for some periods of time systematic risk might be low, and for others very high.

Country Risk Is Not the Same for All Projects The same country risk premium should not apply to every investment in a particular country. Some countries have a better reputation in some business sectors than in others. Hence, the country premium for the more reputable sectors should be lower. This could be the case of investments in the banking sector in Panama, or in bananas in Ecuador. Relatively more stable and consistent government policies should be expected in these sectors given that they are critical sectors of these countries' economies.

Likewise, there could be some activities with higher country risk. A possible example is agriculture, which many nations consider to be a matter of national security. In consequence, governments usually interfere through subsidies, price controls, import quotas, and other measures.

Last, it is feasible, through contracting arrangements, to reduce country risk for certain types of investment,—for example, a joint venture with the local government in a state-controlled sector (e.g., mining). It is reasonable to expect that this would result in less unfavorable interference since such actions would hurt not only the investors but also the government as a partner.

Credit Risk Is Not Equivalent to Country Risk Government bond prices (in hard currency) of developing countries depend on investors' expectations of compliance with the promised payment schedule. Adding the country risk premium to the discount rate assumes that the risk of noncompliance by the government is the right proxy for country risk. This is not accurate in most cases.

7.2.3 An Alternative Approach to Country Risk

Many analysts have become less comfortable with the traditional method of accounting for country risk as described here. This is probably why a number of different alternatives for investment analysis in developing markets have been proposed. We will focus on one of the most recent proposals.

The main intuition behind this approach is that riskier markets should demand higher market risk premiums. Thus, country risk should be taken into account as part of market risk. Therefore, the country risk premium CR should be added to the market risk premium, and not to the risk-free rate (Damodaran 1999a), as follows:

$$E(R_P) = R_F + \beta_P[E(R_M) - R_F + CR]$$

CR is computed through the following procedure:

- A U.S. Treasury bond and a bond in **local currency** with maturities (or durations[4]) comparable to our investment horizon issued by the government of the country under analysis are selected.
- A U.S. corporate bond (in U.S. dollars) with the same credit rating as the government bond of the emerging country (in local currency), and similar maturity, is identified. Since it has the same credit rating, the corporate bond yield should be a good indicator of the yield in hard currency that the (emerging country) government bond should demand. Hence, the excess yield of the corporate bond over the U.S. Treasury bond allows us to infer the country risk premium CR.

The country risk premiums CR computed by this procedure for a group of selected countries as of the end of 1998 are shown in Table 7.7. This procedure is based on the following reasoning:

1. Emerging country government bonds in local currency are more liquid and stable than their hard currency equivalents. Therefore, the credit ratings of the local currency bonds are more trustworthy, and these bonds are a better reference for the determination of the country risk premium.
2. It has been found empirically that the returns of bonds and shares in local currency are strongly correlated. Thus, government bonds in local currency are a good guide for the incremental market risk premium in emerging markets.

Although this is an insightful procedure, in our opinion it has a couple of shortcomings. In the first place, by adding country risk to the market risk premium we implicitly assume that country risk is fully systematic. And we have already explained why we do not agree with this assertion.

In the second place, under the traditional approach the country risk premium was added to the risk-free rate. As an outcome, all projects were subjected to the same level of country risk. In this alternative procedure, country risk is added to the market risk premium. The effect in this case is to tag each investment with a level of country risk that depends on the project's beta. When the beta is zero, there is no country risk. As beta grows larger, country risk increases as well.

---

[4]See footnote 2 in this chapter.

TABLE 7.7

Country	Rating	Country Risk Premium (%)
Argentina	BBB	1.75
Brazil	BB	2.00
Chile	AA	0.75
China	BBB+	1.5
Colombia	A+	1.25
South Korea	AA−	1.00
India	BB+	2.00
Malaysia	A+	1.25
Mexico	BBB+	1.5
Peru	B	2.5
Russia	BB−	2.5
Taiwan	AA+	0.50
Uruguay	BBB	1.75

We think this is not always appropriate. According to this procedure, a low-beta firm, such as an electrical utility, will have lower country risk than another with a higher beta, say, a steel mill. But it is quite likely that the electrical utility will suffer from populist government policies (like delays in adjusting tariffs for inflation) and may in fact face much larger country risk than the steel mill.

There is a variant to this method (Damodaran 1999c). Instead of being added to the market premium, country risk is added to the risk-free rate (much as in the traditional method) but multiplied by a factor lambda (λ) that can vary as follows between zero and one, depending on how much of the project's income comes from exports:

$$E(R_P) = R_F + \beta_P[E(R_M) - R_F] + \lambda CR$$

When exports represent 100% of income (and, supposedly, country risk is nil), λ is zero; λ increases as export income goes down and becomes one when exports are zero.

The problem with this approach is that it focuses country risk exclusively on exports without accounting for national factors (e.g., local currency costs, government interference) that could have a significant effect on operations. Although it could be a good approach for certain situations, we believe it is probably an oversimplification.

We have discussed two models for investment analysis in emerging markets. Both lack theoretical justification, and both affect the discount rate with a country risk premium. There are others that we will not cover; instead, we present a modified version of the CAPM whose main characteristic is that it does not explicitly include a country risk premium in the discount rate.

7.3 A MODIFIED CAPM

We have seen the difficulties associated with quantifying country risk. In addition, we learned that the CAPM poses some special problems when applied to emerging markets. We will use the intuition underlying the CAPM to propose a methodology to tackle these difficulties. We begin by establishing a couple of assumptions.

7.3.1 Assumptions

a. *Diversified Portfolios.* We assume that our project's investors hold well-diversified international portfolios. In consequence, only systematic risk is relevant.[5]

If this assumption is not valid, the impact of the project on investors' portfolios is not homogeneous and the results of the model become less relevant. As we learned, portfolio analysis is the right approach for investment evaluation when investors do not have well-diversified portfolios (see Chapter 5: Personal Investments). Nonetheless, we feel fairly safe in assuming that at least the most significant investors in emerging markets have well-diversified international portfolios.

b. *Hard Currency Consumption Baskets.* The second assumption is that the investors' consumption baskets are denominated in (or at least strongly biased toward) a particular hard currency (e.g., U.S. dollar, Euro, yen).

We consider this to be a reasonable assumption even for developing country investors. This is because the consumption baskets of these investors usually have a large foreign (hard) exchange component and/or the value of the local currency portion is strongly correlated with the prices of imported materials and services.

To summarize, we think that the assumptions of diversified portfolios and hard currency consumption baskets are acceptable at least for the great majority of the most important investors in developing countries.

7.3.2 The Modified CAPM

The modified CAPM model we are about to propose, recognizes that a project's results can be significantly related to two or more markets. For instance, the income (and risk) of an Argentine company exporting to the United States and Brazil must be affected by what happens in these countries. This is why we use a weighted beta for the project.[6,7]

For the sake of simplicity, we will use the U.S. dollar as the relevant hard currency. In other words, we are thinking of investors with consumption baskets that are

---

[5]Often governments restrict the free flow of capital into and out of their countries. But this does not necessarily prevent local investors from holding well-diversified international portfolios, since some will manage to achieve them before the imposition of restrictions.

[6]This adjustment to the CAPM is inspired by some ideas taken from Damodaran (1999a) and Shapiro (1996).

[7]Strictly, beta must be weighted according to the distribution of cash flows. We comment on this topic further on.

dependent on the U.S. dollar. Likewise, we adopt the U.S. stock market as our proxy for the "market portfolio."

Imagine a textile concern with three relevant markets, one of them the U.S. market. The weighted beta is computed in the following manner:

1. The beta of textile companies in the U.S. market $\beta_{t,M}$ is estimated. This can be obtained from a financial information service.[8]

2. Estimate the betas of each local market with respect to the U.S. market. If we name these markets m and n, their corresponding betas will be $\beta_{m,M}$ and $\beta_{n,M}$. These betas can be estimated by regressing the historical returns of (representative) local stock indexes against the U.S. stock market returns.

3. Compute the project beta in each market with respect to the U.S. market, $\beta_{tm,M}$ and $\beta_{tn,M}$, as follows:

$$\beta_{tm,M} = \beta_{t,M}\beta_{m,M}$$

$$\beta_{tn,M} = \beta_{t,M}\beta_{n,M}$$

where $\beta_{t,M}$ is the beta corresponding to the textile business in the U.S. market.[9]

4. Find the weighted beta β_p with the following formulas:

$$\beta_P = \alpha_M\beta_{t,M} + \alpha_m\beta_{tm,M} + \alpha_n\beta_{tn,M}$$

$$\alpha_M + \alpha_m + \alpha_n = 1$$

where the alpha values represent proportional income originating in each market.

5. The modified CAPM is:

$$E(R_P) = R_F + \beta_P[E(R_M) - R_F]$$

where

(a) R_F is the yield of a U.S. government bond in U.S. dollars with maturity (or duration) approximately equal to the project's horizon.

(b) $E(R_M)$ is the expected return of the proxy for the market portfolio, for instance, the S&P 500 Index of the United States.

---

[8]These services offer the values of beta for many companies, each one with specific operational and marketing characteristics, as well as different levels of debt. Thus, it is important to select companies showing high similarities to the one under analysis, and also to adjust for the effect of leverage. This last point will be covered in detail in Part III. Further on we will name some of these services.

[9]In principle, it would be more logical to estimate the betas of the textile business with respect to the local markets (e.g., $\beta_{t,m}$) instead of the U.S. market $\beta_{t,M}$. The trouble is that local betas contain many flaws. More about this further on.

TABLE 7.8

Firm	Metal casting manufacturer in country *RXT**
U.S. beta of metal casting business $\beta_{t,M}$	0.82
Beta of the *RXT* stock market with respect to the U.S. market $\beta_{m,M}$	0.69
U.S. risk-free rate R_F	0.04
Expected U.S. market return $E(R_M)$	0.12

*The firm has 20% of its sales in the local market; the remaining 80% represents exports to the United States.

We have not yet incorporated the impact of financing sources on β_p. This topic is discussed later on (see Chapter 10: Financing in Theory).

A Practical Example Assume a firm with the characteristics shown in Table 7.8. The beta corresponding to the RXT income will be

$$\beta_{tm,M} = \beta_{t,M}\beta_{m,M} = 0.82 \times 0.69 = 0.57$$

The beta corresponding to the U.S. income, $\beta_{t,M} = 0.82$, is used to find the weighted beta, as follows:

$$\beta_P = 0.2 \times 0.57 + 0.8 \times 0.82 = 0.77$$

The expected return is:

$$E(R_P) = R_F + \beta_P[E(R_M - R_F] = 0.04 + 0.77(0.12 - 0.04) = 10\%$$

7.3.3 Comments

The foregoing example elicits some important comments.

About the Indirect Estimation of Beta Publicly traded securities are the natural information source for those interested in estimating beta for a real investment. In developed countries it is a straightforward process to select one or more publicly traded companies in the same (or similar) line of business as the company being analyzed. Then their corresponding betas are obtained from an information service. The project beta should be within the range of these company betas.

However, generally this procedure is not as easily done in developing countries, for several reasons:

- The short history and high volatility of the stock markets in developing countries make it very difficult to estimate average returns with acceptable confidence levels.
- Emerging stock markets tend to be illiquid and, for most securities, long time intervals are usual between one transaction and the next. Thus, information on prices is infrequent and irregular, and many prices (for the periods the securities were not traded)

are unknown. Returns computed from this kind of information are bound to be imprecise; hence observed returns do not accurately reflect real historical returns.

- It is difficult to find companies in many lines of businesses because usually only a limited number of firms are traded in the stock markets. Additionally, the stock indexes are strongly biased toward a few stocks, which are weighted heavily in the market. Therefore, betas do not mirror risk with respect to the market but with respect to a biased basket of securities.

BOVESPA, the main Brazilian (São Paulo) stock index, offers interesting evidence on this issue. As shown in Table 7.9 and Figure 7.1, one stock weights over 38% and just 10 stocks comprise over 80% of the index, which is nevertheless one of the largest stock exchanges in the developing world.

- The betas are influenced by the frequency at which each stock is traded with respect to the average. If the trading frequency of a particular stock is relatively low, in some periods there will seem to be zero return in the series (when the stock is not traded), biasing its beta downward. The contrary occurs when the stock is more frequently traded than the average

Therefore, generally, the best solution for emerging countries is to rely on information from countries with well-developed stock markets, the U.S. market being the most popular point of reference. There are several reasons for this:

1. The vast majority of the largest U.S. corporations have important operations abroad. Up to a point, this qualifies the U.S. market as a reasonable proxy for a global portfolio.

2. The large variety of publicly traded companies facilitates identification of reference firms for practically every conceivable line of business.

3. High liquidity as well as abundant and transparent information assures that price series faithfully reflect real historical market returns.

TABLE 7.9 BOVESPA Composition* (Decreasing Order)

Number	Company	Percent	Cumulative
1	Teles RCTB	38.625	38.625
2	Petrobras	9.572	48.197
3	Eletrobras	6.024	54.221
4	Teles RCTB	5.743	59.964
5	Telesp	5.13	65.094
6	Vale r Doce	3.394	68.488
7	Cemig	3.311	71.799
8	Eletrobras	3.302	75.101
9	Bradesco	2.769	77.87
10	BANESPA	2.273	80.143

*December 1999.

Source: www.bovespa.com.br. Reprinted with permission. © 2000 BOVESPA.com.br.

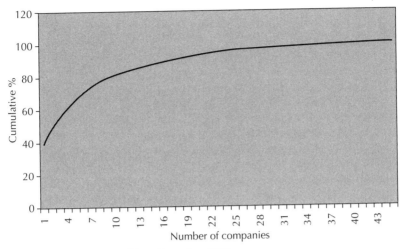

Figure 7.1 BOVESPA composition, December 1999.

Source: www.bovespa.com.br. © 2000 BOVESPA.com.br. Reprinted with permission.

4. Long history and low volatility of the stock market permit a much more reliable computation of average returns.

It is true that the U.S. stock market is the most popular for obtaining reference betas. Nevertheless, it must not be forgotten that other indexes representing a more global portfolio, such as the MSCI, are viable alternatives too.[10]

Two interesting sources of information for the estimation of beta deserve to be mentioned:

www.stern.nyu.edu/~adamodar/New_Home_Page/home.htm

www.reuters.com.

The first one offers the values of beta for different businesses. The second contains the stock index for 30 emerging countries. With them the country's betas with respect to a reference index (e.g., S & P 500, MSCI) can be computed.

The betas for a number of business activities are shown in Table 7.10. Unless otherwise indicated all of them correspond to the United States. The betas of the stock index of a selected group of countries with respect to the MSCI are shown in Table 7.11. Betas from this table are significantly larger than their corresponding correlations (see Table 7.6). This is because $\beta_{i,m} = \rho_{i,m} (\sigma_i/\sigma_M)$ and because the much larger volatility characterizing emerging stock markets makes for a large quotient σ_i/σ_M. As in Table 7.6, the values represent 4–10 years of monthly data up to November 1999.

---

[10]One other possibility is to estimate beta for the investor firm directly, regressing its stock returns against the selected reference index (e.g. S&P 500 or MSCI). However, this would require the investor firm stock to be very liquid to have a long history of public trading, and to have a systematic risk similar to the one of the project being analyzed. These conditions are rarely met.

TABLE 7.10

Sector	Beta*	Sector	Beta*
Advertising	1.07	Machinery	0.71
Aluminum	0.78	Maritime	0.50
Apparel	0.79	Medical services	0.91
Auto and truck	0.65	Medical supplies	0.92
Bank (non-U.S.)	1.09	Metal fabricating	0.82
Beverage (alcoholic)	0.60	Metals and mining (div.)	0.66
Beverage (soft drink)	0.74	Natural Gas (distribution)	0.42
Building materials	0.73	Newspaper	0.76
Cement and aggregates	0.77	Office equipment and supplies	0.81
Chemical (basic)	0.76	Oilfield services/equipment	0.99
Computers and peripherals	1.15	Packaging and container	0.56
Computer software and services	1.26	Paper and forest products	0.66
Copper	0.65	Petroleum (integrated)	0.73
Drug	1.07	Petroleum (producing)	0.70
Drugstore	0.89	Publishing	0.82
Educational services	0.95	Real estate investment trusts	0.70
Electrical utility (eastern U.S.)	0.39	Railroads	0.66
Electrical equipment	0.97	Recreation	0.80
Electronics/Entertainment (non-U.S.)	0.88	Restaurants	0.78
Environmental	0.68	Retail stores	0.96
Financial services	0.83	Securities brokerage	0.91
Food processing	0.68	Semiconductors	1.37
Food wholesalers	0.69	Semiconductor capital equipment	1.62
Furniture/Home furnishings	0.84	Shoes	0.79
Gold/Silver mining	0.53	Steel (general)	0.69
Groceries	0.64	Steel (integrated)	0.72
Home appliances	0.80	Telecom (non-U.S.)	1.00
Home building	0.60	Textiles	0.50
Hotels/Gaming	0.69	Tires and rubber	0.83
Household products	0.79	Tobacco	0.70
Industrial services	0.90	Toiletries/Cosmetics	0.84
Insurance (life)	0.90	Utility (non-U.S.)	0.71
Insurance (property/casualty)	0.80	Water Utilities	0.37
Internet	1.52		

*These betas are "unleveraged," meaning that they have been adjusted to reflect systematic risk without debt (see Chapter 10: Financing in Theory).

Source: Reprinted with the permission of Professor Aswath Demodaran © 1999. www.stern.nyu.edu/~adamodar/ New_Home_Page/home/htm, December 1999. All right reserved.

TABLE 7.11

Country	Beta
Argentina	1.81
Brazil	1.68
Chile	1.35
Colombia	0.57
South Korea	1.11
India	0.08
Malaysia	1.27
Mexico	1.30
Taiwan	1.09
Turkey	0.42
United States	0.75
Venezuela	1.25

Sources: © Reuters 2000 and Morgan Stanley.

Adjustments to Beta

a. *Cash Flow Composition.* Weighted beta was computed according to the proportion of income originating from each market. This was a simplification since, on the one hand, the distribution of costs must also be taken into consideration and, on the other, it is the positive and negative cash flows that are relevant (not income and costs).

The weights of beta (i.e., the alphas) must be calculated to allow for the exposition of each class of cash flow to each market. Let us illustrate with an example.

Suppose the average annual results for the project horizon are as shown in Table 7.12.

Total positive cash flows ($15 million) represent 60% of total (nonnet) cash flows ($15 million + $10 million = $25 million). Total negative cash flows ($10 million) represent 40% of total (nonnet) cash flows ($25 million). The alpha values for each market are given by:

$$\alpha_i = \text{(proportion of positive cash flows in } i\text{) } 0.60$$
$$+ \text{ (proportion of negative cash flows in } i\text{) } 0.40$$

TABLE 7.12

	Results					
	Country A		Country B		Totals	
Cash Flow	$ million	%	$ million	%	$ million	%
Positive	10	66.6	5	33.3	15	100
Negative	8	80	2	20	10	100
Net	2	40	3	60	5	100

Hence,

$$\alpha_A = (0.666 \times 0.60) + (0.80 \times 0.40) = 0.72$$

$$\alpha_B = (0.333 \times 0.60) + (0.20 \times 0.40) = 0.28$$

b. *Operating Leverage.* The project and the reference firms might have different operating leverages. Operating leverage depends upon the mix of fixed and variable costs. The larger the ratio of fixed to variable costs, the larger operating leverage will be. The usual way to measure it is to assess how operating income before financial expenses and taxes varies with changes in sales.

The project and the reference companies might be in the same line of business, but if one of them has higher operating leverage, its income will be more volatile and so will be its systematic risk. Therefore, the project's beta must be adjusted in proportion to the difference in operating leverages.

c. *Business Portfolio Composition.* Many companies are involved in more than one line of business. This is particularly true in emerging countries, with their abundance of diversified conglomerates (see Chapter 2: Consumption, Investments, and Value). In these cases a company beta does not make sense. Instead, a beta for each line of business must be computed and each project evaluated with its corresponding beta.

d. *Liquid Assets.* Many firms confront the possibility of iliquidity by keeping important amounts of liquid assets. This is something we observe in emerging markets, where funding restrictions sometimes oblige firms to develop their own financing sources (see Chapter 11: Financing in Practice). These liquid assets must be treated as a different line of business since they have different risks and betas.

Even after adjustments are made, given the considerable imprecision surrounding the estimation of beta, it is always advisable to evaluate the project for a range of betas around the original estimate. This is even more important in lieu of the recent evidence of fluctuations in the systematic risk of emerging countries (i.e., the Asian crisis). The more uncertain our estimate of beta, the wider the range should be. Naturally, the net present value of the project will not be a single figure but a range of values, as well.[11]

About the Impact of Country Risk Notice that β_P is an average of the project's betas weighted with the cash flows for each market. Additionally, each individual beta results from multiplying the systematic risk of the business in the U.S. market ($\beta_{t,M}$) by the systematic risk of the local market with respect to the U.S. market. Observe that the lower the beta between each local market and the U.S. market, the lower the contribution of the local market to project risk, and vice versa.

---

[11]Up to now we have omitted any adjustment due to differing leverages. This will be discussed in Part III.

If we are prepared to accept that the local stock market betas with respect to the U.S. stock market reasonably reflect nondiversifiable country risk, then in the proposed model, country risk will be automatically factored in by these local market betas. Systematic country risks will be fully reflected by the betas, and the uncertainties associated with the project itself will be incorporated into the cash flow scenarios.

Since, however, it is well known that emerging stock markets are not good proxies of the local economies, country risks are not accounted for adequately through the local stock market betas. We can only hope that as time goes by and local exchanges develop, these bourses will better reflect the local business environment, and their betas with respect to the U.S. stock market will carry a larger proportion of the systematic component of country risks.

At this point the reader will be aware that the main challenge is how the systematic component of country risk can be estimated and incorporated in the discount rate.

Unfortunately, we do not envision a clear-cut solution to this problem, and we must accept a degree of ambiguity in systematic country risk. The only way out is to add this imprecision to the other factors associated with the estimation of beta (discussed earlier) and experiment with different values of this parameter. The less accurately the local exchanges reflect their corresponding economies, the wider will have to be the range of betas. In the end, the assessment of the impact of country risk on the discount rate will rest on the good sense and intuition of the analyst.

Another possibility is to avoid the stock indexes and look for another proxy of the local economy (e.g., the gross national product). The problem with this approach is the difficulty of finding a truly representative indicator that provides data frequently enough to assure a statistically acceptable estimate of beta.

Information Sources Cash flow estimation is more an art than a science. Good projections depend critically on the analyst's experience and the proper use of all available information sources. Some useful web pages with data and information on many countries, as shown in Table 7.13, are suggested as a good starting point for this analysis. Also, as mentioned before in this chapter, the main rating agencies (e.g., Standard & Poor's, Moody's) also offer credit ratings for sovereign debts issued by many emerging countries.

Risk and Flexibility As pointed out earlier, country risk is often manageable. The task for investors in developing countries is to structure investments in such a way that country risk is minimized (hence expected cash flows are maximized). A common country risk management strategy is to build in future project flexibility. Further on we will see how this flexibility can be quantified and its value added to the project's cash flows. See Chapter 9 (The Value of Flexibility) and Chapter 12 (Financing and Value).

As a final comment we point out that the proposed modified CAPM is not a panacea. On the contrary, it still has many of the same flaws of the classic CAPM. These include, particularly, the need to assume that all investors have the same investment horizon and the same expectations and that there are no transactions costs. However, in spite of these important limitations we believe it to be a more appropriate model for emerging markets than the traditional country risk premium approach.

TABLE 7.13

Source	Web Pages	Type of Information
Transparency International	*www.transparency.de*	• Country Corruption Index (CPI) • Bribers Index (BPI)
International Finance Corporation (IFC)	*www.ifc.org*	
The Emerging Markets Companion	*www.emgmkts.com*	• News • Prices and yields of sovereign debt • Credit rankings (Moody's and S&P) • Particular conditions in certain countries • Research
BradyNet	*www.bradynet.com*	
World Bank	*www.worldbank.org*	• Information and research • Statistics
Prof. Roubini	*www.stern.nyu.edu/~nroubini/asia/ AsiaHomepage.htm*	• News • Papers
Prof. A. Damodaran	*www.stern.nyu.edu/~adamodar/ New Home Page/home/htm*	• Country risk indexes • Betas
Prof. C. Harvey	*www.duke.edu/~charvey/ camlinks.htm*	• Country risk indexes
Euromoney	*www.securities.com*	• News and financial information
Reuters	*www.reuters.com*	• Business information
Bloomberg	*www.bloomberg.com*	• Financial data

7.4 CONCLUSIONS

- Despite its considerable limitations, the CAPM remains the most popular model for estimating the expected return of real investments. This is mainly because it is easy to use in practice and because, up to now, no other clearly superior model has been developed.

- When applied it to emerging countries, the CAPM has additional shortcomings: the risks associated with each particular country (i.e., "country risk") must be accounted for, local stock markets are incipient, local companies are very sensitive to foreign influences, and many local investors do not hold well-diversified portfolios.

- The traditional methodology for quantifying country risk is to add to the discount rate the difference in yields between a "risk-free" bond and its equivalent in the developing country.

- We believe the traditional methodology has flaws since, on the one hand, it supposes country risk to be totally systematic while empirical evidence tends to contradict this and, on the other hand, it assumes that governmental credit risk is a good proxy for business country risk. Additionally, it seems that country risk might not be the same for all projects in the same country.

- A modified CAPM is proposed. It assumes that emerging market investors evaluate investment proposals in hard currency. The model allows for income and expenses in different countries and uses a (representative) developed stock market as the proxy for the market portfolio and the basis for the computation of project beta. The correct incorporation of systematic country risk remains a challenge.

- The proposed model is not a panacea. It is just an adaptation of the traditional CAPM to the case of emerging markets.

QUESTIONS AND PROBLEMS

1. Is it true that a country with a socialist and interventionist government must have a larger country risk premium than another country with free market policies?

2. We used a relevant country bond, with a maturity approximately matching the project's horizon, to estimate a country risk premium. Say that we expect country risk to increase and we are considering raising the country risk premium as the project evolves. Is this right?

3. Are the following statements true or false?
   Adding the country risk premium to the discount rate supposes that:
   (a) Country risk is fully systematic.
   (b) Financial markets assess country risk accurately for the length of the project, and this assessment is reflected in country bond yields.
   (c) Investors demand an extraordinary return from the project, which is equal to the difference in yields between the relevant country bond and the developed government bond of reference.
   (d) Country risk impacts all projects in the relevant country in the same way.
   (e) Default risk of the relevant country bond is directly related to the country risk pertinent to the project.

4. Adding the country risk premium to the market risk premium implies that country risk is a function of the project's beta. Discuss.

5. A U.S. company plans to export to a country whose economy's beta with respect to the U.S. market is 0.3. What percentage of its sales must be exported to reduce the firm's beta by half? Use the modified CAPM.

6. According to the modified CAPM, no country risk premium must be included in the discount rate. Does this mean that emerging country volatility is not taken into account?

7. According to the modified CAPM the systematic component of country risk is reflected in the discount rate through the beta of the local stock market with respect to the U.S. stock market (or a developed world index). Is this true?

CHAPTER 8

VALUATION IN EMERGING MARKETS

"The governments of developing countries have played a crucial role in their development."

We have seen how the CAPM can be modified to make it more relevant in the context of developing countries. We now turn our attention to investment valuation in these markets. These comments are valid for **all real investments, including those undertaken by firms and individuals.** However, a complete explanation of this topic would require a more extensive treatment than this chapter will seek to provide.[1]

We begin by explaining how to incorporate inflation and exchange rate considerations into a valuation exercise. Further, we will comment on the impact of subsidies, a common form of government intervention in developing markets. We will also analyze the scenario in which investment funding is restricted. We discuss the relationship between the projection horizon and the terminal value of a project, including the criteria for their determination. We end by commenting on liquidation value and the usefulness of reference indices as a control variable for the computation of net present values.

8.1 INFLATION AND EXCHANGE RATES

So far, we have ignored inflation in all our calculations. If expected inflation is not negligible, however, it must be accounted for in the projected cash flows. When there is no inflation, the purchasing power of a monetary unit remains constant over time; that is, each monetary unit will purchase the same basket of goods and services over a period of time. However, when inflation is positive, we will need more than 100 monetary units in the following year to purchase what can be bought with 100 monetary units this year, and increasing amounts of money as time goes by.

To illustrate, at an annual inflation rate of 20%, the same basket of goods and services that we can obtain for 100 monetary units today will cost.

$$100 \times 1.2 = 120 \qquad \text{in 1 year}$$
$$120 \times 1.2 = 144 \qquad \text{in 2 years}$$
$$144 \times 1.2 = 172.80 \qquad \text{in 3 years, etc.}$$

---

[1]There are several textbooks on investment valuation. Two recommended texts are by Damodaran (1996) and Copeland, Koller, and Murrin (2000).

It can therefore be said that 120 monetary units in one year is equivalent to 100 monetary units in **real terms** because both amounts make it is possible to purchase the same goods and/or services (at different points in time). Similarly, 144 in two years' time and 172.80 in three years' time are also equivalent to 100 monetary units in real terms.

Many analysts account for inflation by multiplying cash flows by an inflation index—imagine a cash flow with a purchasing power of 100 monetary units (i.e., in real terms) in each of the next three years. If it is expected that, say, the consumer price index will increase 10% in the first year, 12% in the second, and 14% in the third, the yearly cash flows are adjusted as shown in Table 8.1. This simple procedure is flawed, however. Projected cash flows represent an aggregation of various components of cash flow (e.g., working capital, labor, sales, rent). On the other hand, inflation indexes are a weighted average of the prices and quantities of a basket of goods and services that can drastically differ from the composition of cash flows. Therefore, the adjustment is very likely to be inexact.

For instance, if we had accounts receivable, inventories, or accounts payable denominated in foreign exchange, working capital would be more dependent on the expected exchange rates than on anticipated inflation.[2] When inflation is high, the cost of labor tends to increase at a rate less than the inflation rate. It is only occasionally that labor negotiations or competitive pressures produce dramatic changes in cost structures. In general, the best way to proceed is to analyze each component of the cash flow separately, and to adjust it according to its particular characteristics.

8.1.1 Type of Currency

We stated in Chapter 7 that investments must be evaluated in terms of a strong currency: in particular, the currency that is most closely related to the investor's consumption basket. Therefore, once every component of the projected cash flows has been adjusted by the expected inflation in local currency terms, the projections must be converted into strong currency based on the expected exchange rates at each point in time. The resulting cash flows must then be discounted at the rate computed in accordance with the modified CAPM.

TABLE 8.1

Year	Cash Flow Without Inflation	Estimated Yearly Inflation	Annual Factor	Cumulative Factor	Adjusted Cash Flow
1	100	0.10	1.1	1.1	110
2	100	0.12	1.12	(1.1)(1.12) = 1.232	123.2
3	100	0.14	1.14	(1.232)(1.14) = 1.4045	140.45

---

[2]In equilibrium this would be irrelevant, since the exchange rate must evolve in step with inflation. The higher the inflation, the faster the devaluation, and vice versa. However, this is rarely the case in many emerging countries, where intervention by government authorities frequently affects the pace of adjustment of the exchange rate to inflation.

However, the estimation of inflation and exchange rates could prove to be problematic. The easiest way to arrive at these estimates is to use a macroeconomic information service (of which there are several in every country). However, we must be cautious with this type of information, for even when it is derived from reliable data, it can be inaccurate. Thus, we must always perform a sensitivity analysis for different levels of inflation and exchange rates in order to assess their effect on the $E(NPV)$.

The interaction between inflation and exchange rates highlights a very important risk: **exchange risk.** If local currency depreciation evolves more slowly than inflation, strong currency cash flows turn out to be larger than their real-term equivalents. This is because their increase due to inflation is larger than their decrease due to devaluation. The contrary occurs when inflation runs slower than devaluation. In the example given in Table 8.1, if the rate of devaluation were 5%, the first year's strong currency cash flow[3] would be:

$$\frac{110}{1.05} = 104.8$$

This is larger than the real value (i.e., 100).

With a devaluation rate of 20%, the value is computed to be 91.7 (110/1.20). This is less than its value in real terms of 100. By performing similar computations for the other cash flows, we obtain the values shown in Table 8.2. When devaluation runs more slowly than inflation, strong currency cash flows increase. The contrary occurs when devaluation increases at a rate higher than inflation.

Disequilibria between the exchange and inflation rates often stem from governments' political motivations and do not have a significant relationship to what generally happens in international financial markets. Hence, it is reasonable to assume that exchange risk is mostly of the nonsystematic type, and therefore it must have a significant impact on only projected cash flows, not on the discount rate.

Many analysts ignore inflation adjustments and currency conversions and arrive directly at cash flow projections in strong currency terms. This approach is valid only

TABLE 8.2

Year	CF in Real Terms	CF with Inflation	Strong Currency Cash Flows	
			Devaluation 5%	Devaluation 20%
1	100	110	104.8	91.7
2	100	123.2	111.8	85.5
3	100	140.4	121.3	81.3

[3]A 1:1 starting exchange rate is assumed. Also, for the sake of simplicity we are assuming no strong currency inflation. If this were not the case, strong currency cash flows would have to be adjusted, dividing them by (1 + strong currency inflation) to make them comparable to real-term cash flows.

when the exchange rate varies in step with inflation. In our example, this would imply that the rate of devaluation would be exactly 10, 12 and 14%, in years 1, 2, and 3, respectively.

This rarely happens in inflationary economies owing to persistent gaps between inflation and the evolution of the exchange rates. However, this simplified approach can be acceptable when inflation does not significantly affect the cash flows, as is the case in projects for which inputs are primarily imported and sales are predominantly for the export market (e.g., most oil and mining projects).

We focused on exchange risk as related to inflation, but there is **convertibility risk** as well. Convertibility risk arises when exchange controls or other restrictions prevent the conversion of the local currency into foreign currency. Since, as exchange risk, it is also the result of policy decisions, convertibility risk tends to be nonsystematic and should have a significant impact on cash flows only, not on the discount rate.

THE EXCHANGE RATE IN ZIMBABWE

The end of the year often tends to be a bad time for the Zimbabwe dollar. Last year the official response to the crisis recalled other emerging market attempts to protect unviable exchange rate pegs. The Central Bank stabilized the currency at Z$ 38 to the U.S. dollar and privately instructed the banks to maintain that rate. Meanwhile President Mugabe blamed "international speculators" for the Zimbabwe dollar crash.

The currency has been battered again in recent weeks. Troubles in the tobacco and mining sectors have stopped foreign currency inflows. But the Central Bank insists to defend the exchange rate and says it has sufficient reserves to cover six weeks of imports. Businesses are not convinced. They have to wait at least eight weeks to buy foreign exchange and travelers needing foreign currency are told to come back in a week.

In the meantime a black market has developed where banks and businesses are selling foreign currency at a "parallel" rate of Z$ 44 to the U.S. dollar. But the Mugabe government is determined to keep the exchange rate at its current level. To help achieve this it borrowed U.S. $150 million from a German bank and is also toying with the idea of tightening exchange controls. Mugabe's determination seems related to the parliamentary elections to be held in April 2000.

Source: "Grim for the Zim", Reprinted with permission of © The Economist Newspaper Limited, London. November 27th 1999. All rights reserved.

Comments In this example we see how (interested) political considerations can have an effect on economic variables. Possibly to ameliorate the inflationary effects (and the unpopular repercussions) of a possible devaluation on the verge of elections, the government is maintaining an overvalued exchange rate.

What are the consequences of this policy on exporters and importers? Is the purchase of foreign exchange at the official exchange rate always going to be transparent? Who wins and who loses? How the population is likely to be affected in the short and medium run? What is the possible impact on investment decisions?

We will come back to the topics of inflation and exchange rates when we deal with working capital in emerging markets (see Chapter 11: Financing in Practice).

8.2 SUBSIDIES

The governments of most countries—developed or not—intervene in the economic affairs of the marketplace. However, intervention by emerging country governments is usually more accentuated. A common policy, for example, is to either interfere with or influence the income and cost structure of projects of certain types. Some of the interventionist policies that governments tend to adopt are discussed next.

8.2.1 Agricultural Subsidies

Despite the increasing globalization of business activities and the growing interdependence among nations, many governments still view agriculture as a special sector that needs to be insulated from foreign competition. Two arguments are commonly advanced to justify this stand. First, for reasons of national security, every country should be self-sufficient in food production to ensure food for its population. And second, agriculture is an integral element of a nation's culture, environment, and landscape, none of which must be tampered with.

It is this thinking that leads governments to assume part of the cost of fertilizers to artificially lower production costs, to set up import restrictions for certain products, allowing local production prices to increase too much, or to sell government-owned agricultural land below market prices. Policies like these tend to introduce price and cost distortions in the economy.

8.2.2 Energy Prices

Governments tend to adopt either the view that energy must be affordable by everybody, hence the government is obliged to assume part of the costs, or that energy is an important source of tax revenue, hence prices should be raised above the market level. In many instances, governments will price energy at differential rates, depending on the customer segment—for example, establishing different pricing structures for agricultural, domestic, and industrial users of energy.

8.2.3 Prices of Public Utilities

It is not uncommon for governments to regulate prices of certain services, such as water supply, telecommunications, public transportation, and garbage collection. Since many of these services are natural monopolies, their regulation is justified.[4] Nevertheless, emerging country governments often go farther and, for instance, lower prices with a

---

[4]Globalization and technology are rapidly transforming public utilities, making these businesses more competitive all over the world. The more competitive they become, the less justified the monopoly argument will be for their continued regulation.

view to appeasing certain politically sensitive groups (e.g., families) and charge higher prices to other groups (e.g., industry). This tends to result either in artificially lower prices for everyone or in one section of society subsidizing another.

It is only when suppliers of such services start taking significant losses, and service quality and reliability are threatened, that governments consider yielding to a price adjustment.

8.2.4 Subsidized Loans

Another route through which governments intervene in national economies is by interfering in financial markets to influence interest and exchange rates (again, to the benefit of some groups and the disadvantage of others). One common practice is stipulating that banks establish mandatory preferential financing schemes for certain activities and/or sectors (e.g., mortgages and agriculture). This causes banks to increase financial costs for the rest of their client base to subsidize the preferred sectors. For further discussion on this issue, refer to Chapter 11, Financing in Practice.

We must be careful when we analyze lines of business that are subject to government intervention of these types—for just as a government establishes these schemes, it can also drastically modify or eliminate them.

The best way to tackle this problem is to evaluate a project both with and without elements that could distort the analysis (e.g., a specific subsidy or tax exemption). The difference between the corresponding $E(NPV)$s will show the effect of each of these policies on the project. If a particular distortion causes a project's $E(NPV)$ to be positive, the project must be accepted only if the distortion is not expected to disappear in the near future and/or if the project's horizon is short.

To illustrate with an example, take the case of an agricultural investor who is offered the following governmental benefits to start a plantain plantation:

1. Raw material subsidies amounting to 10% of market value.
2. A 10% interest rate loan for 80% of the value of the land plus equipment and improvements. Only interest payments are made annually, with the entire principal to be repaid in a single installment at the end of a 10-year period. The market yearly rate for a similar loan would be 15%.

Without the subsidies, the expected cash flow would be as shown in Table 8.3.[5] The $E(NPV)$ of this project is −$39,260 at a 25% discount rate. Since this value is negative the investment proposition is not acceptable. The effect of the subsidies is shown in Tables 8.4 and 8.5. The $E(NPV)$ of the cash flow recorded for an $8000 raw materials subsidy at a 25% discount rate is +$28,560 (Table 8.4). The $E(NPV)$ of the loan described in Table 8.5 at the 15% market rate of interest is +$30,110.

Including the subsidies, the expected net present value of the project is now:

$$E(NPV) = -\$39,260 + \$28,560 + \$30,110 = +\$19,410$$

---

[5]To simplify we disregard taxes.

TABLE 8.3

Expenses	0	Years 1–10	10
Land purchase and sale	−$100,000		$200,000
Equipment and improvements	−$50,000		
Sales		$115,000	
Raw materials		−$80,000	
Other expenses		−$10,000	
Cash flow	−$150,000	$25,000	$200,000

The project's $E(NPV)$ is positive when the impact of the subsidies is taken into account. However, it is important to be aware that the project would be unacceptable in the absence of subsidies. That is, the project cannot be accepted on its own financial merit.

8.3 CAPITAL RATIONING

According to financial theory, the lack of capital never prevents an attractive project from being financed. Whenever an investor does not possess funds, the project can always be sold to another investor who can supply the capital; or investing partners can be found, or a loan can be contracted to complete the requisite funding.

This reasoning is acceptable in advanced economies where financial markets are well developed and it is not very difficult to raise money for interesting business propositions. But it does not hold in emerging markets where the attractiveness of a project is often difficult to convey to other investors (owing to information constraints or moral hazard problems). Further, banks are underdeveloped and tend to demand solid collateral from borrowers, and capital is scarce in general. As a result, investors in developing markets usually face situations of **capital rationing,** and many attractive projects are not undertaken because the necessary funding is not available.

Sometimes investors who have access to several attractive projects are not able to invest in them all owing to lack of funds. In this case, investors must devise a method to choose the right combination of projects. The interested reader can refer to Appendix 8A for such a methodology.

TABLE 8.4 Raw Material Subsidy

	0	Years 1–10	10
Subsidy		$8000	

TABLE 8.5 Loan Subsidy

	Years		
	0	**1–10**	**10**
Subsidy	$120,000	−$12,000	−$120,000

FINANCIAL SUBSIDIES INDIAN STYLE

Indians are keen savers. Indian households save more than 18% of GDP each year, and the rate is rising. Since financial reforms began early this decade. Indians have been investing more in financial assets rather than physical ones such as gold and property. But their choices remain limited: capital controls bar investment abroad, and high interest rates discourage share purchases.

Nearly half of household saving is still in bank deposits, totaling U.S. $177 billion, nearly 10 times the assets managed by mutual funds. Another large chunk U.S. $85 billion is in postal savings and pension funds on which the government guarantees a high fixed return. But the burden of providing that subsidy is now proving too heavy. This, together with a recent ruling exempting mutual fund dividends from taxes (whereas interest on bank deposits remain taxed) is opening the door to private financial intermediaries. Also a bill to liberalize insurance will come up for debate in parliament in December.

The range of private mutual funds is growing. Foreign banks with names such as ANZ Grindlays and ABN Amro have entered the asset management business and several foreign insurers including Sun Life, Zurich, Prudential and Principal, and Standard Life are keen to manage Indian assets.

Source: "Paying Dividends," Reprinted with permission of © The Economist Newspaper Limited, London. November 13th 1999. All rights reserved.

Comments This is a good example of government intervention distorting interest rates. If the government gets out of the business and competition in the financial market heats up, interest rates (lending and borrowing) will surely fall, for two reasons: the subsidy to postal savings and pension funds will disappear and intermediation margins will go down.

Households will get lower returns on their savings, but this will motivate them to buy shares. Firms will benefit both through lower loan interest rates and by having a larger pool of savings, the owners of which are willing to purchase the firms' equities.

All this will certainly benefit the Indian economy.

8.4 HORIZON AND TERMINAL VALUE

It is very important to determine the investment horizon over which the investment will be valued. This horizon is closely related to the value of the project at the end of its horizon, that is, its **terminal** value, computed as the *E(NPV)* of the project's cash flows commencing at the horizon.

When the horizon is longer, fewer cash flows are used to determine the terminal value of the project. The longer the horizon, the smaller the terminal value, and vice versa. In one extreme case, if we take the time horizon to be zero, the terminal value equals the project's present value (excluding the initial investment). If the horizon is not less than the life of the investment, the terminal value is zero.

Zero horizons do not make sense because nothing would be projected. Infinite horizons do not make sense either, since cash flows cannot be estimated for an indefinite time period. An investment horizon equal to the life of the investment does make sense. However, it might be impractical for investments whose life is too long (i.e., 20–30 years), since a considerable amount of financial computation would be involved. Given these considerations, how do we determine the horizon and terminal value of a project?

There are two criteria for the determination of the horizon.

a. *The horizon must be long enough for the project's cash flows to achieve stability.* When evaluating investments, frequently we encounter extraordinary incomes or expenses during the initial years. For instance, when buying new equipment we can expect installation and training costs. Further, there is a learning curve during which production levels are lower than optimal.

Likewise, during the acquisition of a firm one can anticipate significant alterations in income and expenses, liquidation of certain assets, additional capital expenditure, and/or modifications in financial structure. This is especially relevant when the acquired company is undergoing financial difficulties and drastic changes are necessary to reverse the situation.

In emerging markets it is also common to expect periods of uncertain governmental policies that translate into higher cash flow volatility.

It is critical to include these periods of cash flow instability within the horizon. It is only when income and expenses achieve stability that the horizon should be terminated.

b. *The investment horizon must be long enough for the terminal value not to be a very significant percentage of the present value of the projected cash flows (excluding the initial investment).* If we are taking the trouble to make a projection, it is only logical for the project's present value to reflect primarily the projected cash flows, being the present value of the terminal value, a relatively less important component. This is especially relevant in emerging countries, where cash flow volatility can have a significant impact on the project's *E(NPV)*. Our experience suggests that for most projects, the *PV* of the terminal values should not rise above 20% of the expected present value of the projected cash flows.

Let us see how the weight of the terminal value changes with the investment horizon. Assume an opportunity to invest $1 million that produce yearly cash flows of $200,000 for a 10-year period (there are no cash flows after 10 years), as shown in

TABLE 8.6

Year	Terminal Value ($ thousand)	Percentage (%)
0	+1229	100
1	+1152	94
2	+1067	87
3	+974	79
4	+871	71
5	+758	62
6	+634	51
7	+497	40
8	+347	28
9	+182	15
10	0	0

Table 8.6. If the yearly discount rate is 10%, $E(PV)$ will be +$1,229,000. According to our criteria, the horizon for this project should not be less than 9 years.

8.4.1 Terminal Value Estimation

Terminal values can be estimated in three ways. One can start with the present value of asset liquidation or with the present value of a nongrowing or growing perpetuity.

a. Present Value of Asset Liquidation. Once an investment has been made, the option of liquidating it (i.e., selling all or some of the assets) is always available. For example, if we are dealing with a real estate development project, the land can always be sold. Or a firm that has been acquired can always be dismantled and individual assets sold in the open market. What we obtain through this procedure represents the **liquidation value.**

Liquidation value equals terminal value if the investment is liquidated. However, the terminal value has other possibilities, since the investment could continue beyond the horizon. Liquidation will be the most convenient option when the liquidation value is larger than the $E(NPV)$ of the cash flows projected for continuing with the business. Equating the terminal value to the liquidation value is a conservative assumption implying that the business is not viable beyond a certain time horizon. This could be reasonable in highly unstable emerging countries in which long-term business conditions are largely unpredictable.

b. *Present Value of a Nongrowing Perpetuity.* An alternative approach is to take the last cash flow of the projection horizon and compute the terminal value by assuming that this cash flow will remain constant over a number of years. The implicit assumption here is that business conditions will not deteriorate nor improve—they just will stay the same for a very long period of time. A good approximation to this situation is to assume a fixed cash flow forever. Such cash flows extending to infinity are termed **perpetuities.**

For instance, if the last cash flow of the projection was $100 and the yearly discount rate is 10%, it can be shown that the *PV* of a $100 forever at this discount rate is given by[6]

$$PV = \frac{+\$100}{0.10} = +\$1000$$

In general,

$$PV = \frac{CF}{r}$$

where *CF* is the last period's cash flow and *r* is discount rate for the relevant period.
If significant inflation is expected for the currency, the *PV* for the perpetuity is

$$PV = \frac{CF(1 + inf)}{r}$$

where inf is the period's expected inflation.[7]

c. *Present Value of a Growing Perpetuity.* We can also be optimistic and assume that cash flows will grow forever in real terms. In this case the perpetuity's present value is

$$PV = \frac{CF}{r - g}$$

where *g* is the growth rate of the cash flow in each period.
    The most general expression when both inflation and real growth exist is

$$PV = \frac{CF(1 + inf)}{r - g}$$

We must be careful in working with growing perpetuities. As *g* increases, the perpetuity's *PV* increases exponentially. When *g* approaches *r*, *PV* tends to infinity, and the mathematical expression becomes irrelevant. Relatively small increases in *g* can substantially impact the terminal value, pushing the project's *E(NPV)* to unrealistically high levels.

    The most acceptable way to estimate the terminal value depends on the project's own characteristics. The best approach might be to extend the horizon until the maturity

---

[6]Refer to Appendix 8B for the proof of this and other formulas.

[7]Strictly, if expected inflation is positive, the discount rate should increase, though not necessarily in the same proportion.

of the investment is such that either the zero real growth or the liquidation value assumptions become reasonable, and the perpetuity does not significantly impact the project's $E(NPV)$. In addition, growing perpetuities must be avoided, especially in the uncertain environments of developing countries.

8.5 REFERENCES AND ADJUSTMENTS TO NET PRESENT VALUE

At any point in time, the minimum value of an investment is represented by its liquidation value. If the liquidation value is larger than the present value of projected cash flows, the investment's $E(PV)$ will be the liquidation value. If the liquidation value is smaller than the present value of projected cash flows, $E(PV)$ will be the present value of the cash flow projection.

Therefore, liquidation value is an important reference when one is judging the merits of an investment proposal. If the expected value of the projected cash flows $E(PV)$ is less than the liquidation value, the investment must be liquidated. If it is larger, the business must continue. Another important reference is the relationship between $E(PV)$ and certain business indexes such as sales volume and profitability.

8.5.1 Liquidation Value

The first step in computing liquidation value is to obtain the estimated market prices of each asset associated with the investment. Using these as inputs, we prepare an optimal liquidation strategy—the strategy that leads to the largest possible $E(NPV)$. It is important here to not only realize the maximum amount possible for every asset, but also to take into account the timing of the proceeds (the sooner the money is realized, the larger the PV).

The markets for assets, however, can be quite illiquid, depending on the nature, type, and specification of an asset. This is particularly true in developing countries. For instance, it is not uncommon to find only a few (if any) potential buyers of machinery and equipment Therefore, sale prices often must be reduced significantly. These discounts should be taken into consideration in the making of financial projections for the liquidation process.

A similar approach must be adopted when one is accounting for the liquidation of a firm's shares, especially those that are not actively negotiated in the stock exchanges. Again, it is necessary to allow for a discount to estimate the true market value[8] of the assets.

Further, the projected cash flows must also include the costs associated with the process of liquidation. The liquidation value will be the $E(PV)$ of the cash flows corresponding to this process.

As a final point, the liquidating process may display risks that are different from those associated with the original business. Thus, the appropriate discount rate could be different from that of the business in question.

---

[8]An empirical study found that the median of the illiquidity discount for a group of U.S. companies' shares was 33.75% (Silber 1991). This can serve as a useful point of reference.

8.5.2 Index-Based Valuation

The business community tends to give importance to index-based valuation methods. These provide complementary information for assessing the robustness and consistency of the computations against market realities, but they are not a substitute for $E(NPV)$.

These methods are based on indexes of other companies in the same line of business as the firm we are concerned with. Some of the most common indexes are as follows:

- Market price[9]/profits
- Market price/production capacity
- Market price/sales (in units and in strong currency)

The idea is to compare the firm's performance [the firm's $E(PV)$ is used in place of market price] on these parameters vis-à-vis the corresponding indexes for other firms in the industry. Presumably, there must not be large variations between the index values across the firms. Significant differences could be interpreted as a signal that the valuation requires revision, or its assumptions do.

Nonetheless, this approach should be used with caution. These indexes are rarely a good guide for emerging countries where business conditions are dissimilar. Firms dealing primarily with international markets (e.g., cement, mining) might be treated as exceptions to this caveat.

8.6 CONCLUSIONS

- In many emerging markets, inflation and exchange rates are highly volatile and therefore must be taken into consideration when cash flow projections are being made.

- Accounting for expected inflation by using the general price index is a flawed approach, since the project's cash flow components are generally quite different from those of the index. The best approach is to adjust every cash flow component individually.

- In many emerging markets, exchange rate and inflation tend to evolve out of balance. This leads to exchange risk, which can signify either gains or losses for the investor.

- Given the disequilibria between the exchange rate and inflation, projecting cash flows in strong currency directly without considering local inflation, can cause significant errors in most projects. However, such projections can offer a reasonable approximation when the effect of inflation on cash flows is insignificant.

- Barriers to converting local currency into foreign currency lead to convertibility risk. Both convertibility and exchange risk are basically nonsystematic and thus tend to affect cash flows only, not the discount rate.

---

[9]For these indexes to be comparable, it is necessary to adjust for differences in financial leverage (see Chapter 10: Financing in Theory).

- When subsidies are available, the safest way to evaluate the investment is to value the project both with and without the subsidies, to assess the subsidy's impact on $E(NPV)$. This result, in conjunction with our expectations about future government actions, should determine the financial feasibility of the project.
- The time horizon over which a project is evaluated should be long enough for the project's cash flow to achieve stability. In addition, it should be chosen such that the terminal value does not effect the valuation significantly.
- The terminal value is a function of the cash flows commencing at the horizon. We could be conservative and assume the terminal value to be equal to the liquidation value, or we could take a more aggressive stance and assume that cash flows exhibit positive real growth.
- It is not advisable to assume positive real growth of cash flows for computing the terminal value in emerging markets, however, for this practice can distort the project's $E(NPV)$ considerably.
- The liquidation value must correspond to the $E(PV)$ of the cash flows associated with the best liquidation strategy.
- It can be convenient to refer to indexes relating the value of a firm to certain factors (e.g., sales, installed capacity) to validate the result of a valuation. However, these indexes tend to lose relevance in emerging markets.

QUESTIONS AND PROBLEMS

1. Given the projected inflation, exchange rates and cash flows in local currency as shown in Table P8.1. Compute the projected cash flows in strong currency ($).

2. Do cash flows in strong currency increase or decrease in real terms when devaluation evolves more slowly than inflation?

3. Under what conditions is it proper to project cash flows directly in strong currency, without separate adjustments for inflation or exchange rates?

4. What are we assuming when the risks associated with the exchange rate are incorporated not in the discount rate but in the cash flows?

5. As part of a government program to promote small businesses, a firm is offered a $1 million subsidized loan payable in three yearly installments of $300,000, $300,000,

TABLE P8.1

	Year		
	1	2	3
Cash Flows (thousand, local currency)	1000	1000	1000
Inflation (%)	10	15	20
Exchange rates (local currency vs. $)	1000	1050	1100

and $400,000, respectively, at a 10% yearly interest rate. If the market interest rate is 15%, how much is the subsidy worth?

6. What are the two issues that must be taken into account when one is setting the projection horizon of a project?

7. What problem do we encounter when the terminal value is computed as the *PV* of a growing perpetuity?

8. Why, at any point in time, is the minimum value of an investment represented by its liquidation value?

9. Why are liquidation values usually smaller in emerging markets than in developed ones?

APPENDIX 8A

Selection of Alternatives Under Capital Rationing

We will now try to identify the investment alternatives investors must choose when they lack the necessary funds to undertake every investment with a positive net present value.

Assume three projects with the initial investment requirements and *E(NPV)*s at a 10% discount rate as shown in Table 8A.1. None of the projects has a negative *E(NPV)*. Therefore, in the absence of funding constraints, all should be accepted. Further, assume that the investor has only $20,000. In this case, at least one of the projects cannot be executed. Which projects should the investor choose?

The three projects are independent of each other. This means that investing in any of them does not preclude the possibility of investing in another. For example, *A* could be a real estate investment project, *B* a textile manufacturing unit, and *C* the renovation of an existing restaurant facility.

The projects are grouped in a manner that makes each combination of projects exclusive of the others. In other words, investing in a particular set of projects implies

TABLE 8A.1

Project	Investment	E(NPV) (10%)
A	$15,000	40
B	$10,000	20
C	$5,000	5
Totals	$30,000	65

that we cannot invest in any other set of projects. Thus, we can invest in *A* or *B* or *C*, or in *A* and *B*, *A* and *C*, or *A* and *D*, and so on. All the possible combinations with their total investments and *E(NPV)*s are as shown in Table 8A.2.[10]

Combinations *A* and *B*, *B* and *C*, and *A*, *B*, and *C* are not feasible because their investment budgets exceed $20,000. We must choose from among the remaining combinations, the set of projects with the highest *E(NPV)*. This combination is *A* and *C* requiring an investment of $20,000 and yielding an *E(NPV)* of $45,000.

8A.1 MUTUALLY EXCLUSIVE PROJECTS

If some of the projects were mutually exclusive, combining them would not be possible. Thus, combinations containing mutually exclusive projects should be discarded. This would be the case if we were obliged, say, to choose between two machines for metal casting. The purpose would be to choose only one of the machines. If, in our example, *A* and *C* were mutually exclusive, neither this combination nor *A*, *B*, and *C* would be feasible, and the best decision would be to invest only in *A*.

The general procedure for choosing among a group of projects under capital rationing is as follows:

1. List all the projects identifying the required initial investment and *E(NPV)* for each project, as well as the projects that are mutually exclusive.
2. Discard projects with a negative *E(NPV)*,[11] group the remaining projects (excluding the mutually exclusive ones), and compute the associated total initial investment and total *E(NPV)*.

TABLE 8A.2

Combination	Investment	E(NPV) (10%)	Possible?
A	$15,000	$40,000	Yes
B	$10,000	$20,000	Yes
C	$5,000	$15,000	Yes
A and B	$25,000	$60,000	No
A and C	$20,000	$45,000	Yes
B and C	$25,000	$25,000	No
A, B, and C	$30,000	$65,000	No

---

[10]Recall that *NPV* is additive. That is, *NPV* of *A* and *B* = *NPV* of *A* + *NPV* of *B* (see Chapter 2: Consumption, Investments, and Value).

[11]Since these would always decrease total *E(NPV)*, hence would not be attractive under any circumstances.

3. Reject all combinations whose total initial investment is above the available capital and choose the one with the maximum total $E(NPV)$.[12]

When capital rationing is present beyond time zero the problem must be solved through integer programming. Take the four projects, shown in Table 8A.3 with their corresponding E(NPV)s and cash flows over a two-year horizon.

Assume that capital is rationed to a maximum of $130,000 in the initial year and $40,000 in year one.

The problem to solve is

$$\text{Max } E(NPV) = +214X + 27Y + 23Z + 95T$$

subject to

$$-100X - 50Y - 60Z + 0T \geq -130$$

$$+300X + 30Y + 0Z - 350T \geq -40$$

$$X, Y, Z, T \text{ can be only } 0 \text{ or } 1$$

TABLE 8A.3

Project	Cash Flows* 0	1	2	E(NPV)(10%)*
X	−100	+300	+50	+214
Y	−50	+30	+60	+27
Z	−60	0	+100	+23
T	0	−350	−500	+95
Totals	−210	−20	+710	+359

*Amounts in thousands of dollars.

---

[12]The selection can also be made by sorting the groups in descending order based on the profitability index, and beginning from the top of the list, to choose the group with the largest total initial investment, given the capital constraint. The profitability index is found by dividing $E(PV)$ by the amount invested. This procedure is equivalent to the one described in the text.

APPENDIX 8B

Perpetuities

8B.1 PRESENT VALUE OF A NO-GROWTH PERPETUITY

The general formula for the present value of a n-period cash flow C_t discounted at a rate r is:

$$PV = \sum_{t=1}^{n} \frac{C_t}{(1 + r)^t}$$

Suppose C_t constant and equal to C. Also, assume that n tends to infinity. Let us define the following expressions:

$$a = \frac{C}{1 + r} \quad \text{and} \quad x = \frac{1}{1 + r}$$

Then,

$$PV = a(1 + x + x^2 + \cdots)$$

Multiplying by x, we have

$$xPV = a(x + x^2 + x^3 + \cdots)$$

Subtracting the second expression from the first, we write

$$PV(1 - x) = a$$

$$PV\left(1 - \frac{1}{1 + r}\right) = \frac{C}{1 + r}$$

$$PV\left(\frac{r}{1 + r}\right) = \frac{C}{1 + r}$$

$$PV = \frac{C}{r}$$

8B.2 PRESENT VALUE OF A GROWING PERPETUITY

The present value of a growing perpetuity is:

$$PV = \frac{C}{1 + r} + \frac{C(1 + g)}{(1 + r)^2} + \frac{C(1 + g)^2}{(1 + r)^3} + \cdots$$

This is a geometric series of the type

$$PV = a(1 + x + x^2 + \cdots)$$

where

$$a = \frac{C}{1 + r} \text{ and } x = \frac{1 + g}{1 + r}$$

Thus,

$$PV = \frac{a}{1 - x} = \left(\frac{C}{1 + r}\right)\left[\frac{1}{1 - (1 + g)/(1 + r)}\right]$$

For the case in which $r > g$,

$$PV = \frac{C}{r - g}$$

When r approaches g, PV tends to infinity.

CHAPTER 9

THE VALUE OF FLEXIBILITY

"It is possible to know the price of everything, but the value of nothing."

—OSCAR WILDE

Net present value is the cornerstone of investment evaluation. However, it assumes that it is possible to invest only at the beginning of a time period (i.e., one must invest now or never), that investment decisions are irreversible (i.e., once started cannot be modified), and that investors do not have any influence over future cash flows.

In other words, in its simplest form, *NPV* does not allow for any type of flexibility to invest at the most appropriate moments or to alter cash flows along the way. This is not realistic: investors almost always have some leeway before and during the life of a project. We see how it is usually feasible to invest in stages or to abandon certain projects if they turn out to be unfavorable.

Through option theory, this type of flexibility can be quantified and its value added to *E(NPV)* to determine the true value of an investment proposition. This is the topic of this chapter. **Everything we will cover is equally valid for any type of real investment made either by a firm or an individual investor.**

In the discussion that follows, complexity is kept at a minimum level even though the topic itself is complicated. Moreover, the coverage is not comprehensive: only the main ideas are exposed.[1]

A simple example is used to illustrate the effect of flexibility on the value of a project. Also, options are introduced as a financial concept and methods of valuing them are explained. The impact of different parameters on option value is discussed. We differentiate between financial options and those associated with projects. The particular importance of project flexibility in emerging countries is pointed out, and a practical example follows. The link between options and strategic choices is explored. We conclude with some recommendations on project valuation with real options.[2]

The first six sections are a theoretical review. The reader comfortable with option theory can skip them and go directly to Section 9.7.

---

[1]Those who wish to study option theory in greater depth can refer to some excellent textbooks such as Brealey and Myers (1996) and Ross, Westerfield, and Jaffe (1999), or Hull (1997) for a more advanced treatment.

[2]This chapter is partly based on the document Instituto Venezolano de Ejecutivos de Finanzas (1998).

9.1 AN INTRODUCTORY EXAMPLE

We now illustrate the impact of flexibility on a project's value with a numerical example. To facilitate comprehension of this key idea, the example we chose is extremely simple (it actually contains a conceptual flaw, which we will correct later).

Imagine an investment in a pin factory. There is a 50% chance that during the first year of operations things will turn out well, and a 50% chance that they will turn out badly. In the first case we can expect a positive cash flow C_1 of $1 million at the end of the first year. In addition, at this moment the business would have an $E(PV_1)$ of $10 million.

If things turn out badly, the cash flow at the end of the first year C_1 will be $200,000 and the project will have an $E(PV_1)$ of $5 million. The discount rate is 10% per year. This can be demonstrated graphically, as shown in Figure 9.1.

The initial $E(NPV_0)$ will be

$$E(NPV_0) = \frac{1}{1.1}[0.5(\$1000 + \$10{,}000) + 0.5(\$200 + \$5000)] = +\$7363.64 \times 10^3$$

Now suppose we have the option of expanding the capacity of the factory at the end of year 1. If things turn out well, we invest in the expansion and $E(PV_1)$ increases from its original $10 million to $30 million (including the required additional investment at time 1). If things turn out badly there will not be additional investment. This scenario is demonstrated graphically in Figure 9.2.

$E(NPV_0)$ will now be

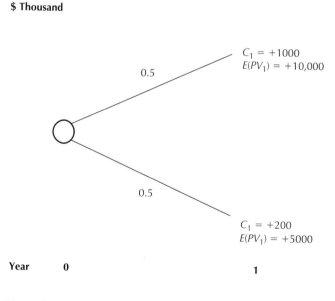

$ Thousand

0.5

$C_1 = +1000$
$E(PV_1) = +10{,}000$

0.5

$C_1 = +200$
$E(PV_1) = +5000$

Year   0   1

Figure 9.1

$ Thousand

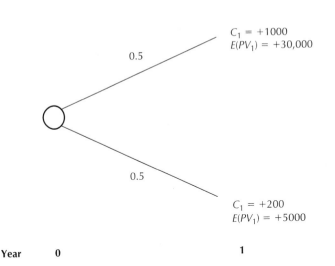

$C_1 = +1000$
$E(PV_1) = +30,000$

0.5

0.5

$C_1 = +200$
$E(PV_1) = +5000$

Year   0   1

Figure 9.2

$$E(NPV_0) = \frac{1}{1.1}[0.5(\$1000 + \$30,000) + 0.5(\$200 + \$5000)] = +\$16454.55 \times 10^3$$

The possibility of expansion if things turn out well enhanced the expected net present value of the project from $7,363,640 to $16,454,550 a $9,090,910 difference. This last figure is the **value of flexibility** associated with the possibility of expanding, in other words, the **value of the option** to expand if things turn out well.

It was mentioned that this example has a flaw. At the end of year 1, uncertainty decreases and we are able to take the most convenient decision given the new information available. This reduction in uncertainty means that the discount rate should be revised. The flaw is that this procedure does not allow for a way to adjust the discount rate. Option theory solves this problem.

9.2 WHAT IS AN OPTION?

Options are financial contracts on the price of an asset. One party to these contracts has a right and the other a duty. The buyer of the option has the right and the seller the duty. For instance, if the buyer of the option has the **right to purchase** one U.S. dollar at the end of one month for 500 monetary units ($500), the seller will be obliged to sell the U.S. dollar at that price if the buyer decides to exercise his right.

The buyer would rather purchase the U.S. currency in the open market if its price in one month is less than $500. But, if this is not so, the buyer will exercise his right. Thus, this option is similar to price insurance, since in no instance would the buyer purchase the U.S. dollar at a price higher than $500. This type of option guaranteeing a **maximum purchase price** is known as a **call.**

Puts are another type of option guaranteeing a minimum selling price. The buyer of a put on 1 U.S. dollar at $500 will be acquiring the **right to sell** the U.S. dollar for $500 at the end of the month. The seller would be undertaking the obligation to purchase the U.S. dollar in case the buyer exercises his right. Only if the market price of $U.S. 1 in one month is less than $500 will the put buyer exercise his right, assuring a **minimum selling price.**

The reference price of the asset is known as the exercise price E, and the time until the option can be exercised is its time to maturity T. In our example, E is $500 and T is one month.

We must differentiate between European and American options. European options can be exercised only at expiration, whereas American options can be exercised at any time before expiration.

9.2.1 Option Value at Expiration

The benefit to the buyer of a call is the difference between the **price of the underlying asset** (e.g., $U.S. 1) at expiration S_T and the exercise price E, as long as S_T is **larger** than E. If S_T is smaller than E, the buyer will not exercise his right and the benefit is zero. The situation of the call seller is a mirror image of the situation of the call buyer, as shown in Figure 9.3.

The benefit to the put buyer equals the difference between E and S_T as long as S_T is **less** than E. If S_T is larger than E, the benefit is nil. Again, the position of the put seller is a mirror image of that of the buyer, as shown in Figure 9.4.

9.2.2 Option Value Before Expiration

Option buyers either get a benefit equal to the difference between S_T and E or do not get any benefit. Option sellers either lose or do not gain. Option sellers will be willing to accept such an unfavorable position only if the seller pays them an amount of money: the option price. This price is the **value of the option before expiration** (C_t or P_t).

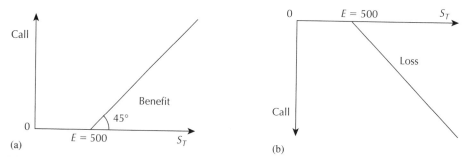

Figure 9.3 Value ($) of the call at expiration: (a) buyer and (b) seller.

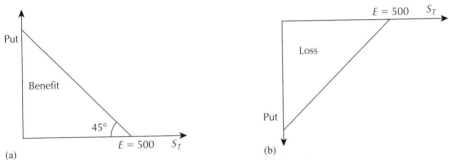

Figure 9.4 Value ($) of the put at expiration: (a) buyer and (b) seller.

In general, American options are more valuable before expiration than their equivalent European options. This makes sense because American options can be exercised not only at expiration like the European ones but also before expiration. This additional right makes them in principle more valuable.[3] For the sake of simplicity, we will focus on European options for the rest of the book.

There are several methods of computing the value of an option before expiration. The first and most famous is the one discovered by Professors Fischer Black and Myron Scholes (Black 1973). Since this important method demands advanced mathematics, however, we will cover it in relatively simple form, focusing instead on a friendlier procedure: the binomial method (Cox & Rubinstein 1979).[4] Let us start with this last model.

9.3 THE BINOMIAL MODEL

The intuition behind this model is to form a **no-risk** portfolio between the underlying asset and its corresponding options. We will use our U.S. dollar example to illustrate. Let us calculate the call value before expiration, assuming the data as in Table 9.1. We introduce two variables: u, which represents the new price of a U.S. dollar in the event of a price increase as a percentage of its current price, and d, its new price in the event of a price decrease as a percentage of its current price.[5] In our example, $u = 1.10$ and $d = 0.90$. The possible values for the call and the dollar are shown in Figure 9.5.

---

[3]The value of an American option can be equal to but never less than its equivalent European one. The values of American and European options are the same whenever early exercise is worthless, as is the case of the call option on a non-dividend-paying stock. For a more detailed explanation of this issue, refer to Hull (1997).

[4]The binomial method is relatively simple mainly because it is based on discrete time intervals, whereas the Black–Scholes model assumes infinitely short intervals (i.e., continuous time), giving rise to differential equations.

[5]In the binomial model it is required that $u > 1 + r > 1$; and $0 < d < 1 < 1 + r$. In addition, $0 < d < 1$ guarantees that the price of the underlying asset will never be negative.

TABLE 9.1

Data	
Initial price of the U.S. \$, S_0	\$490
Monthly risk-free rate, r	1%
Probability of an increase in the U.S. \$ price, q	50%
Percentage price increase of the U.S. \$	10%
Probability of a decrease in the U.S. \$ price, $1-q$	50%
Percentage price decrease of the U.S. \$	10%
Exercise price, E	\$500
Time to maturity, T	1 month

If the U.S. dollar increases by 10%, its value becomes $uS_0 = 490(1.1) = 539$. If the dollar decreases, its value falls to $dS_0 = 490(0.9) = 441$. In the first case, the value of the option is either the local currency equivalent of \$U.S. 1 less the exercise price, or zero, whichever value is larger. Given that $uS_0 - E = 539 - 500 = 39$, the option in this case will be worth 39. If the dollar falls, $dS_0 - E$ is negative, hence the value of the option is zero.

The next step is to form a portfolio with \$U.S. 1 and m calls, such that the value of the portfolio is constant regardless of the price of the U.S. currency. In other words, it is a **risk-free** portfolio. For the final result to be fixed, the value of the portfolio when the U.S. dollar rises must equal the value of the portfolio when the same currency falls. Mathematically,[6] we write:

$$uS_0 - mC_u = dS_0 - mC_d$$

Hence,

$$m = \frac{S_0(u - d)}{C_u - C_d}$$

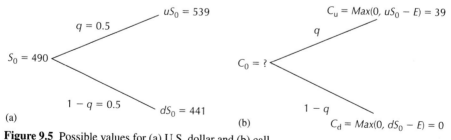

(a)

(b)

Figure 9.5 Possible values for (a) U.S. dollar and (b) call.

---

[6]The call portion in both portfolios has a negative sign, meaning that we buy dollars and sell calls.

TABLE 9.2

Scenario	Portfolio	Result
Favorable	$uS_0 - mC_u$	$539 - 98 = 441$
Unfavorable	$dS_0 - mC_d$	$441 - 0 = 441$

Substituting the values of our example, we have:

$$m = \frac{490(1.10 - 0.90)}{39 - 0} = 2.51$$

Therefore, a long position in \$U.S. 1 together with a short position in 2.51 calls gives rise to the same result in both scenarios, as shown in Table 9.2. This can be demonstrated graphically, as shown in Figure 9.6. Since it is a risk-free portfolio, its present value can be computed by discounting at the risk-free rate. Hence:

$$S_0 - mC_0 = \frac{uS_0 - mC_u}{1 + r} = \frac{dS_0 - mC_d}{1 + r}$$

Or

$$C_0 = \frac{S_0[(1 + r) - u] + mC_u}{m(1 + r)}$$

Substituting the value of m

$$m = \frac{S_0(u - d)}{C_u - C_d}$$

The call formula is obtained for a time to maturity of one month:

$$C_0 = \frac{pC_u + (1 - p)C_d}{1 + r}$$

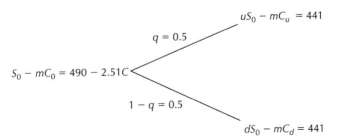

Figure 9.6

where

$$p = \frac{(1 + r) - d}{u - d}$$

$$1 - p = \frac{u - (1 + r)}{u - d}$$

In our example, we have

$$p = \frac{1.01 - 0.90}{1.10 - 0.90} = 0.55$$

$$1 - p = 0.45$$

and the call value will be

$$C = \frac{(0.55 \times 39) + (0.45 \times 0)}{1.01} = 21.24$$

We say that p is the **risk-free equivalent probability.**

The value of the call for longer times to maturity can be obtained by extending this procedure beyond one period. Also, we can use similar reasoning to obtain the value of a put before expiration.[7]

9.3.1 Assumptions of the Binomial Model

The interesting feature about the binomial model is that it permits the computation of option prices by a relatively simple procedure. Nevertheless, this simplicity comes at a price: the need to accept assumptions removed from real life.

The assumptions behind the binomial model are as follows:

Financial Markets Without Transactions Costs. This assumption must be made if we are to have a unique risk-free rate and to be able to create long, short, and fractional positions in any asset at no cost.

No Short Restrictions. The model requires the use of short positions to create risk-free portfolios; hence these cannot be restricted.

Stable Probability Distributions. The model assumes that the parameters of the asset return distributions (e.g., mean and variance) do not vary over time.

Constant Risk-Free Rate. The risk-free rate is constant during the life of the option.

---

[7]Notice that the value of the call, C_0, is independent of q, the probability of a rise in price for the U.S. dollar. This is because the value of an option is based on the feasibility of risk-free portfolios, hence is independent of the investor's risk aversion.

None of these assumptions holds in real life. Because of this, the values obtained through the binomial model are just approximations. Nevertheless, the ability to rely on the binomial method to value options (even approximately) is in itself very advantageous.

Next, we temporarily suspend our consideration of the binomial model to describe the Black–Scholes model.

9.4 THE BLACK–SCHOLES MODEL

The intuitions inspiring the Black–Scholes (Black 1973) and binomial models are identical: to form a no-risk portfolio by combining options with shares and to adjust this portfolio over time.

Nonetheless, Black–Scholes is different because it works in infinitesimal (i.e., infinitely small) periods of time. In such a short span it is assumed that the proportion between calls and stock in the no-risk portfolio stays constant. This implies that there is a linear relationship between the price of the option and the price of the stock, and thus it is possible to build a portfolio free of risk. The expected return on this portfolio will equal the risk-free rate.

Based on this reasoning, a differential equation to price any asset that is a function of the price of another asset can be established. This equation requires for the underlying asset to be actively traded. The equation turns out to be[8]:

$$\frac{1}{2}C_{SS}S^2\sigma^2 + C_SSr + C_t - Cr = 0$$

where

C	price of the asset, the option in our case
S	price of the underlying asset, the stock in our case
σ	instantaneous standard deviation of the price of the underlying asset
r	risk-free rate
C_S and C_{SS}	first and second partial derivatives of the price of the option with respect to the price of the stock
C_t	partial derivative of the price of the option with respect to time[9]

---

[8]This equation is obtained in Appendix 9A of this chapter.

[9]In this equation all variables are independent on the investor's risk aversion. This means that the option is equally valuable for every investor whatever his attitude toward risk. This property is possible because the underlying asset is actively traded and, as in the binomial model, it is always feasible to keep a no-risk portfolio. When the underlying asset is not actively traded, the expected return for the investor on the underlying asset appears in the differential equation. Since this return is a function of the investor's risk aversion, the valuation of the option becomes more difficult.

The final price of the asset depends on the **boundary conditions.** The boundary conditions are the prices of the asset for extreme values of certain variables as the price of the underlying asset and time in our case.

For the special case of a call (European or American) on a non-dividend-paying stock, the boundary conditions are as follows:

$$C_T = \text{Max}(S_T - E, 0)$$

$$C(0) = 0$$

$$\lim_{S \to \infty} C(S) = S$$

These are perfectly reasonable conditions, and they can be spelled out as follows: (1) by definition, the call price at expiration must be either zero or equal to the difference between the price of the asset and the exercise price; (2) if the stock is worthless, the option must be worthless as well; and (3) when the stock price tends to infinity, the price of the call must approach the price of the stock.

It is not common for this type of equation to have a simple solution. Fortunately this one does. The solution is[10]:

$$C = SN(d_1) - Ee^{-rT}N(d_2)$$

where C is the call price, S is the stock price, E is the exercise price of the call, r is the risk-free rate, T is the call's time to expiration, and $N(d)_n$ is the area below the cumulative normal distribution function from minus infinity to d_n:

$$d_1 = (\sigma^2 T)^{-1/2} \left[Ln \left(\frac{S}{E} \right) + T \left(r + \frac{\sigma^2}{2} \right) \right]$$

$$d_2 = d_1 - (\sigma^2 T)^{1/2}$$

$$\sigma^2 = \text{instantaneous variance of the stock}$$

Intuitively, this formula can be interpreted as saying that the price of the call is equal to the stock price less the present value of the exercise price. However, each of these terms is multiplied by a "probability" factor $N(d)_n$.

The Black–Scholes formula rests on the following assumptions:

- Normal instantaneous returns

- No jumps in stock prices

- No cash dividends

---

[10]The solution to the Black–Scholes equation is beyond the scope of this book. The interested reader can refer to Wilmott, Howison, and Dewynne (1998).

- Both variance and risk-free rate constant
- No transaction costs

These are unrealistic assumptions. However, surprisingly, call prices tend to follow the formula quite well. The formula fails significantly only when option prices differ greatly from exercise prices. Constant variance is probably the most critical assumption, since it has been shown empirically that variance is rarely constant and option prices are quite sensitive to changes in variance.[11]

9.4.1 Relation Between Binomial and Black–Scholes Models

As the number of periods within the time to expiration span is increased, the binomial model's risk-free equivalent probability "p" is found[12] to approach 0.5. Through this transformation, option valuation by the binomial model converges toward the Black–Scholes values. When the number of periods tends to infinity, the two formulas are identical.

For the processes to be equivalent and finally converge, the following relationships must hold for the parameters of the binomial model[13]:

$$u = e^{\sigma\sqrt{T/n}}$$

$$d = 1/u$$

$$p = \frac{1}{2} + \frac{1}{2}(\mu/\sigma)\sqrt{T/n}$$

9.5 WHAT DETERMINES THE VALUE OF AN OPTION BEFORE EXPIRATION?

We can infer from the application of both option pricing models that the variables that determine option values before expiration are the price of the underlying asset S_t, the exercise price E, the time to maturity T, the volatility of the underlying asset's price σ, and the risk-free rate r. Let us see how each one can affect the value of calls and puts.

The higher the initial price of the underlying asset S_0 with respect to the exercise price E, the more substantial the potential gain of the call holder and the higher the value of the option. The value of the put will be higher if S_0 is small relative to E.

---

[11]Formulas have been developed relaxing some of these assumptions, including the possibility of cash dividends, nonconstant variance, and jumps in stock prices. Numerical methods for solving the equations associated with complex options have also become quite common (Hull 1997).

[12]In mathematical terms this means that the Markov process behind the binomial model evolves toward what is known as Brownian movement.

[13]Convergence can also be achieved with different values of p. However, the new p's are no longer risk-free probabilities, and the advantages of option pricing by forming risk-free portfolios are lost (Wilmott, Howison, & Dewynne 1998).

Volatility has a symmetrical effect on asset prices. When volatility increases, the asset price can either rise or fall.[14] However, the effect of volatility on option values is nonsymmetrical. When volatility increases, the probability that the asset price will be **above** the exercise price also increases and so does the potential gain of a call holder. On the other hand, the potential loss is not affected, since no matter how low the asset price, the option price can never be below zero. Because of this, the impact of volatility on the value of a call is always positive. An increase in the volatility leads to an increase in the value of the call.

Something similar occurs with the put. An increase in variance increases the probability that the asset price will be **below** the exercise price. Therefore, the potential gain of the put holder increases while his potential loss is not affected, since the put value never can be negative. Thus, variance has a positive effect on put value as well. Variance is generally the most important variable affecting option values.

The span of possible option prices increases with time to maturity. Hence, the longer the time to maturity, the higher the value of the call. Furthermore, since the exercise price is an outflow in the case of the call, the larger the time to maturity, the farther away the outflow and the smaller its present value. Therefore, the call value increases with time to maturity both because of its effect on the possible price range and because of the benefit of a lower present value for the exercise price.

The put is different. Although the positive impact of a larger time to maturity on the price range increases its value as well, the exercise price is in this instance an inflow. Hence, a delay of this income decreases the value of the put. In consequence, the final effect of time to maturity on the value of the put is ambiguous: it increases because of a higher price range but decreases owing to the delay in the exercise price. In sum, we can expect the price of the put either to increase or to decrease with time to maturity.

Finally, the higher the risk-free interest rate, the lower the present value of the exercise price. Since it is an outflow in the call and an inflow in the put, high interest rates will increase the value of the call and decrease the value of the put.

Table 9.3 summarizes the foregoing set of relationships.

TABLE 9.3

The higher the Variable	Option value	
	Call	Put
Asset price	Larger	Smaller
Exercise price	Smaller	Larger
Asset variance	Larger	Larger
Interest rate	Larger	Smaller
Time to maturity	Larger	?

---

[14]This is not exactly true. The price can increase indefinitely but cannot fall below zero. Nevertheless, from a practical viewpoint it is an acceptable approximation for the large majority of underlying assets.

9.6 TYPES OF OPTION

We must separate financial from real options. **Financial options** are generally backed by a contract and traded in the capital markets. Among the best known are options on commodities, such as corn, wheat, coffee, minerals, oil, and orange juice, and options on bonds, foreign exchange, and stocks.[15]

On the other hand, **real options** are mostly implicit (i.e., not contractual). There are two groups of real options. In the first group are those associated with the funding side of an investment. Examples include the possibility of adjusting the provision of funds depending on the results of a project, the option to bankrupt, and the option to exchange debt for equity along the life of a project. We will discuss these options further in Chapter 12 (Financing and Value).

The second group includes options related to investments in real assets, such as the options to postpone or abandon a project, or to develop it gradually. This is the group we will focus on in this chapter.

9.7 FLEXIBILITY IN EMERGING MARKETS

Variance is the usual way to quantify uncertainty, and we saw how variance affects the value of options: an increase in variance leads to an increase in the value of the option. Thus, a project's real options will be more valuable if the uncertainty of its cash flows is high. A project will be more valuable if it has numerous real options and if the uncertainty of its cash flows is high.

As mentioned in Chapter 1. (Financial Theory in Emerging Markets), institutional backwardness, underdeveloped markets, unstable government policies, and economic uncertainty are all sources of risk for emerging market investors. Hence, projects in less developed countries are characterized by high cash flow volatility, and it can be concluded that the real options associated with these projects must represent a significant portion of project value.[16] The option to defer an investment (to be discussed shortly) is probably the most important option of them all.

Uncertainty is not necessarily bad for emerging market investors. The key is to gain a thorough understanding of its real causes and the possible path of volatility, as well as to be able to develop an objective interpretation of the disequilibria that are likely to arise in these environments (e.g., between inflation and exchange and interest rates, or between the intrinsic value and market price of certain assets). This is an important aspect of the business opportunities available in less developed economies.

---

[15]The concept of financial options can be extended to include other contractual arrangements like underwriting new issues of financial instruments and insurance policies.

[16]Recall the two components of risk: systematic and nonsystematic. Only the nonsystematic portion is assured to increase project value through higher cash flow variability (and more valuable real options). The systematic portion has opposing effects: by accentuating cash flow volatility, project value is increased, but by augmenting the discount rate, project value is decreased.

It is not enough to take advantage of these opportunities. At least as crucial is the ability to conceive and embed in investment projects real options of different types, as a way to better manage flexibility in these highly volatile environments. Since the higher the uncertainty, the more valuable the real options and the projects, such an ability is undoubtedly a key factor in doing business successfully in developing countries.

In the following section we use the binomial model to analyze the case of a mining project and illustrate how real options can enhance the value of investment opportunities.

9.8 AN INVESTMENT IN A MINING DEVELOPMENT

Imagine a mining development project. Its $E(PV)$ is $50 million and the initial investment is $55 million. Therefore, $E(NPV)$ equals –$5 million. Under the traditional *NPV* analysis (without considering real options), this project must be rejected.

Does this mean that the project must never be undertaken? What about waiting for a year before making a decision? How valuable would the option to delay this investment for one year be? (We follow the approach of Trigeorgis 1993 in the following example.)

9.8.1 The Option to Defer the Investment

Given the data shown in Table 9.4, we can say that Figure 9.7 represents the likely evolution of the project's present value and mineral prices in a year.[17]

At time 0, when the mineral price is $10, the *PV* of the project is $50 million. At the end of the first year, if the mineral price goes up to $15, the project's *PV* rises to $75 million, and if the mineral price goes down to $6.7 the project's *PV* descends to $33.5 million.

If we have the option to defer the investment for one year, the evolution of *E(NPV)*, adjusted to account for the option *P*, is as shown in Figure 9.8. (As in Figure 9.7, *P* is in millions of dollars.)

TABLE 9.4

Data

Present value of future cash flows V_0	$50 million
Initial investment I_0	$55 million
Upward mineral price movement u	$1.50
Downward mineral price movement d	$0.67
Mineral spot price S_0	$10
Risk-free rate r	5%

---

[17]We could extend the projection for as many years as we wish.

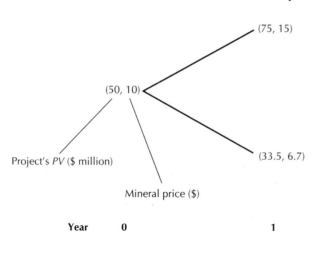

Figure 9.7

Let us explain. If at the end of the first year the mineral price is $15, this means that the present value of the project is $75 million and its $E(NPV)$ $20 million, or $75 million minus $55 million. This is a positive number, so the investment must be undertaken, and NPV at time 1 will be $20 million.

If at the end of year 1 the mineral price goes down to $6.7, the project's PV is $33.5 million and $E(NPV)$ will have a negative value of –$21.50 million, or $33.5 million minus $55 million. This is a negative value, so the best course of action is to not invest in the project, and therefore NPV is $0.

The next step is to compute the risk-free equivalent probability p. Assuming that the project's cash flows are perfectly correlated with mineral prices (quite reasonable in this case), p for the project equals p for mineral prices. Hence:

$$p = \frac{(1 + r) - d}{u - d} = \frac{1.05 - 0.67}{1.5 - 0.67} = 0.46$$

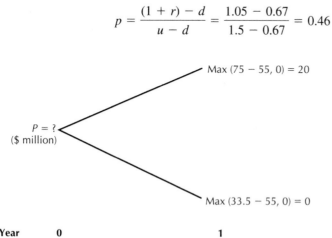

Figure 9.8

The project's adjusted value P will be:

$$P = \frac{(0.46 \times 20) + (0.54 \times 0)}{1.05} = \$8.76 \text{ million}$$

If the investment had been made at the beginning, $E(NPV)$ would have been −\$5 million. If we have the option to defer investment for one year, the net present value becomes +\$8.76 million. Since this last figure is larger, the proper decision is to defer the project.

When deferring, an outflow is being postponed. This outflow is similar to the exercise price of a call. Deferring is equivalent to a call option. The value of the option to defer is the value of the project with the call less the value of the project without the call:

$$8.76 - (-5) = \$13.76 \text{ million}$$

As in every other option, the value of the option to defer the investment is a function of several variables. If the variability in the mineral price or the time to defer were larger, so would be the value of the option.

By deferring we open up a window of opportunity for competitors, who might then take the investment opportunity from our hands. This would result in a lower value of the option (and of the project) as time passes. It is for this reason that the time variable can be crucial in competitive environments when there is the option to defer.

Investment Downturns The option to defer can explain an investment downturn in times of crisis. Volatility generally increases when the economic situation deteriorates. As volatility rises, the value of the option to defer becomes more attractive. After accounting for all the real options attached to existent projects, an investment slump in times of crisis is justified when the appreciation of the options to defer is sufficient to compensate for the increase in project values due to the higher value of all other real options net of any eventual changes in projected cash flows.

9.8.2 The Option to Expand

Going back to our mine development, imagine that there is no option to defer, but once the initial investment has been made we have the option to expand the project by investing more money. What is the value of the project with and without the option to expand? How much is the option to expand worth?

If expansion translates into a 30% increase in the value of the project and the additional investment amounts to \$12 million, the adjusted value will evolve as shown in Figure 9.9. The adjusted value of the project will be:

$$P = \frac{(0.46 \times 85.5) + (0.54 \times 33.5)}{1.05} - 55 = -\$0.31 \text{ million}$$

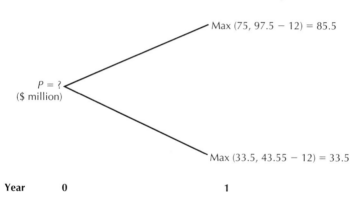

Figure 9.9

Even with the option to expand, the project must be rejected because its adjusted *NPV* remains negative. But the option to expand does increase the value of the project. The value of the option to expand, in this case a call, is:

$$-0.31 - (-5) = \$4.69 \text{ million}$$

We can draw the following conclusion:

- If the project did not have real options, it would be rejected.
- If the only real option were the option to defer, the project should not be rejected but the decision should be deferred for a year.
- If the only real option is the option to expand, the project must be rejected at the outset.
- If we consider both the option to defer and the option to expand, we see that the second option is not valuable enough to make the project acceptable but the option to defer justifies waiting for one year to make the investment decision.

Only two types of real options were illustrated in this example: the option to defer and the option to expand. It is possible to use similar methodology to compute the value of many other options that could be associated with a given project: for instance, the option to invest in stages, the option to invest more slowly or more rapidly, the option to abandon the project at some future time.

9.9 REAL OPTIONS AND STRATEGY

Real options are a key link between finance and strategy. The more an investor is capable of identifying, creating, nurturing, and exercising the real options associated with a project, the more valuable the project will be. Asking the right questions is the starting point (Amram & Kulatilaka 1999):

- What are the drivers of uncertainty and what their magnitudes?
- Where are the decision points?
- What are the opportunities to increase potential gains and decrease potential losses?
- What is the best way to minimize the costs of real options?
- How do the costs of embedded options compare with their expected benefits?

Unfortunately, thinking in terms of real options can be complex, not only because of the difficulties of visualizing every possible option but also because real options tend to be intertwined: each set of options at any point in time creates the opportunity to invest in another set and so on. The result can be a long and complicated chain of options on options over time.[18] Kulatilaka and Venkatraman (1999) propose the typology shown in Table 9.5 as practical way to deal with real options.

9.10 SOME COMMENTS ON VALUING WITH REAL OPTIONS

Our example of real option valuation was very simplistic. In real life we encounter many projects with many time periods, each one of them with different options and even options on options. Only common sense allows for an efficient way to handle these complexities. The key is to weight the true benefit of a more accurate numerical result against the cost of the computational difficulties involved in option valuations.

The investment of time and resources in a more precise estimation of real options will be justified if the project is important and the impact on its value of the real options is significant.

We can think of two extreme cases. If the project justifies a precise valuation, building specific mathematical models (as complex as desired) is appropriate.

TABLE 9.5

Type of Option	Role
Growth options	Imply entrance into loss-leading business operations that may open opportunities to participate in potentially valuable investments in the future
Exit options	Offer a way to reduce potential losses by allowing abandonment of the project.
Staging options	Involve designing investment opportunities by stages when benefits are uncertain, retaining the option to abandon, and at the same time reserving the right to expand at different stages
Sourcing options	Are associated with developing multiple input sources
Business scope options	Are related to the opportunity to change product scope in the future
Learning options	Represent investments in learning new technologies or business models

---

[18]Refer to Pindyck (1998) and Triantis and Hodder (1990) for an examination of the option value of real investments. Refer to Aivaizian and Berkowitz (1998) for a discussion on the investment/financing implications of a flexible production technology.

If an accurate valuation of real options is not justified, we can always use intuition. In particular, we start by computing the project's *E(NPV)* without options. If it is positive, the best bet is to accept the investment, since most probably the real options will only increase the value of the project. If *E(NPV)* is negative we must ask ourselves if its absolute value is larger or smaller than the likely values of the real options. If option values are likely to be more valuable, the project must be accepted. If option values are likely to be less valuable, the project must be rejected.

We conclude this section with some other ideas to be taken into account in valuing real options.

- In many instances identification of the underlying asset can be difficult. The best way to proceed is to choose an asset that is highly correlated with the project's cash flows. In addition, the asset must have a price history that is clear and abundant enough for us to arrive at an acceptable estimate of future variance. Unfortunately, there are not many assets with these characteristics.

- To assess which variables have the most impact on the value of the option one should perform sensitivity analysis. Estimation of these variables must be conducted with special care.

- Competitors, too, have flexibility. As we mentioned, the value of the option to defer could be negatively affected if competitors invest first. The formal valuation of this type of complexity requires game theory.[19]

We come to an end by mentioning two web pages that can be a useful reference for real options:

www.real-options.com

www.puc-rio.vr/marco.ind/main.html

The first contains a considerable number of publications on this topic, and the second deals with real option applications in the oil business.

9.11 CONCLUSIONS

- Traditional *E(NPV)* valuation implies that investments can occur only at time zero, that investment decisions are irreversible, and that investors do not have any influence over cash flows through time. The use of option theory allows us to quantify this type of flexibility, which is very common in real life.

- Options are financial instruments that give their buyers a right and their sellers an obligation. A right to purchase is called a call option and a right to sell a put option.

- The two main methods of option valuation are the binomial and the Black–Scholes models.

---

[19]Refer to Smith and Ankum (1993) and Trigeorgis (1997).

- The simplest method of option valuation is the binomial model. Although its assumptions are somewhat unrealistic, it is still quite useful, but we must be aware that its results are only approximations.

- Option value is a function of the difference between the underlying asset price and the exercise price of the option, the time to maturity, the risk-free interest rate, and the variance of the underlying asset. Variance is usually the most important variable.

- The inherent instability of the economies in emerging markets makes real options there particularly valuable. Maybe the most interesting is the option to defer an investment.

- Identification of attractive investment opportunities together with the ability to design and embed real options in investment projects [to increase their $E(NPV)$] is a key factor in conducting successful business operations in emerging markets.

- It was shown how to calculate the values of the options to defer and to expand. In a similar manner the values of other real options could be computed, such as the option to invest in stages, the option to invest at a slower or faster rate, and the option to abandon a project, among many others. Other interesting options are related to the funding strategy (see Chapter 12: Financing and Value).

- Real options are a key link between finance and strategy. Strategic choices can be viewed as the ability to identify, create, nurture, and exercise real options over time.

- The quantification of real options can become very difficult when many interrelated options are encountered. Therefore, their formal valuation is justified only for important projects or when the number of options is high.

- One of the main problems in the valuation of real options is the identification of an underlying asset whose returns are highly correlated with the project's cash flows.

- The reaction of competitors should be accounted for in the valuation of real options. This is particularly relevant with the option to defer. Game theory can be a useful tool to quantify this type of problem.

QUESTIONS AND PROBLEMS

1. We have a project with the cash flows and $E(NPV)$ values shown in Figure P9.1a. If the project is abandoned, cash flows and $E(NPV)$ values would be as shown in Figure P9.1b.
   Would you be willing to pay $50 million for the option to abandon the project? Use decision trees and assume a 10% discount rate.

2. The strategy of using decision trees to value options has a flaw. What is this flaw?

3. Table P9.3 gives information about the option market in exchange rates between the U.S. dollar and the local currency for the coming month. Use the binomial method to (a) compute how many calls must be in a risk-free portfolio and (b) compute the call price.

4. Why do real options tend to be more relevant in emerging countries than in developed ones?

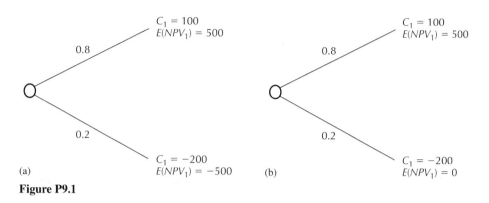

$ Millions $ Millions

(a)
(b)

Figure P9.1

5. We have the investment opportunity for developing an oil field shown in Table P9.5.
   (a) Compute the value of the option to defer the project.
   (b) Decide whether the project must be deferred.
6. How can the competitive environment affect the value of the option to defer a project?

TABLE P9.3

Data

U.S. dollar spot price S_0	$580
Risk-free monthly interest rate r	2%
Upward U.S. dollar movement	20%
Downward U.S. dollar movement	20%
Exercise price (call) E	$600
Time to maturity T	1 month

TABLE P9.5

Data

Present value of future cash flows V_0	$500 million
Initial investment I_0	$600 million
Upward oil price movement u	1.3%
Downward oil price movement d	0.7692%
Oil spot price S_0	$25
Yearly risk-free rate r	6%

APPENDIX 9A

Derivation of the Black–Scholes Equation[21]

9A.1 WIENER PROCESSES

Whenever the price of an asset evolves over time as an independent and identically distributed random variable, it is said to follow a **random walk.** Suppose that asset x changes from a known price x_t at time t to an unknown price a year later (i.e., at $t + 1$). The change of price is represented as follows:

$$\tilde{x}_{t+1} - x_t = a + \phi\, \tilde{\epsilon}_{t,t+1}$$

where a is a constant yearly change, ϕ is the standard deviation of the yearly price change, and $\tilde{\epsilon}$ is a random variable with a standardized normal distribution (i.e., zero mean and unitary standard deviation).

After N years, we have:

$$\tilde{x}_{t+N} - x_t = aN + \phi \sum_{i=t}^{t+N} \tilde{\epsilon}_i$$

Being the result of adding N independent normal distributions, the mean and variance of the summation term are:

$$\text{Mean} = N\mu = 0$$

$$\text{Variance} = N1 = N$$

We perform the following transformation:

$$\tilde{x}_{t+N} - x_t = aN + \phi\sqrt{N} \cdot \frac{\displaystyle\sum_{i=1}^{t+N} \tilde{\epsilon}_i}{\sqrt{N}}$$

---

[21]We follow the approach of Sercu and Uppal (1995).

$$\tilde{x}_{t+N} - x_t = aN + \phi\sqrt{N}\,\tilde{\epsilon}_{t,t+1}$$

If $N \to dt$; then: $dx = a \cdot dt + \phi\sqrt{dt}\,\tilde{\epsilon}$

where $dz = \sqrt{dt}\,\tilde{\epsilon}$ is known as a Wiener process.

A Wiener process is a random walk in infinitesimal time with no constant change and unitary variance. When a nonzero constant change is introduced, we have a **generalized** Wiener process:

$$dx = a\,dt + \phi\,dz$$

9A.2 ITO'S LEMMA

Ito's lemma permits the differentiation of functions containing variables with Wiener processes. Say we have a (nonrandom) function $u = f(x)$ and we wish to differentiate it by means of a Taylor expansion. This expression is obtained as follows:

$$du = f_x dx + \frac{1}{2!} f_{xx}(dx)^2 + \frac{1}{3!} f_{xxx}(dx)^3 + \cdots$$

When $dx \to 0$, $(dx)^2 = (dx)^3 = \cdots = (dx)^n = 0$, and we get the expected result: $du = f_x dx$.

But if x is a generalized Wiener process, we write

$$dx = a\,dt + \phi\,dz \to (dx)^2 = a^2(dt)^2 + \phi(dz)^2 + 2a\phi(dt)(dz)$$

Or $(dx)^2 = a^2(dt)^2 + \phi^2\tilde{\epsilon}^2 dt + 2a\phi(dt)^{3/2}\tilde{\epsilon}$.

When $dx \to 0$, $(dx)^2 = \phi_2\tilde{\epsilon}^2 dt \neq 0$.

Therefore, $du = f_x dx + \frac{1}{2} f_{xx}\phi^2\tilde{\epsilon}^2 dt$.

Observe that:

$$E(\phi^2\tilde{\epsilon}^2 dt) = \phi^2 dt\, E(\tilde{\epsilon}^2) = \phi^2 dt$$

$$\mathrm{Var}(\phi_2 \tilde{\epsilon}^2 dt) = \phi^4 (dt)^2 \mathrm{Var}(\tilde{\epsilon}^2) = 0; \text{ given that } (dt)^2 = 0$$

Hence, the second term in the differentiated expression is not random, and

$$du = f_x dx + \frac{1}{2} f_{xx} \phi^2 dt$$

This is Ito's lemma.

A9.3 THE BLACK–SCHOLES EQUATION

We have a European call with price C as a function of the price of stock S: $C = f(S,t)$.
The stock obeys the following Weiner process:

$$\frac{dS}{S} = \mu dt + \sigma dz$$

Applying Ito's lemma[22], we write:

$$dC = C_S dS + C_t dt + \frac{1}{2} C_{SS} S^2 \sigma^2 dt$$

A risk-free portfolio requires dS to disappear. This is possible by combining a call
with $-C_S S$ units of stock in portfolio p:

$$p = C + (-C_S)S$$

The differential change in the price of the portfolio is:

$$dp = dC - C_S dS$$

Substituting, we have:

$$dp = \left(C_t dt + C_S dS + \frac{1}{2} C_{SS} S^2 \sigma^2 dt \right) - C_S dS$$

---

[22] Notice that S^2 appears in the third term to the right. The reason is that the Wiener process is of
the form dS/S instead of dS. This can be inferred by applying a Taylor expansion on $(dx)^2$.

Being a no-risk portfolio, its yield is:

$$r \, dt \rightarrow dp = pr \, dt$$

Solving, we obtain the Black–Scholes equation:

$$\frac{1}{2}C_{SS}S^2\sigma^2 + C_S Sr + C_t - Cr = 0$$

PART 2 SUMMARY:
FIRM AND INVESTMENT

Whenever investment opportunities have a significant impact on the investor's portfolio, portfolio theory must be used to evaluate investments. However when firms undertake projects, it is expensive and impractical to consult individual shareholders. We therefore need a method that allows managers to make investment decisions independently. This method is the expected net present value maximization rule, used in conjunction with a discount rate consistent with project risk. Expected net present value maximization assumes complete and perfectly competitive markets, as well as the absence of transaction costs.

The smaller the scale of the project in relation to the firm's assets, and the weaker the investment's participation as a stockholder, the more valid is the expected net present value maximization rule. This is because when these conditions hold, the impact of the project on the personal portfolios of investors is not significant.

The CAPM is the most popular model for the determination of the discount rate as a function of project risk. It is based on the assumption that only nondiversifiable risk demands compensation. Among other things, the CAPM assumes that all investors share the same expectations and the same investment horizon.

These are unrealistic assumptions. However, in the absence of an alternative (clearly superior) model, we have no choice but to accept them. The important point to bear in mind is that the more a particular situation deviates from these assumptions, the less reliable will the results of the CAPM be. However, in general, expected net present value is an important piece of information in any valuation.

The reliability of the CAPM is further questionable in the context of developing countries. This is primarily due to such characteristics of emerging markets as the inadequate development of the capital markets, the presence of country-specific economic and political risks, and the sensitivity of the nations in question to economic conditions elsewhere.

A modified CAPM that is adapted to emerging countries is proposed. It takes into account the project's cash flow sensitivities to different markets and incorporates only (a portion of) the country's systematic risk. Nevertheless, the complete identification of the nondiversifiable component of country risk remains an important challenge. The proposed modification does not address all shortcomings and is just an improvement over the existing model (i.e., the CAPM).

In addition to the problems related to country risk and the choice of an appropriate discount rate, investments in developing countries have a series of special characteristics that must be taken into account. In particular:

- Special care must be taken to adjust the different components of the project's cash flow to expected levels of inflation.
- The disequilibria between the rate of inflation and the exchange rate must be estimated.
- Subsidies tend to distort the attractiveness of investment opportunities. Hence, to accurately evaluate investment opportunities with and without these distortions, all subsidies must be identified and viewed separately.
- Possible financing restrictions must be dealt with.
- Depending on the variability of projected cash flows, a proper balance must be found between a reasonable estimate of terminal value and the length of the investment horizon.

Project flexibility is another factor. Given the high volatility of economies in emerging markets, it is particularly important to build flexibility into projects. Flexibility can be (approximately) quantified through option pricing. In fact, the ability to identify the opportunities that come with uncertainty and to incorporate options to increase the value of investment projects is a key factor in doing business successfully in emerging countries. Underestimation of the value of options can produce important valuation errors and miscalculations when one is approaching investment opportunities.

The foregoing issues related to cash flow projections and project flexibility in the context of emerging markets are applicable to any type of real investment whether undertaken by a firm or an individual investor.

PART 3

FINANCING AND INVESTMENT

Chapter 10: Financing in Theory
A theoretical discussion of the optimal level of debt in a firm.

Chapter 11: Financing in Practice
Determinants of the level of debt in emerging markets and proposal of a method for monitoring it.

Chapter 12: Financing and Value
The addition of value in investment opportunities through more flexible sources of financing.

CHAPTER 10

FINANCING IN THEORY

"Equity is soft, debt is hard. Equity is complacent, debt insistent. Equity is a pillow, debt a sword."

— Michael Jensen

So far, we have discussed investment decisions without paying any attention to sources of financing. In a manner of speaking we have assumed implicitly that all financing is from shareholder funds. However, we know that this is not the case. In practice, firms and individual investors contract loans to finance their investments. In this part of the book we center our attention on financing and consider how it can affect investment decisions. As always, the emphasis will be on emerging markets.

We begin by differentiating between the two main sources of financing—debt and equity. We will first consider a simple model without taxes. Finally, taxes and costs associated with the possibility of bankruptcy are factored in to determine optimal leverage.

This is a theoretical chapter. The reader who is acquainted with the theory of capital structure can skip it and proceed directly to Chapter 11.

10.1 FIRM FINANCING

The balance sheet of a firm presents us with a summary of its assets—bank accounts, inventories, accounts receivable, and fixed assets—and its liabilities—debts, accounts payable, and shareholders' net worth (or equity). On the liabilities side we can further distinguish between two account groups: equity, representing funds received from shareholders, and liabilities, representing funds received from creditors.[1]

10.1.1 Debt

Within liabilities, we can differentiate between interest-paying accounts and those with which no explicit costs are associated. Interest-earning accounts are known as **financial liabilities** and comprise primarily bank debts and bonds (in the case of firms with a presence in the capital markets). The rest of the liabilities are mainly debts with suppliers and other accounts related to day-to-day business operations.

---

[1]Henceforth, we will put aside financing considerations at the level of the individual investor and concentrate on the firm, given its much greater relevance. Financing at the individual investor level was briefly covered in Chapter 5: Personal Investments.

183

In performing a financial analysis of a firm's funding, it is advisable to subtract all nonfinancial liabilities from the asset side, leaving just financial liabilities and equity on the liability side of the balance sheet. This facilitates computation of **financial leverage,** which is the ratio between financial and total liabilities (i.e., financial liabilities plus equity). This is the approach we will follow.

10.1.2 Equity

Besides creditors, shareholders are the other group of investors we are concerned with. The funding they provide is reflected mainly in paid-up capital and retained earnings. These funds are remunerated directly, through dividends (in the form of cash or shares), or indirectly through earnings.

Cash dividends are money transfers from the firm to the shareholders and are debited to retained earnings. Stock dividends are not money transfers but simple accounting reclassifications from one account (retained earnings) to another (paid-up capital). Stock dividends materialize in the form of new share certificates. The only way to transform these stock dividends into cash is by selling the new share certificates to a third party.

The impact of earnings on shareholders' returns is indirect. Stock prices vary according to investors' expectations. If the prevailing expectation is that earnings will increase, share prices will rise and stockholders will be able to realize a capital gain by selling shares. If expectations point to a reduction in earnings, investors selling stock will be exposed to a capital loss.[2]

Capital gains are most important in the case of firms with strong investment opportunities (e.g., in their first years of development or when undergoing profound changes). For this reason they feel obliged to reduce cash dividends to a minimum to enable them to reinvest most of their earnings. Cash dividends are more relevant in stable firms that do not possess significant business opportunities and can afford to distribute the bulk of their earnings.

Stockholders can realize capital gains by selling their shares but, **from the firm's viewpoint, equity remuneration takes place only when a cash dividend is paid,** since this is the only true cash transfer from the firm to its shareholders. Capital gains through stock selling should not concern the firm, since these are just private deals among investors trading on their expectations.

10.2 A SIMPLE MODEL

We will now explore the effect of financing sources on debt holders and stockholders, as well as on the value of the firm (Modigliani & Miller 1958).

---

[2]Two comments must be made. First, stock prices fluctuate not only because of earning expectations but also because of changes in perceived risk (and in the discount rate). Second, selling stock to realize capital gains is not straightforward for companies with a closed shareholding structure or in companies whose shares are not frequently traded. In these cases, almost certainly, the shareholder will be obliged to sell at a discount below what would be a fair price in different circumstances.

10.2.1 Debt and Return

Imagine the firm as an entity generating funds from operations and channeling them to debt holders and stockholders. Let us assume that all these funds are in cash and that they are divided into two portions: one for interest payments and the other for cash dividends.

We define the **value of the firm** as the present value of its assets' cash flows discounted at a rate related to the risk level. According to this definition, the value of the firm is not the same as the **value of equity.** The value of equity is the value of the firm less the value of the debt.

Let us take the case of the unlevered firm (i.e., a firm with no debt), whose assets yield $200 yearly forever with a 20% (yearly) discount rate. What is the value of this firm?

Its value V is very easy to calculate, being simply the PV of a perpetuity[3]:

$$V = \frac{\$200}{0.20} = \$1000$$

How much is its equity E worth? Given that there is no debt and all cash flows belong to the shareholders, equity value must be the same as firm value:

$$E = \frac{\$200}{0.20} = \$1000$$

Now let us include debt in the financial structure. Suppose that half the assets are financed by a 10% (yearly) interest rate debt. The cash flows are as shown in Figure 10.1.

At a 10% interest rate, from the $200 operational income, $50 goes to debt holders and $150 to the shareholders. With respect to a $500 equity, this implies a 30% return on equity, a larger figure than our original 20%.

Let us see what happens when leverage varies, as shown in Table 10.1. Observe how return on equity increases with leverage. Why does this happen?

Debt holders have priority over the firm's cash flows, running lower risk than shareholders. Therefore, it is only logical for stockholders to demand a higher return. In addition, an ever larger proportion of operating cash flow is tied to interest payments as

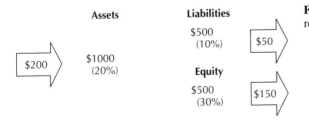

Figure 10.1 Cash flows: debt and returns.

---

[3]This is the financial value of the firm, which is not very different from its market value but can be quite different from accounting value, which is based on historical costs and depreciation policy, among other things.

TABLE 10.1

Equity ($)	Debt ($)	Leverage (%)	Interest (10%)	Dividends ($)	Return on Equity (%)
1000	0	0	0	200	20
800	200	20	20	180	23
500	500	50	50	150	30
300	700	70	70	130	43
200	800	80	80	120	60
100	900	90	90	110	110

leverage rises. Since operating cash flows tend to be risky, this implies a lower probability of compliance with interest payments, hence, a higher probability of bankruptcy.
Thus equity risk increases with leverage. Shareholders will be willing to accept higher
risks only in exchange for higher returns on their investment.

10.2.2 Cost of Capital and Firm Value

The **cost of capital** ρ^* or, more formally, the weighted average cost of capital (*WACC*)
is the weighted average of debt holder and shareholder returns. In our example, for a
50% leverage, the cost of capital is:

$$\rho^* = \left(0.10 \times \frac{500}{1000}\right) + \left(0.30 \times \frac{500}{1000}\right) = 0.20$$

At a 70% leverage level,

$$\rho^* = \left(0.10 \times \frac{700}{1000}\right) + \left(0.43 \times \frac{300}{1000}\right) = 0.20$$

The results are exactly the same. The cost of capital is constant with leverage.
When the proportion of debt increases, the proportion of equity decreases and shareholder risk and return on equity rise to compensate the additional risk. However, the
weighted average of equity and debt returns stays fixed. The reader can verify this by
computing the cost of capital for several debt levels in the preceding example.

The intuition behind this result is the following: since the cost of capital is a
weighted average of debt and equity returns, it is just an indirect way of computing the
return on assets. And the return on assets must be independent of leverage because it is
related only to operational variables such as sales, costs, and nonfinancial expenses.
Under the conditions of this simple example, **return on assets has nothing to do with
the way the firm's operations are financed and is tied only to business risk.** Business risk is then distributed between debt holders and stockholders depending on the interest rate and the proportions of debt and equity.

We said before that the value of the firm was the *PV* of the assets' cash flows discounted at the assets' rate of return. If cost of capital and return on assets are equivalent

concepts and both are independent of leverage, then, under the assumptions we are working with (see Section 10.2.4), **the value of the firm must be independent of leverage** as well.

Another way to visualize this result is to realize that everyone can take debt, deposit money in a bank, or buy debt or shares in the open market to compensate for the effects of the firm's leveraging decision. In other words, the individual investor can achieve any desired risk–return relationship independent of the firm's actions.

Going back to our example, suppose that the firm decides to opt for zero leverage. Hence, return on equity is 20%. Imagine an individual wishing to invest $50 in the company, but as if it were 50% leveraged. The investor's strategy should be to take a $50 loan and purchase $100 of the firm's stock with his own $50 plus the loan proceeds. The result would be as follows:

Proceeds from stock ($)	$100 \times 0.2 = 20$
Cost of the loan ($)	$50 \times 0.1 = 5$
Net gain ($)	15

A $15 gain corresponds to a 30% return on the $50 net investment. This is the same return that would be obtained by purchasing $50 in stock of the same firm, but if it was 50% leveraged.

What would be the right strategy if the company has an 80% leverage? In this case, the return on equity is 60% and purchasing $20 in stock and making a bank deposit of $30 can obtain the equivalent return. Equally, this leads to a 30% return over a $50 investment:

Proceeds from stock ($)	$20 \times 0.6 = 12$
Proceeds from deposit ($)	$30 \times 0.1 = 3$
Net gain ($)	15

If investors can undo any company's leveraging decision to achieve their desired risk–return relationship, then leverage does not matter and must not have any influence on firm's value.

In general, the cost of capital without taxes $\rho*$ is given by the following expression:

$$\rho* = \left(k_D \frac{D}{D + E}\right) + \left(k_E \frac{E}{D + E}\right)$$

where, k_D is the (percent) cost of debt, k_E is the (percent) cost of equity, D is the value of debt, and E is the value of equity.

Since the value of the firm, V, is the sum of the value of debt and the value of equity, we also have:

$$\rho* = \left(k_D \frac{D}{V}\right) + \left(k_E \frac{E}{V}\right)$$

Reordering terms, we get the formula for the return on equity:

$$k_E = \rho^* + \frac{D}{E}(\rho^* - k_D)$$

It must be pointed out that in each of the preceding formulas V, D, and E must be **market (not accounting) values.**

The Risk of Debt Up to now we have (implicitly) assumed that debt risk stays constant irrespective of the level of leverage. But when leverage rises, so does default risk. In this case, both shareholders and debt holders must be compensated, and the cost of debt will increase.

Nonetheless, even though the cost of both financing sources increases with leverage, the proportions of debt and equity adjust in a manner such that the cost of capital does not vary, as shown in Figure 10.2 (Miller 1991).

In the absence of debt, the cost of equity equals the cost of capital and the cost of debt is the risk-free rate. Both costs rise with leverage, while the cost of capital stays constant. It has to be this way because as we mentioned before, the cost of capital is a function of the operating characteristics of the firm and must be independent of leverage (under the current assumptions).

10.2.3 The Estimation of Beta

Assets must equal the sum of equity and liabilities. Therefore, we can think of a firm's assets as a portfolio of these two components. This idea together with beta additivity (see Chapter 6: The Classical Model) allows for a relationship to be found between the expected returns and betas of these three balance sheet components, in the following manner:

$$\beta_A = \left(\beta_D \frac{D}{V}\right) + \left(\beta_E \frac{E}{V}\right)$$

Asset beta β_A is known as the **unlevered beta** and is the key parameter in the computation of the discount rates for real investments. This formula allows us to

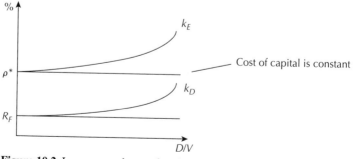

Figure 10.2 Leverage and cost of capital.

TABLE 10.2

Data	
D (market value in $ million)	50
E (market value in $ million)	400
Equity beta β_E	0.9
Debt beta β_D	0.1

calculate asset beta starting from the debt and equity betas, and leverage. This is a very important result, since asset betas are not observable in the marketplace but equity and debt betas are.

Asset betas are usually estimated from debt and equity betas from one or more firms in businesses similar to the one being analyzed. Debt and equity betas are relatively easy to estimate by linear regression of the respective historical returns against whatever is defined as the market portfolio (see Chapter 6: The Classical Model).[4]

We must warn the reader that this formula assumes that **leverage stays constant.** Also, recall that debt and equity must be **market values.**

Let us illustrate with the example of a metal casting company with the data shown in Table 10.2. Applying our formula, we write:

$$\beta_A = \left(0.1 \times \frac{50}{450}\right) + \left(0.9 \times \frac{400}{450}\right) = 0.811$$

Approximating debt beta to zero yields:

$$\beta_A = 0.9 \times \frac{400}{450} = 0.800$$

The result has not changed significantly. This is why the assumption of zero systematic risk (or beta) for the debt is generally an acceptable one.[5]

10.2.4 Assumptions

Let us discuss the assumptions behind the results just obtained.

a. *No Transaction Costs.* This assumption was necessary to ensure that everyone had the same access to financial markets. For example, with transaction costs the possibility

---

[4]Stock betas for numerous companies are permanently computed and updated by many specialized services (e.g., ValueLine).

[5]This is an acceptable assumption as long as the probability of bankruptcy is negligible. We will expand on this topic further on.

of adjusting personal portfolios to compensate for the firms' financing decisions would be costly and could not be valid. Therefore, leverage would not be irrelevant when firm value was being computed.

b. *Perfectly Competitive Financial Markets.* With this condition nobody has advantages in the financial markets. If this were not the case, leverage preferences could differ among market participants and debt levels would not be irrelevant.

c. *No Agency Costs.* This implies that management's sole objective is to maximize shareholders' wealth. Therefore, the financial mix does not have any relation to the particular interests of administrators nor any impact on firm value.

d. *No Taxes.* Neither firms nor individuals pay taxes.

e. *All Cash Flows Are No-Growth Perpetuities.* As we saw, this served to simplify the formulas for the cost of capital and the value of the firm.

Definitely, the first two assumptions are invalid, even more in the developing world where inefficient financial systems proliferate. The third one is not very relevant in emerging markets, since in these countries few firms exist in which shareholders are removed from the important decisions. These three assumptions together with the one about perpetuities will be further discussed in Chapter 11 (Financing in Practice). For the discussion that follows, we release the no-tax restriction.

10.3 WHAT HAPPENS WHEN THERE ARE TAXES?

Let us start by releasing the tax restriction at the firm level. Returning to our last example, assume a 30% corporate tax rate and let us observe what happens with the return on equity when we have 50% leverage, as shown in Table 10.3.

After-tax profits belong to the stockholders. In this case, equity amounts to $500. This profit implies a 21% return on investment, considerably less than the 30% return obtained in the absence of taxes. Taxes make investments less attractive because returns diminish whereas risk remains the same.

TABLE 10.3

Profits and Losses

Income	$200
Interest expense	$(50)
Profit before taxes	$150
Taxes (30%)	$(45)
Profit after taxes	$105

10.3.1 Debt and Cost of Capital

Independence between the cost of capital and leverage ceases to exist with the introduction of corporate taxes. Referring to Table 10.4, let us see what occurs when the firm in our example has zero debt and 50% leverage.

The total income to the universe of fund providers is larger with debt. The higher the leverage, the higher is the interest expense. Since interest expense is deductible for tax purposes, the higher the interest expenses, the lower are the taxes paid. In conclusion, as leverage increases, tax expense decreases and total income goes up. In our example, total income was raised by $15, which corresponds to the amount of taxes saved because of the interest expense (30% of $50).

Let us analyze the situation from a different angle. Without taxes, all operational income ($200 in our example) reached fund providers either as dividends or as interest, depending on leverage.

When debt was zero, return on equity was 20%. As debt went up, so did return on equity. In the case of 50% leverage, return on equity was 30%. That is, the shareholders' compensation for leveraging the firm up to 50% was an additional 10% (30% − 20%).

When taxes are positive, all operating cash flows do not reach fund providers, the difference being taxes paid. Assets still produce $200 our example; but when debt is nil, shareholders get only $140: the original $200 less $60 of taxes. Given that equity is still $1000, this implies a return on equity of 14%, which is 6% lower than in the case with no taxes.

When leverage is raised to 50% shareholders get $105. In relation to the portion they are funding ($500), this amounts to a return on equity of 21%. Now the shareholders' compensation for leveraging the firm up to 50% is an additional 7% (21% − 14%).[6]

Table 10.5 summarizes these results. With taxes, the incremental return on equity, as debt rises, is lower. Given that we kept the cost of debt fixed at 10%, this means that **the cost of capital decreases with leverage.** It can be shown that this conclusion still holds when the cost of debt increases with leverage.

TABLE 10.4 Profits and Losses

	Leverage 0%	Leverage 50%
Income	$200	$200
Interest expense (10%)	$0	$50
Profit before taxes	$200	$150
Taxes (30%)	$60	$45
Profit after taxes	$140	$105
Debt holders' income	$0	$50
Stockholders' income	$140	$105
Total income	$140	$155

---

[6]This is an approximate computation, since the effect of taxes on the value of the firm must also be considered, as we will see later.

TABLE 10.5

Taxes	Return on Equity (k_E %)		Incremental Return (k_E %)
	Leverage 0%	Leverage 50%	
0%	20	30	10
30%	14	21	7

The cost of capital with taxes CC is given by the following formula:

$$CC = \frac{D}{V}(1 - T_C)k_D + \frac{E}{V}k_E$$

where T_C is the corporate tax rate.

The following relationship also holds:

$$CC = \left(1 - \frac{DT_C}{V}\right)\rho$$

where ρ is the return on assets with taxes (which is different from ρ^*, the return on assets without taxes).

Reordering terms, we find the following expression for the return on equity with taxes:

$$k_E = \rho + \frac{D}{E}[(\rho - k_D)(1 - T_C)]$$

We also have the following formula:

$$V = V_u + DT_C$$

where V_u is the value of the firm without debt and with taxes.

This last formula is very interesting because it shows that **the value of the firm rises with debt by an amount equal to DT_C.** This last amount is known as the **tax shield.**

Following, we prove the formula for the cost of capital with taxes CC:
The cash flow L to fund providers is given by

$$L = (X - R)(1 - T_C) + R$$

where X is the cash flow from assets and R is the interest expense.
The first term on the right is the cash flow to shareholders and the second one is the cash flow to debt holders.
Rewriting the expression, we have

$$L = X(1 - T_C) + RT_C = U + RT_C$$

where U is the firm's cash flow without debt.

The value of the leveraged firm V is the PV of L. Then $X(1 - T_C)$ is the firm's cash flow without debt and must be discounted at the assets' return with taxes (ρ) The cash flow to debt R, must be discounted at its cost k_D. Thus,

$$V = \frac{X}{\rho}(1 - T_C) + \frac{RT_C}{k_D} = V_u + DT_C$$

where V_u is the value of the firm with taxes and without debt.

The cash flow from assets must be equal to the cash flows to fund providers. Hence,

$$V_u \rho + T_C D k_D = D k_D + E k_E$$

Dividing by V and rearranging terms, we write

$$CC = \left(1 - \frac{DT_C}{V}\right)\rho = \frac{D}{V}(1 - T_C)k_D + \frac{E}{V}k_E$$

The cost of capital with taxes as a function of leverage is shown in Figure 10.3. Observe that when there is no debt, the cost of capital is ρ. Further, the cost of capital decreases with leverage, but it can never be less than $\rho (1 - T_c)$.

Personal Taxes What really matters is the flow of funds available to investors after all taxes, including theirs, have been paid. We will now incorporate personal taxes into our model.

Assume that tax rates at the individual investor level are T_{pe} for dividends and T_p for interest receipts. It can be shown that in this case, the formulas for the cost of capital, return on equity, and the value of the firm are as follows[7]:

$$CC = \rho\left(1 - \frac{DG}{V}\right) = \frac{D}{V}(1 - G)k_D + \frac{E}{V}k_E$$

$$k_E = \rho + \frac{D}{E}[(\rho - k_D)(1 - G)]$$

$$V = V_u + DG$$

---

[7]The proof of these formulas can be obtained following the same lines as the proof in the case of no personal taxes. The interested reader can refer to Copeland and Weston (1988) or to the original source (Miller 1977).

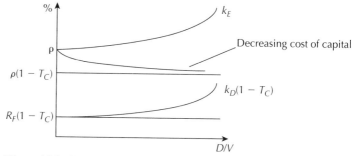

Figure 10.3 Cost of capital and taxes.

where

$$G = 1 - \frac{(1 - T_C)(1 - T_{pe})}{(1 - T_p)}$$

Strictly speaking, personal taxes should be incorporated, but this is not the case in practice. Personal investors usually plan for their real and financial investments after taking into account the effects of their personal tax. Since the situation of every investor is different, it does not make much sense to rely on general expressions like the foregoing.

On the other hand, in dealing with firms whose shareholders are removed from day-to-day investment decisions (which is the case of interest to us), it is impractical to consult stockholders about their personal tax situations. This is because not only are the administrative costs of such consultations high but also, such information is confidential, and out of bounds for management.

For all these reasons we will ignore this complication and assume that the tax effects of investment decisions at the firm level are homogeneous for all shareholders and therefore irrelevant. Henceforth, **when we discuss taxes, we are referring exclusively to corporate taxes.**

10.3.2 Computation of Beta When There Are Taxes

This is the formula for the unlevered beta β_A without taxes:

$$\beta_A = \beta_D \frac{D}{V} + \beta_E \frac{E}{V}$$

This formula includes the value of the firm as a variable. This was not problematic without taxes because the value of the firm was unaltered with leverage. However, this is no longer the case with taxes: the value of the firm increases with the level of debt. Here beta, as a weighted average of equity and debt betas, does not result in the beta of the unlevered firm because it is distorted by the impact of leverage on firm value. Let us see why.

With taxes, the value of a leveraged firm is given by

$$V = V_u + DT_C$$

In addition, V is equal to the sum of debt and equity. Hence,

$$V_u + DT_C = D + E$$

Therefore, the weighted average of the debt and equity betas gives us a beta including both the effect of V_u and the tax shield DT_C, when we are only interested in V_u. This problem is easily solved applying beta additivity to both sides of this equation and solving for the unlevered beta (Ross, Westerfield, & Jaffe 1999):

$$\beta_A \frac{V_u}{V} + \beta_D \frac{DT_C}{V} = \beta_D \frac{D}{V} + \beta_E \frac{E}{V}$$

Getting rid of V and replacing V_u with the following expression,

$$V_u = D + E - DT_C = E + D(1 - T_C)$$

we get

$$\beta_A = \frac{\beta_E E + \beta_D D(1 - T_C)}{E + D(1 - T_C)}$$

If for the sake of simplicity we assume the beta of debt to be zero, this formula is reduced to

$$\beta_A = \frac{\beta_E E}{E + D(1 - T_C)}$$

Like the rest of the formulas in this chapter, these formulas require market values for both debt and equity. Additionally, we must remember that we are assuming here that **the tax shield is a nongrowing perpetuity.**

Setting the corporate tax rate at 30%, let us find the unleveraged beta in our example. Applying the (first) formula, we write

$$\beta_A = \frac{(0.9 \times 400) + (0.1 \times 50 \times 0.7)}{400 + (50 \times 0.7)} = \frac{363.5}{435} = 0.836$$

If the beta of debt were zero,

$$\beta_A = \frac{0.9 \times 400}{400 + (50 \times 0.7)} = 0.827$$

Again, there is no significant difference between these results, and the assumption of no systematic risk for the debt is still an acceptable one.[8]

10.4 THE COSTS OF FINANCIAL DISTRESS

The preceding results lead us to a conclusion that does not reflect reality: if managers maximize firm value and firm value increases with leverage, then the optimal leverage should be achieved at the maximum level possible. But this is not what we see in real life. Instead, many firms are reluctant to take on too much debt. What does this mean? Are managers wrong to be intimidated by high levels of debt?

As we mentioned before, the higher the debt, the larger the portion of operating cash flows that must be earmarked to service it. Since operational cash flows are risky, the probability of default rises with leverage. When employees, suppliers, customers, and others with an interest in the firm perceive a significant risk of bankruptcy, new costs that compromise the profits of the firm arise. These costs grow with leverage and are known as **costs of financial distress** (*CFD*s).

*CFD*s originate in the direct and indirect costs of bankruptcy.

10.4.1 Direct Costs of Bankruptcy

The direct costs of bankruptcy depend mainly on the type of firm and its network of contracts.

From a strict viewpoint, bankruptcy just means that the property of the firm's assets is transferred from the stockholders to the debt holders. For this to materialize, it is necessary to hire experts of all kinds: valuators, lawyers, financial specialists, and so on. The cost of all this depends on the type of business we deal with. For instance, the bankruptcy of a pharmaceutical firm requires the valuation of specialized machinery and patents. This is a difficult undertaking, whereas a mortgage foreclosure is just a very simple legal procedure.

Additionally, bankruptcy costs increase when the contractual structure of the firm is complex. This is because complicated and costly negotiations are generally required to untangle the different contractual rights.

Creditors realize that the higher the likelihood of bankruptcy, the more likely is it that the firm will have to incur these costs. This results in a reduction of the value of the firm. Thus, the direct costs of bankruptcy depend as much on the costs associated with bankruptcy as with the probability of its taking place.

10.4.2 Indirect Costs of Bankruptcy

Besides costs directly associated with bankruptcy, there are other costs originating from sectors with an interest in the firm:

---

[8]Refer to footnote 5.

TABLE 10.6

Assets	Liabilities and Equity	
Cash	$200 Liabilities	$950
Other assets	$800 Equity	$50
Totals	$1000	$1000

Managerial and Operational Difficulties The likelihood of insolvency has implications for the firm: suppliers reduce shipments and restrict credit conditions; key employees leave the company; clients start dealing with competitors; and bankers reduce credit lines and ask for better guarantees. In this situation, and faced with strong pressure, managers tend to underperform. This translates into additional costs that reduce the value of the firm.

Agency Costs Another outcome of the likelihood of bankruptcy is that managers and shareholders will start facing incentives to decrease the value of the firm. Some of the possible conducts are as follows.

a. *Riskier Decisions Are Taken.* It seems odd for shareholders to be inclined to take riskier decisions during a financial crisis, but it can happen.

Think of a firm with $1000 in assets of which $200 is available to be invested in a risky project, as shown in Table 10.6. The firm has debts for $950, and equity is $50. Suppose the risky project has two possible outcomes at the end of one month: a positive cash flow for $500 if things turn out well, or a zero cash flow if things do not turn out as wished. If things turn out well, the balance sheet shown in Table 10.7 will be obtained. If things turn out poorly, the balance sheet shown in Table 10.8 will be obtained. In the first case, the whole benefit ($300) favors shareholders. In the second case, shareholders lose the small amount of equity that they still possess ($50), but the bulk of the loss is borne by creditors.[9]

This effect in favor of shareholders and against creditors will be more important the larger the risked amount, the higher the risk, and the larger the leverage.

TABLE 10.7

Assets	Liabilities and Equity	
Cash	$200 + $300 Liabilities	$950
Other assets	$800 Equity	$50 + **$300**
Totals	$1000 + $300	$1000 + $300

---

[9] If the probability of gains is large enough, the shareholders may even be inclined to undertake negative $E(NPV)$ projects.

TABLE 10.8

Assets		Liabilities and Equity	
Cash	$200 − $200	Liabilities	$950 − **$150**
Other assets	$800	Equity	$50 − $50
Totals	$1000 − $200		$1000 − $200

b. *Good Projects May Be Rejected.* Imagine the same firm. The investment is also $200 but there is no risk involved, and the project will produce a safe positive cash flow of $500 in one month. Assume that at the end of the month, a $600 debt becomes due. If the project is accepted, the managers will be handing out $200, but at the end of the month they will end up with zero cash (the same situation if the project were not accepted) since the entire proceeds of the project will be appropriated by creditors. Naturally, managers will not be enthusiastic about this business proposition, even if highly profitable.

In general, the tendency to reject profitable investment opportunities will depend on the project's profitability and the timing of cash flows for both the project and the firm's debts.

c. *Moral Hazard.* In anticipation of losing all their equity, shareholders may fall into patterns of unethical conduct to the detriment of creditors. For instance, improper cash dividends might be distributed, or the shareholders might arrange to acquire some assets of the firm for themselves at below-market prices. As a preventive measure, creditors usually set up some restrictions and increase controls on the firm's operations. All these steps result in a reduction in the firm's value.

We have seen that when leverage increases, on the one hand, the tax shield reduces the cost of capital and, on the other hand, the costs of financial distress increase. Therefore, there must exist a level at which the cost of capital is minimized and leverage is optimal.[10] This can be demonstrated graphically, as shown in Figure 10.4.

Unfortunately, the costs of financial distress are very difficult to estimate and, consequently, the computation of optimal leverage in this manner is out of reach for all practical purposes. Therefore, the ideas exposed throughout this chapter serve more as a conceptual reference that as an applicable real-life procedure.[11]

To conclude, let us update our formula for the value of the leveraged firm by subtracting the present value of the costs of financial distress (*CFD*):

$$V = V_u + DT_C - PV(CFD)$$

---

[10]Optimal leverage corresponds to the point at which the marginal cost of financial distress matches the marginal benefit of the tax shield. This point depends on the actual shape of these two functions. For a detailed explanation, refer to Barnea, Haugen, and Senbet (1980).

[11]For an interesting effort to estimate the costs of financial distress, refer to Opler, Saron, and Titman (1997).

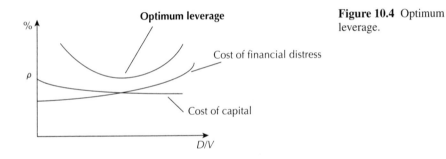

Figure 10.4 Optimum leverage.

We have covered the most relevant financial theory with respect to capital structure. In the next chapter we will examine firms of different types and will propose a practical method for leverage determination and monitoring, with a focus on emerging markets.

10.5 CONCLUSIONS

- Financial liabilities are those that demand interest payments.
- For the purposes of financial structure analysis, we rearrange the liability side of the balance sheet so that it contains just financial liabilities and equity.
- The value of the firm is defined as the *PV* of operational cash flows discounted at a rate consistent with risk level. The value of equity equals the value of the firm less the value of the debt.
- The cost of capital originates from asset returns and depends basically on business characteristics.
- When there are no taxes, and no transaction or agency costs, and markets are perfectly competitive, both the cost of capital and the value of the firm are constant with leverage.
- Ignoring personal taxes, when there are corporate taxes, the cost of capital decreases and the value of the firm increases with leverage. This increase in firm value is known as the tax shield.
- The discount rate for real investments is a function of unlevered beta. Unlevered beta is computed from the equity and debt betas of firms in businesses similar to that of the firm being analyzed.
- When there are taxes, unlevered beta differs from the weighted average of the debt and equity betas, and its computation requires a more elaborate expression in lieu of the effect of the tax shield on firm value.
- When leverage increases, so do the costs of financial distress. These costs originate primarily from direct bankruptcy costs, operational difficulties, and agency costs.
- Theoretically, optimal leverage is determined by the point at which the marginal benefit of the tax shield matches the marginal costs of financial distress.

QUESTIONS AND PROBLEMS

1. Why does return on equity increase with leverage?

2. When there are no taxes, the cost of capital is not affected by leverage. Why?

3. We have the information about firm XYZ shown in Table P10.3. Someone wishes to invest $100,000 in XYZ stock but as if the firm had a 20% leverage. How much must be invested in equity and how much in debt? Assume no taxes.

4. Compute the equity beta of a firm that is leveraged to 30% of its (asset) market value and has an unleveraged beta of 0.8. Assume no taxes and that the beta of the debt is zero.

5. Why does the cost of capital decrease when the firm pays taxes?

6. Solve Problem 4, assuming a 20% tax rate.

7. Why is the equity beta in Problem 6 smaller than the equity beta in Problem 4?

8. How are the tax shield and the costs of financial distress used to determine optimal leverage?

TABLE P10.3

	Assets	Liabilities
Amount ($ million)	100	50
Return (%)	30	20
Return ($ million)	30	10

CHAPTER 11

FINANCING IN PRACTICE

"There are no right answers. Only answers that can be better or worse depending on what will actually happen in the future."

In the preceding chapter we established the theoretical foundations of the optimal level of debt. We will now discuss the determinants of leverage in greater detail, with an emphasis on emerging market realities.

We explain the defining factors behind debt as a source of financing and discuss risk management techniques as a tool to control cash flow volatility. The particular conditions that affect leverage and are prevalent in emerging countries are also discussed. We finish by proposing a practical procedure for monitoring the debt ratio that is particularly suited to the environment of developing countries.

11.1 THE DETERMINANTS OF LEVERAGE

In Chapter 10 we stated that the costs of financial distress are tied to bankruptcy costs, operational and managerial difficulties, and agency costs. Now we will be more specific and examine the attributes of the firm to get a better understanding of these costs and optimal leverage.

In practice, the costs of financial distress and the optimal debt ratio depend on various factors related to cash flow instability, the firm's goods and services, asset characteristics, organization, growth potential and, of course, tax considerations (Shapiro 1992).

11.1.1 Cash Flow Volatility

For a given debt ratio, the more unstable the cash flows, the larger the probability of default. Therefore, firms with high cash flow volatility should have low levels of leverage.

11.1.2 Goods and Services of the Firm

In Chapter 10 we mentioned that one indirect bankruptcy cost stemmed from the possibility of a firm's customers beginning to deal with its competitors. The likelihood of this happening is related to the attributes of the firm's goods and services. The main elements to take into consideration here are as follows.

a. *Future Relationships.* When we buy a banana, we exchange money for fruit. It is possible for us to buy again from the same grocer, but this type of transaction ends when we pay the price, and the sale is independent of any future relationship between buyer and seller.

When purchasing a refrigerator, an automobile, or any other durable asset on the other hand, the buyer has a strong interest in the seller's ability to supply parts and other maintenance services. This is quite different from the banana transaction, since here the act of purchasing the asset automatically creates an implicit obligation of the seller toward the buyer. If there were room for suspicion that the seller might not stay in business long, the buyer would probably prefer to deal with a competitor.

b. *High Costs of Change.* A similar argument obtains in the case of a company selling software that requires costly training. If the company is likely to disappear, users will surely prefer to do business with a financially stronger competitor to avoid paying for training that soon will be useless.

c. *Low Transparency of Attributes.* When we purchase an airplane ticket, we do it trusting that the airline equipment is properly maintained. We would be reluctant to purchase a ticket from a financially troubled airline lacking the necessary funds to comply with this crucial obligation.

All firms commercializing products or services with one or more of the aforementioned characteristics must make sure that their debt levels are manageable under reasonable circumstances. If not, they run the risk of losing their clientele.

11.1.3 Types of Assets

The key point here is the degree of ease with which the firm's assets can be sold in case of liquidation. Illiquid asset markets can impose significant discounts in prices and larger losses for debt holders and stockholders. Consequently, the greater the difficulties for asset liquidation, the lower the debt ratio should be.

Another, not less important aspect has to do with the role of assets in the firm's operations. Companies with high ratios of fixed to total assets (i.e., with high operating leverage) are more vulnerable to a fall in income, especially if sales are volatile. Thus, high operating leverage and instability in income recommend low levels of leverage.

11.1.4 Organization

The following elements must be taken into consideration with regard to organizational attributes.

a. *Contractual Relations.* In Chapter 10 we pointed out that complex contracting arrangements between interested parties (i.e., suppliers, customers, employees, managers, bankers, etc.) make it costly to untangle the rights and obligations of every party in a bankruptcy case. Hence, the more complex the contractual structure, the higher direct bankruptcy costs will be.

b. *Dependency Relations.* This is a special case of the contractual relations issue. It is common for many companies to set up exclusive relationships with suppliers and/or clients, resulting in chains of firms that are formally autonomous but in reality are intimately linked. For instance, this has been the case between many automobile manufacturers and their suppliers of electrical equipment, brakes, windshields, and so on.

Although reliance on such arrangements can be an advantageous strategy, the resulting dependency makes each party reluctant to establish such a relationship with a counterpart suspected of having financial difficulties.

In some oligopolistic markets (common in developing countries), such dependency relationships are frequently not voluntary. It is usual to find clients who are strongly linked to a supplier of goods and services crucial for their operations. Again, if the supplier were to be suspected of insolvency, the clientele would establish closer ties with a competitor.

c. *Specific Human Resources.* Firms likely to become bankrupt find it increasingly difficult to retain specialized professionals with limited employment opportunities, for whom changing jobs is particularly costly.

The more intense the contractual and dependency relationships and the more exposed the firm is to specialized personnel, the lower the debt ratio should be.

d. *Agency Problems.* In Chapter 2 (Consumption, Investment, and Value) we explained how the personal interests of management play a major role in investment decisions when the stockholder structure is disperse and shareholders are not actively involved in the administration.

The main reason is that usually, a significant proportion of management compensation depends on company profits, closely tying managers' wealth to the welfare of the company. In other words, being highly dependent on compensation, upper management income tends to be undiversified and highly correlated to the firm's risk.

As an outcome of this situation, there are two possible dysfunctional managerial conducts. The first and more common conduct occurs when the company is stable. The second, less common and more dramatic conduct, can occur when the company has a large amount of debt with an insufficient asset base and is, therefore, about to enter bankruptcy.

In the first instance (i.e., when the firm is stable) management is generally reluctant for the firm to take much debt because this would increase risk for the company and the risk of management's (undiversified) personal portfolios. In the extreme case, management could keep the firm at a ridiculously low debt ratio, allowing the accumulation of excess cash flows. In turn, these cash flows may be dissipated on projects of dubious profitability that are, nonetheless, beneficial to managers' sense of image, power, and prestige.

Fortunately, the possibility for management to act with such independence is an exceptional case in emerging markets, given that the overwhelming majority of companies remain tightly controlled by a group of dominant shareholders.[1]

---

[1]However, it is not unusual to find dominant shareholders also occasionally promoting unwise projects with the same purpose of enhancing their image and social prestige.

The second type of conduct (observed when the company is highly indebted and about to fail) is the opposite one: management may try to take even more debt to invest the proceeds into highly risky projects. If things turn out well, enough money could be made to avert or postpone the crisis. If not, the company will fail, but there will be extra time to prepare for the upcoming crisis. This is similar to the tendency of stockholders to accept highly risky projects in highly leveraged firms (as discussed in Chapter 10: Financing in Theory).

It is noteworthy that in the second type of conduct, the incentives for both management and shareholders point to the same perverse direction, namely, to diminishing firm value at the expense of creditors. Thus, the argument for managerial independence ceases to be relevant and, in fact, this is a valid situation in developing countries (as opposed to the first conduct).

11.1.5 Growth Potential

Rapidly growing companies generally find it difficult to finance their (abundant) business opportunities from internally generated revenues. Thus, they have no choice but to issue debt or equity. In this case, the inability to raise funds is particularly costly because many attractive projects must be abandoned. But there are not many financiers eager to lend money (even less so to heavily indebted firms). Therefore, external financing must come primarily from shareholders. In sum, high barriers to external financing and significant growth opportunities recommend a conservative debt ratio.

11.1.6 Taxes

We cannot forget to mention the corporate tax rate. In principle, high tax rates imply larger tax shields and increase the attractiveness of debt. However, in the end, this depends on the prevalent tax legislation, and we will discuss its implications in Section 11.2.2.

11.1.7 The Dynamics of Leverage

We have talked about debt as a static concept, as if once management decides the debt ratio, it remains constant. In real life, leverage is not constant but oscillates around what could be considered to be an "optimal" (or desired) level. The reason for this is that besides the direct financial costs (such as dividends and interest expenses), each financing source has particular issuing costs that must be taken into consideration.

There are two types of issuing cost: those associated with the issuing process itself, such as commissions and legal expenses, and those associated with **asymmetrical information.**

The costs of asymmetrical information arise from the informational differences that exist between management and fund providers. For instance, a firm raising new equity must persuade shareholders of the attractiveness of the projects to be financed with the new funds. In contrast, bank loans do not often require many explanations, given that they are less risky than stock (i.e., they have higher priority in a bankruptcy) and tend to be backed by some kind of guarantee.

Management establishes an order of preference for various financing sources—retained earnings, debt, and stock—depending on the issuing costs of each (Myers & Majluf 1984).

> *Retained Earnings.* Using retained earnings to finance projects neither imposes any direct issuing costs nor requires major explanations to stockholders. Hence, it is the least costly source and the one management tends to turn to first.
>
> *Debt.* Debt is the second less expensive source, given that its costs of asymmetrical information are lower than the costs of stock but higher than those associated with retained earnings.
>
> *Stock.* Higher informational and issuance costs make stock the most expensive funding source.[2]

As shown in Figure 11.1, the mere existence of issuance costs causes actual leverage to oscillate around desired leverage. The more significant the issuance costs, the more pronounced will the oscillations tend to be.

11.1.8 Risk Management

Up to now we have assumed that volatility is a given fact that we cannot affect. In reality, however, this is not so. Frequently we can reduce volatility and, in this way, gain the option of increasing leverage.

Risks to Consider The more relevant risks in the developing world are inflation, exchange, and financing risks.

a. *Inflation Risk.* Inflation impacts both the firm's inflows and and its outflows, which therefore must be synchronized in such a way that the net effect of inflationary changes

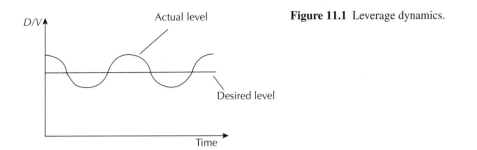

Figure 11.1 Leverage dynamics.

---

[2]An interesting implication of this line of argument is that leverage might be a function of firm's growth and profitability. The more profitable the firm and the less significant its growth opportunities, the more projects will be financed from retained earnings, and the lower the amount of debt that will be issued; in consequence, leverage will be lower. On the other hand, when profitability is low and investment opportunities significant, leverage will be higher.

on the firm's net worth is minimal. The correlation between the operating margin (i.e., operating income less operating expenses) and inflation is an important consideration. The firm's net worth increases with inflation if the correlation is positive. Net worth will grow in real terms only if the operating margin increases faster than inflation. This could be the case of a distributor of goods with a high local content. On the other hand, the outcome will be unfavorable if the correlation between the operating margin and inflation is low or negative. For instance, the regulated tariffs of an electric utility might not be adjusted fast enough to compensate for the negative effect of inflation on expenses.

b. *Exchange Risk.* Exchange risk is associated with operating flows in different currencies. Exchange rate fluctuations could have an important impact on the firm's net worth.

The correlations between operating flows and exchange rates must be taken into account. If an operating flow in local currency is positively correlated with a specific exchange rate, it will behave partially as a flow in that foreign currency. The higher the correlation, the more the similarities to a foreign currency flow.

Exchange rate lags are a common phenomenon in the developing world. Many of these countries' economies are highly dependent on imported goods and services. When the local currency is devalued, the prices of these goods and services rise, pushing inflation up. Exchange rate lags occur when local monetary authorities try to control inflation by devaluing the local currency too slowly. This translates into overvaluation and a reduction in the cost of imports (and inflation).

A less expensive exchange rate also makes debts in foreign currency more attractive. However, this advantage is risky and transitory: sooner or later the exchange rate will shift toward a reasonable equilibrium. Most of the time there is a sudden devaluation, and the firm's net worth is affected considerably. The more positive the difference between assets and liabilities denominated in foreign exchange, the less unfavorable will the impact be.

Last we must recall convertibility risk (see Chapter 8: Valuation in Emerging Markets). Convertibility risk appears when conversion of the local currency into foreign currency is curtailed or is permitted only at a controlled (and unfavorable) exchange rate. Maximizing financing in local currency can ameliorate this problem.

c. *Financing Risk.* We face financing risk whenever timely financing at a reasonable cost is not readily available. This situation can be avoided through banking arrangements and by diversifying funding sources. Further on in this chapter and in Chapter 12 (Financing and Value) we will come back to this topic.

The two most common risk management strategies are profit stabilization and operating leverage reduction.

Profit Stabilization Profit stabilization serves to reduce sales volatility and/or the cost of sales volatility. There are at least two ways to accomplish this. The first is through long-term sales (or purchase) contracts that assure the corresponding cash flows for a period of time.

The feasibility of this strategy is dependent on the possibility of supply disruption in the country (or countries) where the firm is present. Disruption of key supplies affects operations and sales, and makes compliance with long-term contracts unpredictable. Hence, this kind of arrangement is practical only for short periods of time. This eventuality can be fairly common in many emerging countries where, for a variety of reasons, governments impose controls (e.g., import quotas, exorbitant duties, foreign exchange restrictions) that can have a significant impact on supply chains.

Designing financing instruments that are highly correlated with certain income or cost streams is a second way to stabilize profits. Imagine, for example, an oil-producing company issuing debt whose interest rate is a function of oil prices. If oil prices go up, so will the firm's income and financing costs. If oil prices go down, the firm's income and financing costs will go down as well. Thus, more stable profits will always be the final result.

This strategy will be convenient as long as issuance costs are reasonable. Issuance costs can become unbearable when one is trying to place these instruments in a highly illiquid and undeveloped emerging capital market, mainly because potential buyers are likely to be unwilling to take them at reasonable yields (see Chapter 12: Financing and Value).

Volatility can be managed through standardized financial instruments, too, such as the futures, options, and swaps commonly available in advanced countries. These instruments, which allow the transfer to third parties of risks associated with certain price fluctuations (e.g., the firm's sales and/or supplies), reduce profit variability.[3]

Reduction of Operating Leverage The higher the operating leverage, the more sensible are company profits to income fluctuations. Thus, if operating leverage can be diminished, profit volatility will be also reduced. Replacing fixed costs with variable costs reduces operating leverage. A popular method of accomplishing this is by outsourcing.

Risk Management and the Individual Investor Imagine an investor with an important portion of his wealth invested in a family firm and, thus, with an undiversified and relatively risky portfolio. Selling part of the company shares and investing the proceeds in other assets is a possible method of increasing diversification and reducing risk (see Chapter 5: Personal Investments). Nevertheless, this could imply significant transaction costs, especially in the illiquid financial environments of most developing countries. An equally important consideration is the possible loss of control resulting from the sale of shares to outside parties.

Risk management is an alternative method of reducing/transferring risk and could allow the investor to improve his portfolio without having to sell part of the family company.

To summarize, the desirable debt ratio (around which actual debt oscillates) can be established, in principle, depending on the interaction between taxes and the characteristics of the firm and its businesses. Besides, the desirable debt ratio can be increased through risk management techniques, which can also be useful for managing

---

[3]Options were treated in Chapter 9 (The Value of Flexibility). In this book futures and swaps are not discussed. The interested reader can find good expositions of these topics in many texts on corporate finance such as Brealey and Myers (1996), or Ross, Westerfield, and Jaffe (1999).

undiversified portfolios. Risk management measures will be advisable depending on their costs in relation to their benefits in terms of lowering volatility.[4]

11.2 LEVERAGE IN EMERGING MARKETS

All that was said about leverage before is equally valid in emerging markets. However, in these countries we must take into account other important factors as well.

11.2.1 Economic and Institutional Climate

We know that the economic climate in emerging countries tends to be uncertain. External shocks and governmental intervention create high and unpredictable volatility. There are lapses of relative stability followed by periods of uncertainty so intense that any forecast longer than a few weeks is quite unreliable.

Leverage is tied to volatility. If volatility is difficult to predict, so will the debt ratio be. Therefore, emerging market firms should exercise much more caution about assuming debt than is necessary for their counterparts in developed countries.

Another noteworthy aspect is the frequent disequilibrium between inflation and interest rates. Sometimes interest rates fall so much that they become negative in real terms. At other times they rise to very high levels. Because of this it might not be advisable to keep a stable debt ratio. Instead, firms must be prepared to adjust leverage up or down rapidly, depending on the level of interest rates. It is for this reason that an important success factor in some emerging markets is the availability of alternative funding sources (debt or equity) that can be tapped rapidly at any time.

Something similar occurs with debts in hard currency, since exchange rates are also likely to be out of balance with inflation and interest rates. So debt in hard currency can be a good idea at times and not at others. Again, a high dosage of manageability is required to be able to adjust the debt profile quickly. Only export companies with reliable sources of hard currency can be advised to maintain this type of long-term commitment.[5]

Figure 11.2 reveals how dramatic the disequilibria between interest and exchange rates can be by showing the path of local interest rates expressed in U.S. dollars for 90-day bank deposits for four emerging nations. Observe that local interest rates for this group of countries not only fluctuated considerably but also were often negative.

Bankruptcy constitutes another important factor. In many emerging countries bankruptcy laws and procedures can be cumbersome and arbitrary. Hence, bankruptcy costs end up unfairly distributed. Also, it is not rare for liquidation to be the only reasonable way out of a financial crisis.

---

[4]The more volatile the cash flows, the more valuable the real options associated with a project (see Chapter 9: The Value of Flexibility). Risk management reduces cash flow variability, hence the value of real options. This is an often hidden cost of risk management (Chang 1997).

[5]When there is no significant convertibility risk and local currency income has a stable and strong correlation with the exchange rate, long-term commitments in hard currency can be justified, too.

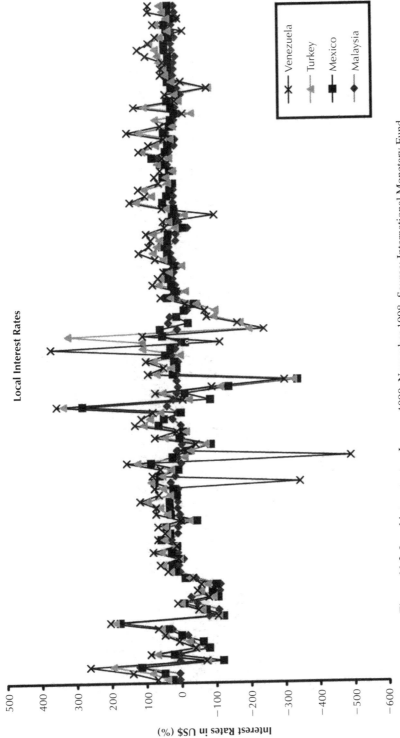

Local Interest Rates

Figure 11.2 Local interest rates: January 1990–November 1998. *Source:* International Monetary Fund.

11.2.2 Taxes

Thus far, we have mentioned corporate taxes on profits only. However, in many countries there are other corporate taxes that can impact the benefits of leverage significantly. In particular, in developing countries that have experienced high inflation, taxes can sometimes eliminate the benefits of the tax shield.

The inflation tax existing in some Latin American countries is a case in point. According to this tax, each balance sheet item is classified as either "monetary" or "nonmonetary." High rotation items like accounts receivable, accounts payable, and bank debt are monetary. More stable items such as fixed assets, inventories, and equity are nonmonetary. The nonmonetary items must be inflation adjusted, whereas the monetary ones need not. Firms pay a tax on their supposed "profits" due to a favorable impact of inflation on their balance sheets. The tax is computed on the difference between the adjusted items in the asset and liability sides. Let us illustrate by the example shown in Table 11.1.

For a (government-designated) inflation index of 20%, the adjustment is:

$$(\$800 \times 20\%) - (\$500 \times 20\%) = +\$60$$

This implies that the firm will pay taxes on an inflationary "profit" of $60. Notice that if equity had been $800 or higher, the adjustment would be either zero or negative and there would be no inflationary tax. Thus, the larger the equity (and the lower the debt), the smaller the inflationary tax. In conclusion, the direction of this tax incentive is the opposite to the one of the traditional tax on profits.

11.2.3 Capital Rationing

The majority of emerging market companies face significant barriers when they attempt to access funds rapidly and at reasonable costs; in other words, their sources of capital are rationed. The interaction of capital rationing with other market particularities brings up important implications about firm leveraging.

Investment Opportunities In dealing with capital rationing, untapped debt capacity gives the firm access to the necessary funding to undertake unanticipated investment opportunities. This is true both in developed and developing countries. However, in this last group capital rationing can become critical enough to have particular relevance.

TABLE 11.1

	Assets	Liabilities
Monetary	$200	$500
Non monetary	$800	$500 (equity)
Totals	$1000	$1000

Untapped debt capacity comes at a price: not taking full advantage of the possible tax shield. This is the price to be paid in exchange for having the possibility of investing in those attractive projects that might come up in the future. Untapped debt capacity must be large if the future investment opportunities are perceived to be numerous and attractive and the capital rationing strict.[6]

Cartels   Cartels proliferate in emerging countries. One common tactic of these firms is to gain market share by ousting a competitor, even if it means taking losses in the short run (e.g., lowering prices below variable costs). Competitors with weaker financial positions will be the first to suffer the consequences of such tactics. Therefore, when there is capital rationing, in oligopolistic markets, the debt ratio of every firm must be a function of the debt ratio of the other firms in the same market.

Undiversified Portfolios   Investors with a high share of their portfolios tied in one firm and facing capital rationing have the following dilemma:

1. To decrease portfolio risk by reducing the firm's debt ratio.
2. To increase leverage as much as possible and invest the proceeds in other businesses, thus decreasing risk through operational diversification.

Selecting the better of these two strategies depends on the level of interest rates and on the relative abundance of investment opportunities. If real interest rates are high and investment opportunities scarce, the first strategy will be more attractive. If real interest rates are low and business opportunities abundant, the second strategy will be more appropriate.

Another possibility is to sell the firm's stock (partially or totally). The validity of this tactic is determined by the transaction costs of selling the shares and by how important it is for the investor to maintain control over the firm's operations (see Chapter 5: Personal Investments).

Working Capital Considerations   Ill-conceived governmental policies and inefficient markets can have an important influence on the operating efficiency of firms in emerging countries. Since adjustments in the amount and composition of working capital can influence the firm's financing mix significantly, factors related to working capital management are particularly relevant. We will comment on some.

a. *Suppliers.* When there are just a few suppliers, the firm risks interruptions and quality problems in its supplies. In consequence, it is sometimes necessary to keep larger inventories.

b. *Inflation.* Inflation can have favorable effects on some items such as fixed assets, inventories, and accounts payable. It can also have unfavorable effects on items like

---

[6]In personal or quasi-personal firms, untapped equity or debt capacity at the shareholder level is another possibility.

accounts receivable and cash balances. These asymmetries can impact the optimal composition of the balance sheet.

c. *Government Policies and Regulations.* Government meddling in the economy can take many forms. We will refer to one of them: price controls. Governments can establish **price controls** for many reasons: as an attempt to reduce inflation, as an action against monopolistic practices, to benefit certain sectors (and to inconvenience others), and so on. Price controls can impact the optimal levels of inventory. When a price increase is anticipated, purchases accelerate and inventories rise. Exchange rate controls are among the most popular. As with other prices, when devaluation is anticipated, inventories denominated in foreign currency accumulate, whereas these inventories are reduced if a revaluation is expected.

In sum, as in the more advanced countries, leverage is basically a function of the firm's attributes. However, given the much higher volatility of emerging market economies, **the desirable debt ratio in emerging markets tends to be lower than it is in the developed countries.**[7] Furthermore, high economic uncertainty in emerging markets requires firms to build in considerable **financial manageability** and to be prepared to quickly adjust the amount and profile of their debts depending on circumstances. Long-term commitments must be minimal unless backed by stable hard currency income.

The desirable level of leverage at each point in time is a function of macroeconomic equilibria (or disequilibria) and must seek value maximization by weighting:

1. The cost of debt and its possible tax benefits.[8]
2. The costs and benefits of risk management tactics.
3. The costs of financial distress.
4. The investment opportunity set and the likelihood of aggressive conduct from (oligopolistic) competitors.

Besides these considerations, to the extent that members of management can act independently of stockholders, the personal agendas of the former must be factored in. Also, in the case of personal and quasi-personal firms, the effects of leverage on the investor's portfolio must be accounted for.

---

[7]The historical evidence may be different, having many emerging market firms with higher debt ratios than their developed country counterparts. Nonetheless, this anomaly probably can be explained by stockholder portfolio considerations, government financing subsidies (explicit or implicit), or simply by irresponsible management of the financial structure.

[8]The cost of debt must take into account not only interest payments but fees, commissions, and other possible expenses. The actual cost of debt is found by computing the internal rate of return of the corresponding cash flow (including all costs).

11.3 A PRACTICAL DETERMINATION OF LEVERAGE IN EMERGING MARKETS

The determination of optimal leverage is not a simple undertaking in emerging markets. This is due to the number of variables that must be factored in, the prevalent economic uncertainties, and the difficulties of quantifying certain elements. In this section, we offer a practical procedure for monitoring the desired level of debt in these markets.

11.3.1 Value of the Unlevered Firm

A valuation model for the firm must be prepared to start with. Operating cash flows (without financial debt) must be estimated, taking under consideration macroeconomic variables as well as the firm's likely evolution. Next we ascertain the parameters to which cash flow and firm value are sensitive (e.g., sales units and prices, inflation, exchange rates, interest rates).

Based on these results, and given the horizon for which we wish to plan debt, cash flows are estimated and the value of the unleveraged firm is computed for (at least) three scenarios: optimistic, expected, and pessimistic. The higher the volatility, the wider the dispersion among these scenarios will be.

Let us illustrate with a simple example. A firm is planning its debt level for the upcoming year. The asset discount rate after taxes is 16%. Operating cash flows (without financial debt) for the next four quarters, their *PVs*, and (unleveraged) firm values for each scenario are shown in Table 11.2.

11.3.2 Debt Ratio

To compute the debt ratio, we will work not with the value of the firm but with the operating cash flow *PVs* for the next four quarters because we are defining leverage just for the upcoming year (it will probably change at the end of that period). The underlying assumption is that the leverage decision taken now will be independent of the leverage decision to be taken one year from now (or at least that one decision will not have a significant effect on the other).

The length of the horizon is a function of volatility. The higher the volatility, the shorter the horizon, and vice versa. We chose one year in our example, but if volatility

TABLE 11.2*

| | | | Quarterly Cash Flow | | | |
| | | PV of | | | | |
Sceneraio	Firm Value	Cash Flows	1	2	3	4
Optimistic	+ 10,000	+ 807.83	+ 150	+ 200	+ 250	+ 300
Expected	+ 5,500	+ 468.32	+ 100	+ 120	+ 140	+ 160
Pessimistic	+ 2,500	+ 198.93	+ 50	+ 50	+ 60	+ 60

*All amounts are in thousands of dollars.

diminishes in the future we will plan the debt ratio for lengthier periods and leverage will be more stable.

The next step is to identify the least favorable operating cash flow in the pessimistic scenario. In our firm, it is +$50,000 in the first two quarters. We want to establish leverage based on the riskier period of time; since dispersion (and volatility) is larger in the second quarter, this is the one will work with.

Suppose the tax rate is 30%, the interest rate is 8% yearly (or 2% quarterly), and only interest, not principal, is paid during the period of analysis. In addition, assume that cash flows are normally distributed in every period and that the probability of a result worse than $50,000 in the second quarter is 5%.[9] Using the standardized normal distribution (see Chapter 5: Personal Investments), the implicit standard deviation of the operating cash flows in the second quarter can be estimated as follows:

$$\alpha = \frac{x - \mu}{\sigma} \Rightarrow \sigma = \frac{x - \mu}{\alpha} = \frac{\$50 - \$120}{-\$1.65} = \$42.4 \times 10^3$$

Now we must decide how much of the $50,000 we are willing to put side to service the debt. Say that we want a 99% probability for the cash flow to be sufficient (or a 1% probability of default). Debt service I can be computed by the following formula:

$$\alpha = \frac{I - \mu}{\sigma} \Rightarrow I = \mu + \alpha\sigma = +\$120 - \$2.33 \times \$42.4 = +\$21.21 \times 10^3$$

At the 2% quarterly interest rate this corresponds to a debt of,

$$D = \frac{\$21.21}{0.02} = \$1060.5 \times 10^3$$

In relation to the expected present value of the unleveraged firm of $5.5 million this is equivalent to a 19.3% leverage.

What is the new expected value of the firm? It is given by its unleveraged expected value plus the present value of the tax shield $PV(TS)$ less the present value of the costs of financial distress $PV(CFD)$. For the time being, let us forget the costs of financial distress and focus on the other two components.

The expected value of the unleveraged firm is $5.5 million. Each quarter, the tax shield equals the interest multiplied by the tax rate. Thus, $PV(TS)$ is a series of $6360 ($21,210 × 30%) quarterly, discounted at 2% (the cost of debt). The result is $24,230, meaning an effect of leverage on expected firm value (before CFDs) of:

---

[9]A more formal analysis could be done. Monte Carlo simulation could be used to estimate the probability distributions for unleveraged firm values and for the cash flows. In this manner the distributional assumptions would be more realistic, and it would not be necessary to assume a probability of cash flows below the one for the pessimistic scenario. The interested reader can refer to Hull (1997) for an introduction to Monte Carlo simulation.

$$V = \$5500 + \$24.23 = \$5524.23 \times 10^3$$

Depending on tax legislation, expected firm value may or may not increase with debt. If it does not increase, then leverage is determined exclusively by the *CFD*s, meaning that the firm should not have any debt (or that, at most, debt should be taken only to the point at which the *CFD*s start being significant).

Since expected firm value increases with debt in our case, it is clear that the tax shield is positive and the firm should always be leveraged. In our example, the debt level was estimated for a 1% probability of default. In the end, however, the debt ratio will depend upon the *CFD*s, the impact of possible risk management strategies, and the desired financial manageability.

Costs of Financial Distress The costs of financial distress are difficult to quantify. At most we can estimate the costs of some events likely to come up in a crisis situation, such as the need to take costly loans in a rush, changes in credit terms from suppliers, or a fall in sales, and compare them with the tax shield benefit.

The question to be answered in our example is how big the costs of financial distress should be for a debt level of $1,060,500 to start being inconvenient. This will happen when the expected present value of the costs of financial distress $E[PV(CFD)]$ begin to surpass the $PV(TS)$.

In our example $PV(TS)$ is $24,230 and the probability of default is 1% (in the riskier quarter).[10] Thus, the debt will start being inconvenient when

$$E[PV(CFD)] = 0.01PV(CFD) \geq PV(TS) = \$24,230$$

The debt starts being too high when $PV(CFD)$ reaches $2,423,000, an amount much higher than the debt itself of $1,060,500. Such a high value seems quite improbable and thus, we could claim that at least this level of debt is justified.

Let us see what happens with a debt level corresponding to a 5% probability of default. This probability implies a debt service equal to the full $50,000 cash flow and a debt level of $2.5 million ($50,000/0.02). $PV(TS)$ would be $57,120 and the corresponding (maximum) present value for the costs of financial distress $PV(CFD)$ would be $1,142,320, 46% of the principal. Still a significant figure but much smaller than the previous one ($2,423,000).

We could perform similar computations for many debt levels to gain sense of their effect on the cutoff point for the costs of financial distress. The end result of this exercise will be a debt level we feel comfortable with.

Up to now we have considered only the tax shield and the costs of financial distress. Now, other decision parameters will be factored in. For our example we will suppose a debt level of $2.5 million (corresponding to a 5% probability of default) as a starting point.

---

[10]This is a simplification, since default can occur at any time and not only during the riskier quarter. Therefore, $E[PV(CFD)]$ could be actually higher.

Risk Management We saw earlier how risk management tactics can reduce cash flow volatility, permitting higher leverage and a higher tax shield. However, risk management is costly. Thus, its convenience must be assessed by weighting the impact on the expected value of the firm of both a higher tax shield and the costs of each risk management tactic.

Suppose our firm arranges with some important clients for a number of units of merchandise to be sold in the future. These units will be priced below their market value but never lower than a minimum preestablished price. An improvement in future cash flows in the pessimistic scenario is to the benefit to the firm. The countervailing cost is the price reduction.

Say this arrangement improves cash flows in the pessimistic scenario as shown in Table 11.3. Thus, for a 5% probability of default, debt service increases to $70,000 (quarterly). This implies a debt level of $3.5 million ($70,000/0.02) and a PV(TS) of $79,960. This last figure is $22,840 larger than the last we obtained ($79,960 − $57,120).

A price reduction was the cost paid for this improvement. If the negative effect of this price reduction on the expected value of the firm is smaller than $22,840, the arrangement is a good deal and the debt should be raised to $3.5 million (to take full advantage of the tax shield). The arrangement must not be signed if the effect of the price reduction on firm value is larger than $22,840.

Financial Manageability Financial manageability becomes critical if oligopolistic behavior is aggressive, investment opportunities significant, and capital rationing strict. Financial manageability is achieved by maintaining a gap between the capacity to contract debt *(debt capacity)* and the amount of debt that is actually taken.[11] Therefore, the decision here is how large this gap should be.

Coming back to our example, let us say that we feel comfortable with a gap of 20%. That is, we want to take permanent debt up to 80% of our debt capacity. Then, permanent debt will depend on the debt capacity we manage to develop in the financial markets.[12] Let us see what happens for different debt capacities and then consider the costs and benefits of financial manageability.

a. *Debt Capacity Below $3,125,000.* Eighty percent of this amount is exactly the same as our starting debt level of $2.5 million. Since permanent debt is pegged at $2.5 million and is below our risk management adjusted level of $3.5 million, the debt level is determined by the manageability condition. Without being able to take advantage of the

---

[11]Financial manageability can be achieved too by investing in liquid assets, though it is a costly strategy given that the return on these assets is lower than the cost of debt or equity. However, it might be justified if a strong restriction of financing sources is anticipated in the near future.

[12]Debt capacity is determined by the firm's relationship with banks, financial markets, and other possible financing sources. We will expand on this topic in the next chapter (Financing and Value). Additionally, as mentioned before, some degree of financial manageability can also be kept at the shareholder level in personal and quasi-personal firms.

TABLE 11.3*

	Firm Value (Unleveraged)	PV of Cash Flows	Quarterly Cash Flow			
			1	2	3	4
Before	+2500	+198.93	+50	+50	+60	+60
After	+3400	+271.53	+70	+70	+80	+80

*Amounts in thousands of dollars.

OUTSOURCING CAPITAL

For a large chunk of its own equity Winnipeg-based United Grain Growers (UGG) substituted the imposing capital of the world's second larger reinsurer: Swiss Re. According to Prakash Shimpi, a finance wizard at the reinsurance company, the trick is to overcome the myopia that stops finance directors seeing that capital can come from a number of sources, both on and off the balance sheet.

UGG trades grain grown by western Canada's farmers. So usually the biggest risk to its profits has been a drop in grain volumes. "If we have a drought my pipeline is pretty damn empty," says Brian Hayward the chief executive, "so we have to keep a lot more capital as a buffer."

Swiss Re realized two things. First that UGG's main risk has no correlation with many of its other risks, such as fire or worker's compensation liabilities. And second, that even a bundle of all of UGG's risks had little or no correlation with the millions of risks that Swiss Re faces around the world. So, Swiss Re offered to insure the entire business of UGG (including the likelihood of a fall in grain volumes) knowing that it needs to set aside less capital than UGG did.

Source: "Outsourcing Capital," Reprinted with permission of © The Economist Newspaper Limited, London. November 27, 1999. All rights reserved.

Comments Here we can see how a risk management decision can have an impact on capital structure. UGG was able to decrease its equity in exchange for a stream of premium liabilities in the future. This is reasonable as long as the premium stream is not too high and is steady enough to compensate the reduction in UGG's cash flow volatility.

Observe that UGG is simply exchanging an uncertain cash flow (stemming from grain volume variability and other insurance-type risks) for another uncertain cash flow (the premium stream) with less variability and (presumably) lower expected value. The implicit assumption here is that the reinsurer has a more diversified portfolio than UGG's owners and the addition of UGG's risks demands a relatively smaller compensation. Therefore, the reinsurer is able to benefit its client and make money at the same time (see Chapter 5: Personal Investments).

Why are UGG's owners likely to be less diversified than Swiss Re's shareholders?

enhanced tax shield, the risk management arrangement (i.e., the future sales contract) is not justified.[13]

b. *Debt Capacity Between $3,125,000 and $4,375,000.* For this range, the debt level would be between $2.5 million and $3.5 million. Here the manageability condition also holds, but to take advantage of a debt level above $2.5 million, the future sales arrangements must be signed. However, they must be modified to match the incremental debt stemming from these contracts with the permanent debt coming from the manageability condition.

For instance, a debt capacity of $4 million would imply a permanent debt of $3.2 million and a quarterly debt service of $64,000 ($3200 × 2%). The future sales arrangement must be targeted to bring the cash flow of the pessimistic scenario only up to $64,000 and it is not necessary to incur the additional cost of increasing it to the original $70,000.

c. *Debt Capacity Larger than $4,375,000.* Here, permanent debt from the flexibility restriction is larger than both $2.5 million and $3.5 million. Therefore, we should take full advantage of the future sales arrangement and increase permanent debt to $3.5 million. Observe that we will have more financial manageability because the 80% debt capacity utilization target will never be reached. This will place the firm in a stronger position to defend itself against eventual competitor aggressions.

d. *Costs and Benefits of Financial Manageability.* However, financial manageability has costs and benefits. The benefits stem from the enhanced access to investment opportunities that otherwise would not be possible owing to financing restrictions (including the contingency of having to react to possible aggressive actions by competitors).

There are two types of cost: direct costs and opportunity costs. Direct costs are fees and other disbursements associated with credit facilities or other financing arrangements necessary to increase debt capacity. In case (c) in our example, debt capacity was above target and, though it made the firm stronger, the question we must ask ourselves is whether this advantage is worth the additional (direct) costs of a larger-than-needed debt capacity. Were this not the case, it might be necessary to cut debt capacity and increase debt utilization up to the original 80% level.

In cases (a) and (b) the manageability restriction held and capacity utilization was the targeted 80%. However, here another cost comes up: the opportunity cost of not taking advantage of the higher tax shield that was feasible in lieu of other considerations (i.e., the costs of financial distress and risk management mechanisms). Should we go above the 80% target?

Managerial Agenda When stockholders are not directly involved in the administration and management acts with considerable independence, management may have the power to set up the debt ratio according to its interests. If this debt ratio were lower than

---

[13]This is true as long as the future sales contracts do not carry other advantages for the firm.

the one determined by the procedure described, then the actual debt level will be established by the managers.[14]

Portfolio Considerations Recall that most emerging market firms are possessed to a great extent by small shareholder groups. If the shareholder base is concentrated, we should complement this analysis with an evaluation of the impact of the leveraging decision on the personal portfolios of significant shareholders. This evaluation could eventually result in an adjustment of the firm's debt level (see Chapter 5: Personal Investments).

Naturally, the permanent debt level must be periodically revised to reflect the flow of new information. Periodicity will depend on business climate volatility. The higher the volatility, the more frequently the leverage decision must be revised, and vice versa. Additionally, we must recall that the actual debt level at any point in time will be a function of the adjustment costs associated with the different financing sources.

11.4 COST OF CAPITAL AND DISCOUNT RATE IN EMERGING COUNTRIES

In Chapter 10 we gave the following formula for the value of the firm V with taxes and before consideration of the costs of financial distress:

$$V = V_u + DT_C$$

Firm value V_u is the present value of operating cash flows discounted at the asset discount rate after taxes and without debt (ρ). The other term is the present value of the tax shield $PV(TS)$ corresponding to taxes saved every period (because of interest expenses) discounted at the cost of debt. In this formula $PV(TS)$ equals DT_C because the debt is assumed to be a constant perpetuity. Nevertheless, in general, this is not the case, and it is necessary to discount the tax shield period by period.

We will comment on the tax shield and firm value computations from the preceding formula. Let us start with the tax shield.

11.4.1 Value of the Tax Shield

The cash flows corresponding to the tax shield must be discounted at the **market** cost of debt. But this rate is not always the same as the **actual** cost of debt: perhaps because the market cost of debt has changed, or the actual cost of debt may be subsidized.

---

[14]The trend in most developed countries is to make an important portion of upper management compensation dependent on the stock price or other parameters reflecting shareholder net worth. This with the purpose of better aligning management's behavior, with stockholders' interests offsetting this type of conduct, at least partially. Nevertheless, the effectiveness of such incentives must be questioned, since many managers have found a way to adjust them to their personal interests through derivative financial schemes (*The Economist* 1999c).

Changes in the Cost of Money Imagine a company that a year ago took a 12% yearly interest loan. However, the cost of money has changed, and if the company wishes a similar loan now it will have to pay 15% interest. The discount rate to be applied to the tax shield must be now 15% instead of the original 12%. The reason is that the relevant discount rate is not the historical one but the one that will prevail from the moment the valuation is performed. This could be an important point when the cost of money suffers wide fluctuations, as is usual in many developing countries.[15]

Cost of Money Subsidies Frequently, developing country governments like to intervene in their economies with the purpose of promoting certain business activities considered important (see Chapter 8: Valuation in Emerging Markets). One popular form of intervention is through loans at preferential interest rates. To illustrate, let us consider an agricultural concern having a 10% yearly interest rate government loan with the cash flows as shown in Table 11.4. For a tax rate of 30%, the tax shield will be as shown in Table 11.5.

At first sight it seems that *PV(TS)* must be obtained by discounting the tax shield cash flow at the 10% loan rate. But this is not so. The correct discount rate is the one

TABLE 11.4

	Year			
	0	**1**	**2**	**3**
Principal	+100			−100
Interest		−10	−10	−10
Total	+100	−10	−10	−110

*All amounts are in thousands of dollars.

TABLE 11.5*

	Year			
	0	**1**	**2**	**3**
Interest		−10	−10	−10
Tax shield		+3	+3	+3

*All amounts are in thousands of dollars.

---

[15]This is not as valid when loans are at variable interest rates. In such cases, changes in the cost of money will affect debts only up to the moment when the interest rate is adjusted.

corresponding to the market cost of money. If the market rate were 12%, *PV(TS)* would be:

$$PV(TS) = +\frac{3}{1.12} + \frac{3}{(1.12)^2} + \frac{3}{(1.12)^3} = +\$7.21 \times 10^3$$

We comment next on the computation of firm value from the formula for the value of the leveraged firm.

11.4.2 Cost of Capital and the Value of the Firm

In Chapter 10 we introduced the following formula for the cost of capital with taxes:

$$CC = \left(1 - \frac{DT_C}{V}\right)\rho = \frac{D}{V}(1 - T_C)k_D + \frac{E}{V}k_E$$

The formulas for the cost of capital and the value of the leveraged firm suggest two manners of finding the value of a firm: by discounting operating cash flows after taxes at the cost of capital *CC*, and by adding the present value of the tax shield to the value of the firm without debt. The second procedure is known as **adjusted present value.**

The two procedures seem to be equivalent, but beware that this is not the case (Inselbag & Kaufold 1997).

When one is discounting at *CC* it is assumed that the proportion of debt and equity stays fixed throughout the horizon. But this is rare, especially in emerging market companies suffering frequent changes in leverage. Thus this approach is likely to be flawed.

Adjusted present value looks like a good solution. After all, in this method the *PV* of operating cash flows is computed separately from *PV(TS)*, allowing the debt (originating the tax shield) to evolve independently over time. Thus there is no requirement to keep leverage fixed.

However, generally we want to value the firm with a stable debt ratio starting at some point in the future, and this is where the adjusted present value approach fails. When leverage stabilizes, debt levels stem from the value of the assets, which are themselves determined by the operating cash flows. Hence, part of the future interest expense and the tax shield are a function of and will be as risky as the operating cash flows. Then, the right thing to do is to discount this riskier portion of the tax shield at the (after-tax) unleveraged rate ρ, not at the cost of debt. However, this can be very cumbersome, and *CC* offers an advantage under these circumstances. It can be shown that discounting at *CC* automatically takes into account the risk stemming from changes in leverage.[16]

Summarizing, adjusted present value must be used when leverage is unstable; *CC* is used when we are confident that the debt ratio will be fixed.

---

[16]The proof is given in Inselbag and Kaufold (1997).

11.5 CONCLUSIONS

- For every firm, desirable leverage is a function of cash flow volatility, the firm's goods and services, asset composition, organizational issues, and growth potential.
- Actual leverage is dynamic and oscillates around desirable leverage, depending on the adjustment costs of the different financing sources.
- Cash flow volatility can be reduced, and the optimum debt level increased, through costly risk management techniques. Additionally, risk management can be useful to better manage undiversified portfolios.
- High and changing volatility, macroeconomic disequilibria, tax legislation, and capital rationing can seriously affect desirable leverage in emerging markets.
- Capital rationing is particularly important because of its impact on the firm's ability to undertake attractive investment opportunities, and to react appropriately against possible competitor aggressions. Furthermore, capital rationing is also relevant to defining debt ratios for personal and quasi-personal firms.
- Desirable leverage tends to be lower in emerging markets. Besides, in these countries it is often necessary to build in a high level of financial manageability.
- A methodology for the determination and monitoring of desirable leverage in emerging markets was proposed. The intuitive approach is to tackle each relevant variable separately, starting with the tax shield and the costs of financial distress, followed by risk and financial manageability, and ending with the effect of managerial interests and the specificities of personal and quasi-personal firms.
- The more volatile the economy, the more frequently desirable leverage must be revised.
- While desirable leverage is unstable, the present value of a firm's cash flows must be computed by adding the present value of the tax shield to the present value of the operating cash flows (after taxes). Once desirable leverage has stabilized, present value must be computed by discounting cash flows from operations (after taxes) at the cost of capital.

QUESTIONS AND PROBLEMS

1. How does operating cash flow volatility affect leverage?
2. How does the ratio between fixed and total assets affect leverage?
3. What is the relation between the diversification of management's portfolio and firm's leverage?
4. Why do high-growth companies tend to have low leverage?
5. Why might it not be convenient to keep leverage at the optimal level at every point in time?
6. Profit stabilization and the reduction of operating leverage are ways of reducing cash flow volatility, allowing a higher optimal level of debt. Why are these strategies not always implemented?

7. In the presence of capital rationing, how is leverage affected when
   a) there are numerous investment opportunities?
   b) the firm is in an oligopolistic market?

8. Let us refer to the example used in this chapter to illustrate the determination of leverage (see Section 11.3). A firm is planning its debt level for the upcoming year. The asset discount rate after taxes is 16%. Operating cash flows (without financial debt) for the next four quarters, their *PVs* and (unleveraged) firm values in $ thousands for each scenario are as shown in Table P11.8.

   Suppose a 20% tax rate and a yearly cost of debt of 24% (6% quarterly).

   As before, cash flows are normally distributed, and the probability of a result worse than $50 thousand in the second quarter is 5%.

   (a) How much must the debt be for a 99% probability that the second quarter cash flow will be sufficient?
   (b) What is the value of the firm before costs of financial distress for the debt level determined in part (a)?
   (c) How large would the costs of financial distress have to be for this leverage to start being inconvenient?

9. At what rate must the tax shield cash flows be discounted?

10. Why must adjusted present value be used when leverage is unstable, and the formula for the cost of capital after taxes when we are confident that the debt ratio will be fixed?

TABLE P11.8*

| | | | Quarter | | | |
| | | | Cash Flows | | | |
Senario	Firm Value	Cash Flow *PVs*	1	2	3	4
Optimistic	+10,000	+807.83	+150	+200	+250	+300
Expected	+5,500	+468.32	+100	+120	+140	+160
Pessimistic	+2,500	+198.93	+50	+50	+60	+60

*All months are in thousands of dollars.

CHAPTER 12

FINANCING AND VALUE

"Marx and Adam Smith did not share many ideas, but both agreed, for very similar reasons, that the corporate form of organization did not function properly. Both were skeptical that such an organization could be efficient and fair as long as ownership and control were kept separated."

We started our discussion on leverage in Part III stating that under certain conditions, debt does not have any effect on the value of the firm. Then we saw how, in a more realistic world, when taxes, financial distress, risk management possibilities, and financial market inefficiencies are accounted for, the opposite conclusion is reached: that leverage can indeed be a convenient way to add value. We ended Chapter 11 by proposing a practical guide for establishing and monitoring the desirable debt ratio for emerging market firms.

Up to now our reasoning was based on the assumption that the leverage decision was the result of exogenous variables stemming from the economic and business climate, and that we could react only to these variables. We will now learn that this is not the case: we can adopt a proactive stance, and value can also be added by building flexibility into the financial strategy.

We will focus on two topics. The first one refers to specific projects and the manner in which value can be created through financing schemes that can be adapted to project results over time. The second topic refers to the firm's long-term financing strategy and the manner in which good planning can gradually reduce capital rationing (and add value) by opening up new sources of funding.

12.1 THE VALUE OF FINANCIAL FLEXIBILITY

Value is added when managerial decisions can be taken either before or during the life of a project (see Chapter 9: The Value of Flexibility). Something similar happens when the financing decision can be revised as project results are revealed over time. We illustrate this with an example. To understand this concept clearly, however, a basic comprehension of option theory, and particularly the binomial model, will be necessary. (The reader who does not feel comfortable with this theory is urged to review Chapter 9.)

Take the case of a project with the characteristics shown in Table 12.1. (We follow the approach of Trigeorgis 1993 in this example). The project has a two-year horizon

TABLE 12.1

Data	
Present value of future cash flows V_0	$100 million
Initial investment I_0	$90 million
Upward movement u	2
Downward movement d	0.5
Yearly risk-free rate r	10%

and will be financed by $60 million in equity and $30 million in debt. For the sake of simplicity, we assume no taxes and that the cost of debt equals the risk-free rate (this last restriction will be lifted later on). Let us compute $E(NPV)$ for each, shareholders and debt holders. Their sum will add up to the project's total $E(NPV)$.

The risk-free equivalent probability p is

$$p = \frac{(1 + r) - d}{u - d} = \frac{1.1 - 0.5}{1.5} = 0.4$$

Project value over time is as shown in Figure 12.1.

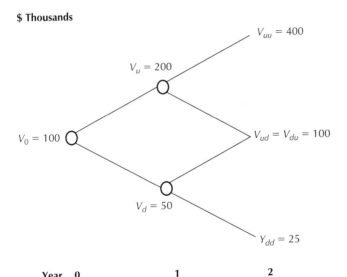

$ Thousands

$V_{uu} = 400$

$V_u = 200$

$V_0 = 100$

$V_{ud} = V_{du} = 100$

$V_d = 50$

$Y_{dd} = 25$

Year   0   1   2

Figure 12.1

12.1.1 Full Capitalization from the Beginning

If financing is not flexible, the entire investment must be made at the beginning. Under this scenario shareholder value E_{xx} at any node at the end of the second year will be given by the following formula:

$$E_{xx} = \text{Max}[(\text{value} - \text{debt})_{t=2}, 0]$$

For instance, if project value increases for two years in a row, its value at the end of the second year V_{uu} is \$400,000 and shareholder value E_{uu} is

$$E_{uu} = \text{Max}[(400 - 36.3)_{t=2}, 0] = +\$366.7 \times 10^3$$

The term in brackets represents the difference between project value at year 2 (V_{uu}) and the original \$30,000 debt plus interest at a 10% yearly rate (\$30 × 1.1 × 1.1 = \$36,300).

Computing the corresponding values for all the possibilities at year 2 we get the result as shown in Table 12.2. Notice that when project value is \$25,000 bankruptcy is declared, debtors take possession of the assets, and the shareholders are left with nothing. Hence, shareholder value is zero. This is their worst possible outcome, since shareholder value can never be negative.

Using the binomial model, we compute shareholder value when project value increases at year 1:

$$E_u = \frac{pE_{uu} + (1-p)E_{ud}}{1+r} = \frac{(0.4 \times 363.7) + (0.6 \times 63.7)}{1.1} = \$167 \times 10^3$$

When project value decreases at year 1:

$$E_d = \frac{pE_{du} + (1-p)E_{dd}}{1+r} = \frac{(0.4 \times 63.7) + (0.6 \times 0)}{1.1} = \$23.16 \times 10^3$$

Shareholder value at year 0 will then be:

$$E_0 = \frac{pE_u + (1-p)E_d}{1+r} = \frac{(0.4 \times 167) + (0.6 \times 23.16)}{1.1} = \$73.36 \times 10^3$$

TABLE 12.2*

Project Value		Debt	Shareholder Value	
V_{uu}	400	36.3	E_{uu}	363.7
$V_{ud} = V_{du}$	100	36.3	$E_{ud} = E_{du}$	63.7
V_{dd}	25	36.3	E_{dd}	0

*Amounts are in thousands of dollars.

$ Thousands

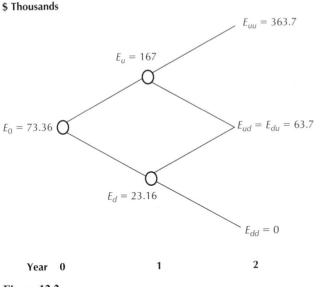

$E_{uu} = 363.7$

$E_u = 167$

$E_0 = 73.36$

$E_{ud} = E_{du} = 63.7$

$E_d = 23.16$

$E_{dd} = 0$

Year   0   1   2

Figure 12.2

This can be demonstrated graphically, as shown in Figure 12.2. The shareholder's initial investment is $60,000; therefore, their $E(NPV)$ is $13,360 ($73,360 − $60,000).

At any point in time the value for the debt holders will be the debt or the value of the project, whatever amount is **smaller.** Doing the computations for each scenario, we get at the end of the second year the result shown in Table 12.3.

Using the same formulas, we obtain the debt holder values for year 1:

$$D_u = \frac{pD_{uu} + (1-p)D_{ud}}{1+r} = \frac{(0.4 \times 36.3) + (0.6 \times 36.3)}{1.1} = +\$33 \times 10^3$$

$$D_d = \frac{pD_{du} + (1-p)D_{dd}}{1+r} = \frac{(0.4 \times 36.3) + (0.6 \times 25)}{1.1} = +\$26.84 \times 10^3$$

TABLE 12.3*

	Project Value	Debt	Debt holders' Value	
V_{uu}	400	36.3	D_{uu}	36.3
$V_{ud} = V_{du}$	100	36.3	$D_{ud} = D_{du}$	36.3
V_{dd}	25	36.3	D_{dd}	25

*Amounts are in thousands of dollars.

The value of the project for the debt holders will be:

$$D_0 = \frac{pD_u + (1 - p)D_d}{1 + r} = \frac{(0.4 \times 33) + (0.6 \times 26.84)}{1.1} = +\$26.64 \times 10^3$$

This can be demonstrated graphically, as shown in Figure 12.3. Subtracting their initial $30,000 investment we get a negative $E(NPV)$ for the debt holders of $-\$3,360$.

The $E(NPV)$ for the overall project will be $13,360 - \$3,360 = +\$10,000$. This is exactly the difference between the expected value of the project ($100,000) and the total initial investment ($90,000). This result was expected, since the value of the project must be the same, independent of how its benefits are distributed between debt holders and shareholders.

Since the $E(NPV)$ for the debt holders is negative, the project is bad business for them. Under such conditions, debt holders raise the cost of debt to the point at which they get a fair return for their investment. The increase in the cost of debt comes from the shareholders, who then get a lower $E(NPV)$. But this is just a transfer from one party to the other; the project value remains exactly the same ($+\$10,000$).

12.1.2 Financing in Stages

Imagine that the project is financed in two stages, as shown in Table 12.4. Total investment increased from $90,000 to $95,000 ($40,000 + $55,000), since the investment delay has a financial cost that we assume to be equal to the risk-free interest rate (10%). Further, assume that the $11,000 loan at the end of year 1 is disbursed only if at that point the result of the project is favorable. Applying the binomial model gives the result shown in Table 12.5.

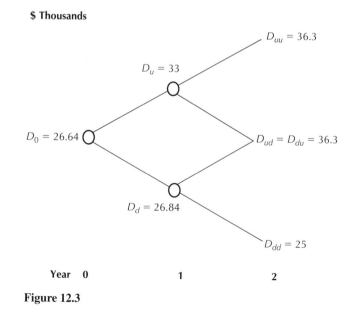

$ Thousands

$D_0 = 26.64$

$D_u = 33$

$D_d = 26.84$

$D_{uu} = 36.3$

$D_{ud} = D_{du} = 36.3$

$D_{dd} = 25$

Year   0   1   2

Figure 12.3

TABLE 12.4

	Beginning of Year	
	1	2
Equity	$20,000	$44,000
Debt	$20,000	$11,000
Total	$40,000	$55,000

Now, E_{ud} and E_{du} are not equal. In the initial case, first-year results are favorable and the $11,000 loan is disbursed, whereas in the second case, first year results are unfavorable and there is no loan.

Let us calculate shareholder's $E(NPV)$ at the end of year 1:

$$E_u = \frac{(0.4 \times 363.7) + (0.6 \times 63.7)}{1.1} = \$167 \times 10^3$$

$$E_d = \frac{(0.4 \times 75.8) + (0.6 \times 0.8)}{1.1} = \$28 \times 10^3$$

Shareholders can decide whether to make the second $44,000 disbursement. They will do it only if $E(NPV)$ is positive. This option demands that we adjust the previous results depending on their decision.

In the case of E_u, $E(NPV)$ if the new investment is made will be $123,000 ($167,000 − $44,000). Being a positive value the adjusted value $Aj(E_u)$ will be $123,000, as well. Mathematically,

$$Aj(E_u) = \text{Max}[(167 - 44), 0] = \$123 \times 10^3$$

In the case of E_d, the new investment is larger than the value of the project for the shareholders. Hence, the disbursement will not be made and the adjusted value $Aj(E_d)$ will be zero. Mathematically,

$$Aj(E_d) = \text{Max}[(28 - 44), 0] = 0$$

TABLE 12.5*

Project Value		Debt	Shareholder Value	
V_{uu}	400	36.3	E_{uu}	363.7
V_{ud}	100	36.3	E_{ud}	63.7
V_{du}	100	24.2	E_{du}	75.8
V_{dd}	25	24.2	E_{dd}	0.8

*Amounts are in thousands of dollars.

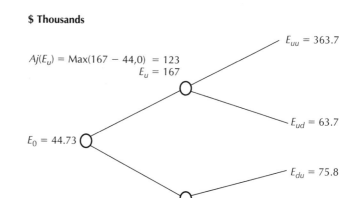

$ Thousands

$$Aj(E_u) = \text{Max}(167 - 44,0) = 123$$
$$E_u = 167$$

$$E_{uu} = 363.7$$

$$E_{ud} = 63.7$$

$$E_0 = 44.73$$

$$E_{du} = 75.8$$

$$E_d = 26.84$$
$$Aj(E_d) = \text{Max}(28 - 44,0) = 0$$

$$E_{dd} = 0.8$$

Year   0   1   2

Figure 12.4

Therefore, the value of the project for the shareholders will be,

$$E_0 = \frac{(0.4 \times 123) + (0.6 \times 0)}{1.1} = \$44.73 \times 10^3$$

This can be demonstrated graphically, as shown in Figure 12.4.

Upon subtracting the initial $20,000 investment, $E(NPV)$ for the shareholders turns out to be $24,730.

Finally, let us compute $E(NPV)$ for the debt holders. The values at the end of the second year will be as shown in Table 12.6. Based on these results we obtain values of $33,000 and $22,000 for D_u and D_d, respectively. In the case of D_u debt holders disburse the second $11,000 loan installment and the adjusted value $A_j(D_u)$ is $22,000. Thus, $E(NPV)$ for the debt holders is:

$$D_0 = \frac{(0.4 \times 22) + (0.6 \times 22)}{1.1} = \$20 \times 10^3$$

TABLE 12.6*

Project Value		Debt	Debt Holders' Value	
V_{uu}	400	36.3	D_{uu}	36.3
V_{ud}	100	36.3	D_{ud}	36.3
V_{du}	100	24.2	D_{du}	24.2
V_{dd}	25	24.2	D_{dd}	24.2

*Amounts are in thousands of dollars.

This can be expressed graphically, as shown in Figure 12.5.

By subtracting the original $20,000 loan, we get an $E(NPV)$ equal to zero for the debt holders. This makes sense since, in this case, there is no chance for the debt holders to lose money. Therefore, the fair interest rate will be the risk-free rate (i.e., 10%).

By adding up shareholder and debt holder value, we obtain a value for the overall project of $24,730 ($24,730 + $0), which compares favorably with the corresponding figure when there was no financing flexibility ($10,000).

Let us discuss the logic behind these results. When there is financing flexibility, the probability of the debt holders losing money is reduced. Likewise, project value for the shareholders also increases, since they have the option of not continuing if results are unfavorable. Then, the expected net present value for the whole project must be higher.

Flexible financing is not necessarily designed in such a simple manner. It is possible to devise more complex schemes—for instance, to allow for options to exchange debt for equity, or equity for debt, to restrict certain benefits (e.g., dividends), or to vary the cost of debt with the project results. And this type of financing does not have to be tailor-made. Hybrid financial instruments, part debt and part equity, increasingly available in emerging financial markets, can also be employed. Examples include convertible stock, convertible debt, preferred stock, callable bonds, and warrants.

12.2 FINANCING STRATEGY

The present value of operating cash flows (including real options) is the key determinant of firm value. Nevertheless, to take advantage of investment opportunities, it is necessary to come up with the required funding to finance them. Every company faces this problem, and it is a critical issue for emerging market firms because capital rationing is so significant in their environments.

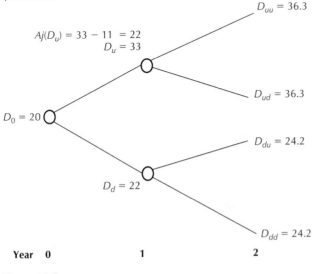

$ Thousands

$D_{uu} = 36.3$

$Aj(D_u) = 33 - 11 = 22$
$D_u = 33$

$D_{ud} = 36.3$

$D_0 = 20$

$D_{du} = 24.2$

$D_d = 22$

$D_{dd} = 24.2$

Year   0   1   2

Figure 12.5

The less developed a financial market, the more accentuated will the capital rationing problem be. Also, the more numerous the investment opportunities, the more damaging will the consequences of capital rationing be. By preventing the realization of many attractive projects, strict capital rationing combined with abundant investment opportunities can reduce considerably the chances of enhancing the value of a firm.

But where do investment opportunities arise? They can originate both within the firm and outside it. Opportunities originating outside the firm depend on business climate. A prosperous and growing economy will undoubtedly offer many more investment opportunities than one that is stagnant or depressed. Opportunities coming from within the firm depend on managerial ability to identify the most promising strategic directions, focus human and financial resources in those areas, and take full advantage of opportunities once they arise. As discussed earlier (see Chapter 9: The Value of Flexibility), this particular managerial ability is critical to the success of projects in environments with frequent economic disequilibria and diffuse information, characteristics often found in emerging markets.

A company that faces capital rationing and wishes to grow and take advantage of business opportunities has no choice but to initiate a process to expand its financing sources. We can distinguish three phases in such a process[1]:

1. Reliance on personal or family resources
2. Entry into the local capital market
3. Entry into international capital markets

We will comment on each of these phases. However, since this topic is not entirely in consonance with the primary orientation of this book, our coverage will be cursory.

12.2.1 The Personal or Family Firm

Small individual or family-owned firms[2] tend to rely on bank debt and equity for sources of financing.

Bank Debt Bank debt as a financing source has two constraints: the amount of debt that a particular firm can actually take and the ability of local banks to satisfy the demand for loans.

The amount of debt that a firm can take depends primarily on its attributes and on the business climate. A firm's ability to borrow has a ceiling beyond which further financing requires new equity funds.

The ability of a local bank to lend is a function of its size in relation to the firm. When the firm is relatively small, local bank financing is not a limiting factor. But this

---

[1] In practice it is possible to expand the financing sources up to a certain point in a different way by combining financial and industrial groups, as has been done by so frequently in Japan, South Korea, and Germany.

[2] We will talk of personal or family firms as relatively small ones. However, there are many sizable firms around the world that still can be considered in this category.

is not the case when the firm develops and its financing needs outgrow the capacity of local banks. This is a common occurrence in emerging markets. Hence, it is not unusual to find that larger local (personal or family) companies may have borrowing needs that exceed the lending capacity of the local banks. At this point, equity finance is the only way out.

The Limits of Equity Financing Equity financing comes from two sources: retained earnings and fresh capital. The evolution of retained earnings depends in turn on profits and cash dividends. The larger the profits and the lower the cash dividends, the more rapidly will the shareholder's surplus grow.

Profits are mainly a function of business climate and managerial competence. A successful management performance is the most we can hope for.

Cash dividends and fresh capital may or may not be relevant in this type of firm. If the firm is the main source of income for the shareholders, paying out cash dividends could considerably weaken the firm's net worth. To the extent that the shareholders have other sources of income, cash dividends become less important and management has more leeway to adjust them to the firm's financing needs.

Similarly, shareholders will be less reluctant to contribute fresh capital, and management will be in a better position to ask for it, when the firm does not comprise a significant proportion of the shareholder portfolio (i.e., the amount to be disbursed is relatively small).[3,4]

The financing possibilities available to this type of firm are quite limited. This is not particularly relevant if the available financing is balanced with investment opportunities. However, when new businesses demand increasing amounts of funds, capital rationing begins to hurt. When this occurs, the firm is obliged to enter the next stage of financing development.

12.2.2 Entry into the Local Capital Market

When bank debt and equity are exhausted, the firm must issue bonds in the local capital market.

Bond Issuance Asymmetrical information is the main problem associated with issuing bonds in the capital market. This problem arises because investors are much less informed than bankers about the firm's day-to-day operations, hence tend to worry about how management will use the funds, and whether the planned investments are as attractive as promised. Other issues of concern entail the competence of the management team, its trustworthiness, and the risk of default.

---

[3]Cash dividends are irrelevant in the absence of taxes, transaction costs, barriers in the financial markets, and perfect access to information. The proof of this statement appears in Appendix 12A. Nevertheless, these are unrealistic assumptions everywhere (particularly in emerging markets).

[4]Another consideration is the impact of cash dividends and fresh capital on the risk–return characteristics of shareholder portfolios. Naturally, the impact will be more significant when the firm comprises a significant proportion of the investor portfolio.

Most participants in emerging financial markets are unsophisticated. This generally results in placement at reasonable yields of only the simplest financial instruments. This is an important consideration when it becomes necessary to issue bonds in these markets.

For all these reasons the first bond issues tend to be low-risk, simple ones. The more straightforward way to achieve this is by reducing maturities and/or attaching attractive guarantees. For instance, it is common for the first issues to be of a very simple instrument like commercial paper (maturing in less than a year) and to set up some kind of safe collateral (e.g., bank guarantees, accounts payable from solvent clients, prime real estate).

Bonds with longer terms, fewer guarantees and, eventually, more complexity are issued later on, as the firm's reputation as a responsible borrower is established.

Financing Strategy as an Investment A good reputation in the financial markets is the key to opening up new sources of funding. But building this kind of reputation requires time and a well-thought-out process that must be closely monitored by management. This is, in effect, a "financial marketing" plan that can be as important as other plans for the marketing of the firm's goods and services, or maybe more so.

The cost of raising financing is another factor. Preparing and distributing a new bond issue demands considerable managerial effort and implies disbursements (marketing expenses, legal expenses, consultant fees, underwriting fees, bank commissions, etc.) that may be very significant. Especially in the initial issues, the magnitude of these costs is sometimes so high that at first sight it seems not to make much sense to proceed further. However, these expenses must not be seen as fully applicable to the current bond issue. A good portion of them must be thought of as an investment in reputation building that will pay back by reducing financing costs in the medium term.

It is not enough to develop debt-funding sources in the local capital markets. Sooner or later, a maximum acceptable level of leverage is reached and new equity capital is required. At this point the firm has no option but look to the possibility of opening up the shareholder base.

Opening up the Shareholder Base; Control Implications Information asymmetries are a much more critical consideration in the raising of new equity capital than with respect to debt. Once the funds have been provided, new shareholders have little control over their destiny, nor any assurances of future dividends or share prices. Hence, the return on their investment becomes highly unpredictable. In comparison, by having a contractual right to a preestablished payment schedule, bondholders enjoy a far less risky position. It is at this point that the firm's investment in reputation starts to pay off. If the company enjoys a good image in the financial markets, it should not have major trouble attracting new shareholders.

The implications of going public on managerial control are likely to be more relevant than informational asymmetries when the firm is opening up the shareholder base. The control issue is not a major problem while the dominant shareholders keep an absolute hold on the company's operations. It is likely to become a major obstacle, however, as new shareholders and professional managers take more and more control.[5] When ceding control, the dominant shareholders perceive:

- A loss in power and image before society
- A loss of power associated with managerial control itself
- The loss of perks and other managerial benefits
- The loss of privileged managerial information on business opportunities

These losses may be sizable, and reluctance of the dominant shareholders to cede managerial control is to be expected. Yet, nondominant shareholders have a different position. They lose nothing when control passes to the hands of professional managers and/or a wider caucus of shareholders. On the contrary, from their viewpoint they benefit from going public. On the one hand, since the firm's shares are openly traded in the stock market, they now face lower transaction (illiquidity) costs when they buy and sell shares. And, on the other hand, the mere fact that cash can be easily raised by selling stock makes them less dependent on cash dividends and allows more flexibility for the firm to dispose of retained earnings to finance investment opportunities. These differences of opinion between the two groups of shareholders can lead to potentially paralyzing conflicts.

Nevertheless, even when all these problems are overcome, at this point the firm still remains dependent on the local capital market. This is dangerous, since emerging countries are so sensitive to local economic and political affairs and to the vagaries of international capital flows that the pool of financial resources could either explode or drain in a short period of time (see Chapter 1: Financial Theory in Emerging Markets). Thus as long as it is focused locally, the firm is exposed to high uncertainty with respect to its financing sources.

High volatility of financing sources and significant investment opportunities can combine to make the local capital market insufficient. Now the firm must consider a new stage of financial development: entrance to the international financial markets.

12.2.3 Entry into International Capital Markets

The first logical step at this stage is to borrow from international banks. This step does not warrant discussion. The next step is to go through the route of **private placements.**

Private Placements A private placement takes place when financial instruments are negotiated directly with a limited number of investors such as multilateral institutions, mutual funds, investment funds, or other international investors. When managers are dealing with a small group of sophisticated people, information asymmetries are

---

[5]As long as legislation permits, the loss of control upon going public can be ameliorated (at least in the medium term) by restricting certain rights on the new stock, particularly voting rights. The better the firm's reputation in the financial markets, the smaller will be the incremental expected return (in relation to the full rights stock) of the holders of this restricted stock.

reduced and the complexities of the instrument do not constitute a problem. Presumably, lower levels of information asymmetries will result in lower financing costs.

Additionally, easier communications with fund providers also allows for greater flexibility to negotiate changes in the event of financial difficulties.

However, private placements come with a hidden cost. Since they are acquired by a limited number of investors, the liquidity of these instruments is much lower than that of a public instrument. To the extent that investors value the option of selling these instruments before maturity, they will demand a liquidity premium, which will increase the cost of the issue. Therefore, private placements will be profitable as long as the reduction in yield due to lower information asymmetries more than compensates for the increase in yield due to greater illiquidity.[6]

Liquidity and maturity are intertwined. The larger the maturity, the lower the liquidity, and vice versa. Thus, private placements will be more attractive for bonds than for shares and for short-term bonds than for long-term ones. Summarizing, private placements will be more convenient under the following conditions:

1. Significant information asymmetries exist.

2. Early liquidation is less relevant for investors.

3. The maturity period is shorter.

International Issues If investment opportunities are large enough, after a while it is necessary to go deeper into international financing sources. It is logical to issue bonds and then stock.[7] Information asymmetries are significantly greater in the international context. Renewed managerial efforts and higher expenses are necessary to cope with these informational obstacles. However, as in local financial markets, a good part of these efforts and disbursements must be added to the cost of future issues. In addition, as more issues are made in the future, expenses will be lower and unitary costs will gradually diminish.

At this point, international investors have the following main concerns about the issuing firm:

- The attractiveness of the firm's investment opportunities
- The competitiveness of the firm at a global level
- The legal framework of the issue[8]

---

[6]The illiquidity problem can be dealt with through an agreement binding the firm to go public within a predetermined period of time. This will not be costly for the company as long as the decision to go public, and the timing of this move, are already part of the firm's plans.

[7]At least in the initial stages, stock issues are usually arranged in the form of American depository receipts (ADRs) or global depository receipts (GDRs). These are instruments backed by a predetermined number of shares deposited in a bank trust.

[8]Owing to underdevelopment of judiciary systems in emerging market, issues are frequently subject to the legislation of a developed nation.

- The quality of the organization
- The organization's relationship with minority shareholders
- The quality and reputation of management

The process of opening up new financing sources has another important cost. The expanding presence of new fund providers separates the original shareholders from the company's operations in an increasing degree. Hence, agency costs rise as the independence of the firm's management is augmented. This is the price to be paid not only to access wider sources of funds, but also to capture the benefits of an organization that is exposed to international financial markets. The benefits that arise are several:

- Realization of the firm's full potential
- Improvement of the capital rationing constraint
- Cash dividends are less restrictive to financial policy
- Higher liquidity for the firm's financial instruments, especially stock
- Enhanced stock prices, due to greater liquidity and smaller information asymmetries
- Increasingly lower issuing costs, due to economies of scale in financing
- Greater formality and better controls on management and the firm's financial results

Investment banks are a key factor in the opening up of new financing sources. Their main contributions are to give financial advice, to provide the capacity to distribute the firm's securities in the capital markets, and to lend the positive effect of their image to promote the amelioration of informational asymmetries. This last point is particularly crucial when one is accessing international financial markets. Of course, investment banks are costly, and the firm's ability and willingness to pay for their services must be evaluated in each instance.

The role of international rating agencies (e.g., Standard & Poor's and Moody's) is also important. The more favorable the classification obtained from these agencies, the lower the costs and the wider the sources of financing. Company modernization and investment in financial marketing can have a positive impact on credit rating classification over time, as well (see Chapter 7: A Modified CAPM for Emerging Markets).

Mergers and Acquisitions Economies of scale in operations and financing can also be obtained by merging or being absorbed into a larger organization. Nevertheless, this act has more to do with strategic considerations than with finance. Although the capital rationing problem can be solved in this manner, gaining competitive advantages is by far the main reasonable justification for mergers and acquisitions.

As a result of globalization, an increasing number of companies are losing their national character and amalgamating into multinational organizations. Integrating into a larger entity can be an attractive (and sometimes inevitable) strategy for many firms in developing markets that find it difficult to survive on their own in an ever more competitive environment. The challenge for stockholders and managers in emerging country firms in general is to strengthen their companies and nurture their negotiating power as much as possible to be prepared for the moment integration becomes inevitable, if indeed it ever does.

Entering International Capital Markets by Various Paths This three-stage process of financial development is not a rigid one. It is quite possible for a family-controlled firm to issue international securities and ignore the local capital market, to be merged into a multinational organization before experimenting with commercial paper locally, or to go public in the international markets without having tapped the local market. In other words, this is a flexible process that can be adapted to suit each firm's characteristics.

12.3 CONCLUSIONS

- Financing opportunities are not static. It is possible to turn them into sources of value for the firm.
- One possibility is to devise flexible financing schemes, where funding is contingent on the project's results. In this manner, debt holders can avoid losses and shareholders have the option of continuing to invest or not at different points in time.
- Flexible financing schemes are particularly attractive for the volatile environments of emerging countries.
- In principle, financing flexibility can be quantified through option theory.
- Capital rationing together with an abundance of investment opportunities makes it important for many emerging market companies to open up their funding sources as a primary means of enhancing the value of their firms.
- Three stages can be envisioned when it becomes necessary to open up financing sources: the small company financing itself exclusively from local banks and its own shareholders; entry into the local capital market, and entry into the international capital markets.
- Integration into a multinational organization is a last possible phase in the financial development process.

QUESTIONS AND PROBLEMS

1. Refer to the example on flexible financing of this chapter and recalculate the value of the project for both stockholders and debt holders if the financing is structured as shown in Table P12.1.
2. What are the main financing barriers for emerging market family firms that have not been opened to the capital markets?
3. What are the main financing barriers for emerging market family firms once they have opened to the local capital markets?
4. What is usually the main barrier facing family firms when they open up their shareholding structure?

TABLE P12.1

	End of Year	
	1	2
Equity	$20,000	$22,000
Debt	$30,000	$22,000
Total	$50,000	$44,000

5. Why might dependence of emerging market family firms on the local capital markets be risky?

6. Give the main advantage and the main disadvantage of private placements.

APPENDIX 12A

The Conditions for Cash Dividend Irrelevance

Imagine a firm with the balance sheet (market values in $ thousands) as shown in Table 12A.1. Assume that paid-in capital is represented by 300 shares, with a nominal value of $1 each. Retained earnings are as large as paid-in capital. Hence, the book value for each share is $2. A stockholder owning 3 shares will have a total book value of $6 (3 × $2).

Say the company pays a $1 cash dividend for each 3 shares. The balance sheet after the dividend is paid is shown in Table 12A.2. The book value per share will be now:

$$\text{Book value per share} = \frac{\$500}{300} = \$1.67$$

TABLE 12A.1

Assets		Liabilities	
Cash	$200	Debt	$500
Other	$900	Paid-in capital	$300
		Retained earnings	$300
Totals	$1100		$1100

TABLE 12A.2

Assets		Liabilities	
Cash	$200 − $100 = $100	Debt	$500
Other	$900	Paid-in capital	$300
		Retained earnings	$300 − $100 = $200
Totals	$1100 − $100 = $1000		$1100 − $100 = $1000

After the dividend has been paid, the shareholder who owns 3 shares will have the same 3 shares with a new book value plus cash:

$$\text{Book value} = 3 \times 1.67 = \$5$$

$$\text{Cash} = \$1$$

The total is $6, exactly the same amount he had before the dividend. Therefore, we can conclude that the cash dividend is irrelevant.

Notice that this conclusion requires three conditions:

1. Taxes, both before and after the dividend, do not make the situation different either for the firm or for the shareholder.

2. There are no transaction costs that make it costly to transform shares into cash, or vice versa, so that the shareholder is not indifferent between possessing cash or shares.

3. The dividend does not convey information of any kind.

PART 3 SUMMARY:
FINANCING AND INVESTMENT

Debt and equity are the two basic sources of financing. Debt has a priority claim on operating cash flows hence is less risky than equity and demands a lower return. Both the return on debt and the return on equity increase with leverage. However, in perfectly competitive markets and in the absence of taxes, transaction costs and agency costs, the weighted average cost of debt and equity (i.e. the cost of capital) remains constant and is equal to the return on assets. This makes intuitive sense, since the true engine of a firm's return must be the characteristics of its business, not the way it is financed.

Under the foregoing assumptions, the value of the firm (defined as the expected present value of its future cash flows including the business opportunities) does not change with leverage, either. Additionally, unlevered beta (which is necessary for the estimation of the discount rate) is simply a weighted average of the debt and equity betas.

When corporate taxes are factored in, the cost of capital decreases and firm value increases with leverage. But this beneficial effect has an upper limit because when the level of debt rises, the associated costs of financial distress must be dealt with. These costs, which appear when debt reaches uncomfortable levels, originate in expected bankruptcy costs, agency costs, and managerial and operative difficulties.

Moreover, when corporate taxes are present, unleveraged beta is no longer a simple weighted average of the debt and equity betas. Rather, the impact of taxes on firm value must be accounted for before beta is estimated.

The desirable level of debt for every firm depends on the following factors:

The volatility of its cash flows

The characteristics of its goods and services

The characteristics of its assets and organization

Its potential for growth

The tax regime

Besides, volatility can be reduced and leverage increased through risk management mechanisms (albeit at a cost). In addition, the amount of debt is not stable but oscillates around its desirable level depending on the costs associated with the different sources of financing. The combination of all these factors defines the most convenient debt level for every firm at each point in time.

Owing to the high volatility prevailing in emerging markets, the desirable level of debt for firms in these countries tends to be smaller than that for their counterparts in the more advanced nations. Furthermore, economic uncertainty demands that developing country firms allow for considerable flexibility in adapting the amounts and sources of financing as circumstances vary. Long-term financial commitments in foreign exchange must be kept to a minimum, unless backed by stable hard currency income.

Additionally, at every moment, desirable leverage for emerging market firms is a function of the country's macroeconomic situation and must seek for an adequate balance of the following factors:

The possible tax benefits of leverage

The costs and benefits of risk management mechanisms

The costs of financial distress

Investment opportunities

Possible aggressive actions by competitors

To the extent that management can act independently of stockholders, the managers' personal agendas must be factored in. Also, in the case of personal or quasi-personal firms, it is necessary to take into consideration the effects of leverage on the risk–return characteristics of the investor portfolio.

A procedure for the determination and monitoring of desirable leverage in emerging markets is proposed. The idea is to tackle the factors, one at a time, beginning with the tax shield and the costs of financial distress, followed by risk management, financial manageability, the managerial agenda, and the special characteristics of personal and quasi-personal firms.

Leverage does not depend exclusively on what is happening around the firm and changes in business conditions. Adding flexibility to financing opportunities can also influence the debt ratio.

In this respect, two areas were covered. The first one is concerned with the design of financing strategies that can be gradually adjusted to business results. These strategies add value by reducing the probability of default and bounding the losses due to unfavorable results to stockholders. These schemes offer considerable room for creativity. However, hybrid financial instruments, comprising part debt and part equity, increasingly available in emerging financial markets, can also be employed. Examples include convertible stock, convertible debt, preferred stock, callable bonds, and warrants.

The other way to add value from the financing side has to do with long-term financing strategy. The purpose here is to set up a plan for gradually reducing capital rationing and the firm's cost of capital. From this perspective, the evolution of the firm can be envisioned in three stages: the first in which financing sources are restricted to local banks and existing stockholders, the second in which the local capital market is accessed, and the final phase in which international financial markets are tapped. Another possibility is the integration with a global company, permitting not only new sources of financing, but also a wider business scope.

Opening up new financing sources takes time and money. Not only do managers have to focus an important part of their effort on this task, but significant investments must be made in advertising campaigns, fees, legal expenses, and so on. A well-thought-out "financial marketing" plan can often be more important than other marketing plans developed for the firm's goods and services.

CHAPTER 13

FINAL REMARKS

"If you want to understand something, try to change it."

In this chapter we summarize the more relevant ideas of the book and integrate the different pieces of information to create a practical framework for finance students and practitioners in developing countries

Financial models have been conceived generally within the context of advanced countries. They are intended to simulate the actions of investors, consumers, and other economic agents in these markets. Given the complexities of human behavior, this ambitious undertaking can be achieved only by making certain assumptions. However, these assumptions are at best, marginally reflective of reality. Therefore, this leads us to question the validity of financial models.

During the last decades a new branch of finance termed behavioral finance has developed. Its purpose has been to better comprehend the investors' decision processes. Behavioral finance has been successful in identifying certain conducts that are inconsistent with some of the assumptions usually made in financial theory. Among its most relevant findings are those relating to the instability of preferences and the way in which investors handle information, as well as group pressure as a relevant variable in some decision processes.

Emerging countries display one or more of the following characteristics:

- Uneven wealth distribution
- Underdeveloped markets
- Scarcity and unreliability of financial information
- Institutional backwardness
- Predominance of cartels and monopolies
- Unstable governmental policies (often not conducive to economic growth)
- Highly volatile economic variables (accentuated by growing financial globalization—more about this shortly)

These characteristics lead us to question further the relevance and applicability of financial models in developing countries.

In the preceding chapters we reviewed the main principles of financial theory and their application to emerging markets. As a result, four key ideas emerge within the context of emerging economies:

243

1. What are the value drivers of investment opportunities and what can be done to enhance them?
2. What are the main considerations for projecting cash flows?
3. Which methods are most appropriate for valuing investments?
4. How can leverage affect investment decisions?

A brief discussion of each of these topics follows.

13.1 THE VALUE OF INVESTMENT OPPORTUNITIES

The attractiveness of an investment opportunity is based on a match between the competitive advantages the investor possesses (whether the investor is an individual, a promoter, or a firm) and the factors critical for a project's success. One of the most interesting aspects of investing in developing countries is that the **competitive advantages necessary for success in a particular project are not always the same as those required for success in developed countries.** This will be our first point of discussion in this section.

Further, the characteristics of developing countries contribute to the creation of highly volatile economic environments. Although at first glance this tends only to subtract value, a closer examination suggests that **market volatility presents ample opportunity to add value to investment opportunities.** The second point of discussion in this section pertains to this issue.

13.1.1 Competitive Advantages

In discussing competitive advantages, we differentiate between financial investments, such as shares and bonds, and real investments like projects, firms, and specific business opportunities.

Financial Investments Financial markets in developed countries have numerous participants and move enormous amounts of capital. Information flows rapidly and regularly and tends to reach all participants. Consequently, prices of financial instruments adjust quickly to new information, making it difficult to obtain extraordinary returns on financial investments.

The situation, however, is different in emerging markets. The lack of liquidity in financial markets and their generally underdeveloped nature allow for manipulation of prices of financial instruments. In addition, fresh financial information is almost always monopolized by a relatively small number of investors, who tend to control most of the wealth. Therefore, the investors with access to the right information and sufficient capital can occasionally benefit from extraordinary returns (and positive net present values) on financial investments.

Emerging financial markets have been increasingly exposed to the investment actions of the large investment funds in developed countries. Relatively unimportant (and not always well-conceived) decisions taken in the main financial centers of the world frequently end up causing large amounts of capital to enter or leave the financial markets of emerging countries in short periods of time. On the one hand, this brings economic unstability. On the other, there are large fluctuations in prices and returns of financial instruments above and below what could be considered to be their final equilibrium levels. This opens up another opportunity of extraordinary returns to well-informed investors with the ability to identify the right time to buy or sell.

To conclude, investors have a greater likelihood of obtaining extraordinary returns on financial investments in emerging markets than in developed countries.

Real Investments Competitive advantages possessed by the investor make it possible to obtain extraordinary returns on real investment projects. These advantages tend to be project specific: particular knowledge, distinctive organizational capabilities, or other differentiating qualities on the basis of which investors can create value.

Possessing the right competitive advantages and capabilities is a valid issue in both developed and developing countries. However, emerging market investors often require competitive advantages specific to the sociopolitical environment. Environmental advantages are necessary to overcome problems that arise from market, institutional, and judiciary failures. And, frequently, environmental advantages can be more important than even traditional competitive advantages.

The rise of the "diversified conglomerates" in developing countries is a means of nurturing crucial environmental advantages. These organizations ease relationships with governmental bodies and facilitate bank financing, hiring of (scarce) qualified human resources, and contracting with suppliers, clients, and other third parties.

To summarize, although traditional competitive advantages are important, environmental advantages are meaningful as well and can often be crucial to business success in developing countries.

13.1.2 Value Creation

The high volatility associated with emerging markets substantially increases the value of real options (those associated with projects). These options originate with the possibility of adapting decisions to realized cash flows or to available sources of finance during the course of the project. They add value if additional investments and financing are contingent on project results. The ability to incorporate this kind of flexibility in investing in a developing country project is a key success factor.

Some examples of real options are as follows:

• The option to defer or expand a project
• The option to invest in stages or change the speed of investment flows
• The option to abandon a project

Real options can be valued (approximately) through option pricing theory, but computations become difficult when an appropriate underlying asset cannot be identified and/or when many interrelated options are encountered. Therefore, although real options must always be accounted for, their valuation is justified only for important projects or when the number of options is high.

New Financing Sources Financial strategy is another way to add value. The idea is to implement a plan that gradually eases capital rationing and decreases the cost of capital for the firm. Value is added as a growing number of investment opportunities become feasible.

In this respect, the evolution of the firm can be visualized in three phases:

- The first phase, in which financing is limited to local banks and existing shareholders
- The second phase, during which the firm opens up to the local capital market
- The third phase, in which international financial markets are approached

Another possibility is the integration with multinationals, allowing for expansion into new markets, as well.

Accessing new sources of financing is a lengthy process that requires considerable managerial effort as well as the investment of substantial amounts of money (in advertising campaigns, fees, legal expenses, etc.). The process has to be well thought out and carefully managed. In addition, a well-developed financial marketing plan can be as important as, if not more important than, a regular marketing plan for the firm's product or service.

13.2 COUNTRY RISK AND CASH FLOW ESTIMATION

Here we will consider the incorporation of country risk into investment decisions, and other issues related to the projection of cash flows.

13.2.1 Country Risk

Traditionally, country risk is quantified as the difference between the yield of a risk-free instrument from a country of reference (the United States) and its closest equivalent in the relevant country. This difference is known as "country risk premium."

The country risk premium is added to the corresponding discount rate in the country of reference (obtained from a financial model, e.g., CAPM) to determine an adjusted discount rate. This could be thought of as an adjustment to the risk-free rate in the country of reference. The higher the risk premium in a particular country, the higher is the discount rate.

However, this traditional approach is flawed for three reasons, which we touch on in the subsections that follow.

Country Risk Is Not Totally Systematic and Is Unstable Adding the country risk premium to the risk-free rate, hence to the discount rate, implicitly assumes that country risk is fully systematic or not diversifiable.[1] However, evidence suggests that public stock returns in developing and developed countries are not highly correlated. To the extent that these returns are truly representative of the local economies, it seems that at

---

[1]An explanation of systematic or nondiversifiable risk is given in Section 13.3.2.

least a good portion of country risk is diversifiable. Additionally, country risk (and its systematic and unsystematic components) can change considerably over time as well.

Country Risk Is Not the Same for Every Project Not all investments in a country have the same country risk. If a country's reputation in a certain economic activity is better than for the rest of its economy, that activity should have a lower country risk premium. Likewise, for some other economic activities the country risk premium could be higher. Through contracting arrangements it is also feasible to decrease country risk for certain types of investment (e.g., associated with the local government).

Credit Risk Is Not Equivalent to Country Risk Developing countries' government bond prices (in hard currency) depend on investors' expectations of compliance with the promised payment schedule. Adding the country risk premium to the discount rate assumes that the risk of noncompliance by the government is the right proxy for the country risk of the particular investment. This might not be accurate in most cases.

Instead of simply adding a country risk premium to the discount rate, the appropriate step would be to try to identify the nondiversifiable component of country risk and incorporate only this portion in the discount rate. Nevertheless, in many cases, this step might be easier stated than performed.

13.2.2 Other Issues

We will now cover issues related to inflation and exchange rates, subsidies, and investment horizons and terminal values.

Inflation and Exchange Rates Inflation and exchange rates are highly volatile in many developing countries, depending as they do on fiscal and monetary policies. Thus the risks associated with these factors are to a great extent diversifiable, and their effects must be taken into account basically in the cash flow projections (not in the discount rate).

It is not sufficient to factor in inflation merely by multiplying cash flows by a price index. The results from such an exercise are likely to be fraught with error because cash flow constituents rarely match the components of the price index basket. Instead, each individual component of the cash flow must be adjusted separately, based on its unique characteristics, and then added up to obtain the nominal cash flow for each period. Next, these must be translated into hard currency at the expected exchange rates.

Government intervention in developing countries usually results in misalignment between inflation and exchange rates. This leads to "exchange risk" and to the potential for benefits or losses for investors. Given this disparity, projecting cash flows directly in hard currency at expected exchange rates without accounting for inflation may be very inaccurate for many projects. Nevertheless, when inflation has a negligible effect on cash flows, as might be the case in some mining or oil projects, the approximation may be quite good.

When there are barriers to exchanging the local currency, into hard currency, we encounter "convertibility risk." As with inflation and exchange risk, convertibility risk is basically diversifiable and thus should impact mostly cash flows, rather than the discount rate.

Subsidies Investment propositions affected by subsidies should be evaluated with and without the subsidy. These results, and the expectations about future government actions, should be used to guide project decisions. If the net present value is negative without these subsidies, and, if it is likely that the subsidies will be eliminated or modified significantly in the near future, the project must most likely be rejected, or accepted only if the horizon of concern is short.

Horizon and Terminal Value As a result of government policies or other causes, it is common to anticipate extended periods of anomalous cash flows for many projects in developing countries. In these cases the horizon must be long enough to permit cash flows to achieve a certain stability. It is also necessary for the weight of the terminal value not to be too significant in the present value of the project. If this is not the case, the valuation exercise ceases to make much sense.

Terminal value depends on the cash flows that initiate at the horizon. The most conservative approach would be to assume that the terminal value is equal to the liquidating value. The most optimistic approach would assume a positive real growth rate for cash flows from this point on. Assuming, a positive real growth rate generally is not advisable because doing so can significantly distort the net present value of the project. In emerging countries, where it is so difficult to visualize too far into the future, it is better to err on the conservative side for long-term estimates.

13.3 VALUATION METHODS

We consider two possible valuation methods: portfolio theory and net present value.

13.3.1 Portfolio Theory

Portfolio theory is recommended when the opportunity in question, whether it is a real or a financial investment, has an important impact on the investor's portfolio. The impact is important when the possible risk and return combinations on the efficient frontier are altered significantly and it is very costly for the investor to readjust his portfolio buying or selling securities. In this scenario, the risk and return combinations with and without the investment opportunity and accounting for the readjustment costs of the portfolio are compared, and then a portfolio decision is arrived at.

Debt must be considered to be a short position, whereas real investments should be regarded as regular instruments with restrictions on the minimum amount to be invested. These last restrictions curtail diversification. Therefore, in each case, the investor must evaluate whether the loss from less diversification is compensated by a higher expected return.

The need to work with utility functions is the main shortcoming of portfolio theory. We propose instead to use the normal probability distribution and statistical confidence intervals to account for investor's preferences. That is, given a certain probability of, say 5%, the corresponding "minimum" return for this probability level is computed for each portfolio under consideration. The preferred investment strategy is selected by comparing the minimum returns for each portfolio against its expected returns. Although this is not a theoretically rigorous procedure, it can be justified on the grounds of practicality.

There is another problem with portfolio theory. Estimating parameters (expected returns and covariance matrices) on the basis of historical returns is, to say the least, somewhat unrealistic in emerging countries whose economies are prone to dramatic changes. The situation is even worse with respect to real investments (e.g., personal or quasi-personal companies), where parameters like covariance with other assets are difficult to infer.

The only way out is to perform a sensitivity analysis by varying the parameters and altering the assets in the portfolio. In this manner the investor is able to assess the effect on risk and return of different asset combinations and can make investment decisions with a better sense of the consequences.

In assessing a real investment, it is also convenient to calculate its net present value. The net present value can serve as a reference point to help appreciate the result of the investment proposition, as if a firm with a well-diversified shareholder base was considering it.

13.3.2 Net Present Value

Net present value is the appropriate procedure for evaluating investments without a significant impact on the investor's portfolio, as is the case in firms with a very fragmented shareholder base. The assumption here is that any possible effect of the investment proposition on the investor's risk and return set will be insignificant.

The method consists in discounting projected cash flows at a rate consistent with project risk. The most popular model for estimating this discount rate is the capital asset pricing model. The CAPM assumes that only nondiversifiable or systematic risk (that part of risk which is correlated with the most diversified portfolio, known as the "market portfolio") demands an expected return from the investor. This model is based on unrealistic assumptions—particularly that there are no transaction costs and that all investors have the same time horizon and expectations and hold the market portfolio.

The validity of the CAPM is questionable in the context of countries with emerging markets, given the inefficiencies of their financial markets and the vulnerability of their economies. Despite this, we must accept the CAPM for what it is. Not only is it a practical tool, but also, for now, there is no indisputably superior model available to us.

Nevertheless, with the objective of making the CAPM better applicable to developing countries, we propose a modified CAPM by assuming that emerging market investors hold well-diversified portfolios and that their consumption is fundamentally in hard currency. These assumptions can be considered to be acceptable, at least from the standpoint of the majority of the more important investors, given that globalization has eased the access to financial instruments of all kinds on a global scale. Besides, a substantial proportion of these investors' consumption is either in imported goods or in local goods with a strong imported component.

The proposed model ignores the country risk premium and works with a beta that accounts for the risks of the different markets in which the firm does business. This beta is affected by the beta of the local stock market with respect to the (selected) market portfolio. If the local stock market truly reflects the local economy, this beta will carry the systematic component of country risk. If this is not so, the only way out is to choose a different indicator for the local economy and/or to perform sensitivity analyses for a range of values of beta.

Given the inherent weaknesses of emerging stock markets, it is recommended that the beta of the line of business under analysis be estimated from a well-developed financial market (such as the United States). However, in doing so, we implicitly assume that the computed beta is similar to the beta of its counterparts in the developed market. In many instances this is an invalid simplification and needs to be corrected through certain adjustments.

The proposed method is not a panacea but a simple improvement on a model that is itself very limited, that is, the CAPM. As we suggested while discussing portfolio theory, it is convenient here as well to rely on sensitivity analysis. Further, it is important to remember that the results of this exercise serve only as a useful point of reference and should in no case comprise the only basis for the investment decision.

13.4 FINANCING DECISIONS

Every investment requires resources to finance it. Financing strategy does not give rise to complications for the individual investor since, as we mentioned before, debts are factored in as short positions in financial instruments. But at the firm level, financing has special relevance for the role of income taxes and the tax shield on the cost of capital (and the discount rate). In principle, a proper equilibrium must be sought between the tax benefits and the costs of financial distress associated with leverage.

In general, the desired leverage is a function of operating cash flow volatility, the type of goods and services of the firm, the characteristics of its assets and organization, the growth potential, and the tax rate. It is also possible to implement risk management mechanisms, at a cost, to increase leverage. In addition, agency considerations, mainly those related to management, must be taken into account. Finally, the debt level is not fixed but oscillates around a target, depending on the adjustment costs of the different financing sources. The combination of all these elements defines at every time the most convenient leverage for every firm.

13.4.1 Leverage in Emerging Markets

Ceteris paribus, given the high volatility associated with emerging markets, desirable levels of leverage tend to be lower here than in the developed world. In addition, macroeconomic and political uncertainties make it necessary for companies to build greater flexibility into the capital structure, to allow for rapid changes in the amount and type of debt at any point in time. Long-term debt commitments in hard currency must be kept at a minimum unless backed by stable hard currency income (or, if local currency income shows a stable correlation with the exchange rate and convertibility risk is negligible).

Besides the need for financial flexibility, the appropriate degree of leverage in emerging markets is also a function of macroeconomic conditions at each point in time and must seek to maximize firm value by assessing the following factors:

The general characteristics of the firm, especially cash flow volatility

The possible fiscal benefits of leverage

The benefits and costs of risk management measures

The costs of financial distress

Investment opportunities and possible financial aggressions by competitors

Managerial and portfolio considerations

A Method for Leverage Monitoring We propose a method for determining and adjusting leverage in emerging markets. The core idea is to tackle each associated variable separately—beginning with the tax shield and the costs of financial distress, and followed by risk management, financial flexibility, and other considerations.

Initially, operating cash flows (excluding debt) must be projected for different scenarios. Based on the most pessimistic scenario, the debt service is statistically determined to ascertain a tentative level of debt. This debt level is adjusted first by comparing eventual tax benefits against the possible costs of financial distress. Second, risk management measures are factored in and their cost is balanced against the possible benefit of a larger tax shield. This helps us to arrive at a new adjusted level of debt. After the investment opportunity set and the likelihood of financial aggression by competitors have been taken into account, the percentage of debt capacity to be committed on a permanent basis is determined. Finally, management interests and portfolio considerations are considered to determine the desired level of debt.

Cost of Capital and Firm Value The cost of capital after taxes can be estimated as a weighted average of the costs of debt and equity. The value of a leveraged firm equals the value of the same firm with no debt plus the present value of the tax shield (in the absence of costs of financial distress). This suggests two ways of computing the value of the firm: First, by discounting after-tax cash flows at the cost of capital, and second, by adding the present value of the tax shield to the value of the firm without debt. The second procedure is known as "adjusted present value." At first sight the procedures appear to be equivalent, but that is not the case.

The main problem in discounting at the cost of capital is that it is implicitly assumed that the proportions of debt and equity remain fixed throughout the horizon. This rarely happens anywhere, especially in emerging market firms that face frequent changes in desirable leverage.

The adjusted present value seems to solve this problem. When the present value of operating cash flows is computed separately from the present value of the tax shield, the debt originating the shield can evolve independently without having to stay at a fixed proportion.

But adjusted present value is problematic whenever the proportion of leverage stabilizes. When this happens, debt levels are linked to changes in the firm's assets and thus to operating cash flows. Therefore, part of the interest payments and the tax shield are at the same risk level found in the unleveraged firm and must be discounted at the unleveraged cost of capital (not at the interest rate). The advantage of discounting at the cost of capital arises precisely when the proportion of leverage stabilizes, since it can be shown that it takes into account automatically the risk associated with changes in the level of debt.

In conclusion, the adjusted present value method must be used for the periods during which the proportion of debt is unstable. The cost of capital method is best employed when debt starts to evolve together with the assets of the firm.

Answers to End-of-Chapter Questions and Problems

CHAPTER 1: FINANCIAL THEORY IN EMERGING MARKETS

1. While each model is incomplete, the more models we study, the clearer these relationships become. Once we have grasped several models, we can begin visualizing economic relationships as they exist in reality. It is certainly an ambitious task to try to understand complex investment decisions, but it is better to subject them to the rigors of a modeling exercise than to rely purely on intuition.

2. It appears that financial models should give consideration not only to relevant information, but also to the environment in which decisions are made.

3. We cannot categorize a country within the ranks of the developing world by strictly applying the key attributes we have listed. It can be said only that emerging countries tend to display some or all of these characteristics in some measure. In contrast, developed countries do not share these characteristics. In spite of its long-standing political stability, other problems typical of the developing world are present in Mexico, including low educational and income levels and an uneven wealth distribution.

4. The magnitude of the Brazilian financial system makes financial theory more applicable in Brazil than in other smaller emerging countries. However, the same cannot be said in relation to most developed nations, since Brazil's financial markets still suffer certain problems, such as institutions that are not fully developed, exacerbated sensitivity to foreign capital flows, and a small number of companies dominating most transactions in the stock exchanges.

CHAPTER 2: CONSUMPTION, INVESTMENTS, AND VALUE

1. Investment decisions are really (deferred) consumption decisions. Since consumption gives us satisfaction, investing requires giving up this satisfaction. A potential investor will not be willing to invest if expected profits do not compensate for the loss of satisfaction from consuming less. In this manner, investment and consumption are intertwined.

2. Not necessarily. The satisfaction from consumption activities varies at different points in time. People vary in their time preferences. For example, some might enjoy consuming more now than a year from now, while others might enjoy consumption more after the end of their productive years. Thus, consumption and investment preferences have a lot to do with our place in time.

3. The investor will almost always be worse off. Nevertheless, this depends on his consumption basket. If it is composed mainly of goods and services denominated

in U.S. dollars, an investor will be considerably harmed. But the more the consumption basket is tied to the ruble and the less to the U.S. dollar, the smaller will be the damage.

4. At first sight Scenario B seems more attractive, since it produces a better result in the most likely scenario and has less variability between the other two scenarios. However, the decision really depends on how conservative the investor is. A relatively less conservative investor who was willing to risk less favorable outcomes in the two worst scenarios to get a better result in the good one might choose A, whereas a more conservative investor might instead lean in favor of B.

   Another consideration is the likelihood of each scenario. For instance, if the good scenario were almost certain most investors will end up choosing A over B.

5. Because the market interest rate is the only link between these two decisions. Since this rate is an observable parameter, it can be concluded that the investment decision is always the same and has nothing to do with investor's preferences, whereas the consumption and savings decisions are personal and rest on the preferences of each individual. Everyone will agree on the optimal investment level but will most likely disagree on how much to save and consume. However, every individual makes saving and consumption decisions by means of the financial market, without affecting the investment decision on which all consent.

6. (a) In the first case NPV holds and A will be preferable to B as long as

$$NPV_A > NPV_B$$

   or

$$-700 + \frac{X}{1.12^2} > 5868.9$$

$$X > 8240$$

   (b) In the second case the best decision is not obvious depending on how much the investor wishes to consume in each period and on how much consumption he is willing to forego at the end of year 1 to increase consumption at the end of year 2.

7. It is true that access is practically the same for all investors. However, on the one hand financial resources that make their way to the stock exchanges are modest and, on the other hand, the distribution of income is generally unequal. As a consequence, financial resources are not only scarce but also localized within a small investor base. Further, financial information is usually concentrated among the few who control the bulk of wealth; the materials available to most people tend to be incomplete, outdated, and inaccurate.

   The outcome of this situation is that in these financial markets few participants, holding privileged information, manage significant amounts of capital (at least relative to the size of the market). This setting offers numerous opportunities to obtain extraordinary returns by buying or selling securities at attractive prices. In addition, the possibility of moving large amounts of capital into and out of the market at short notice allows the profitable manipulation of prices.

8. Not necessarily. It depends on how relevant environmental advantages are as opposed to the competitive advantages of the business itself.

9. When one or more shareholders face barriers to borrowing, some of them may prefer lower investment and higher dividends, while others may choose higher investment and lower dividends. Differential borrowing access can certainly engender stockholder clashes that could threaten the growth of the firm and even its survival.

CHAPTER 3: THE IMPACT OF RISK

1. X must be less than or equal to 210.

2. When the relationship between *NPV* and utility is linear.

3. If the lives and amounts invested are the same, the project with the higher expected return must necessarily be the one with the largest *E(NPV)*. Hence, these decision rules will be equivalent.

4. When the amount invested in each investment opportunity is not bounded (from above or below).

5. (a) False, (b) True, (c) False.

6. Because the standard deviation is not always a reliable measure of risk. For instance, in the $E(R) - SD$ space it is possible to select against an opportunity that is best for all possible scenarios.

7. Because it has the same $E(R)$ and smaller SD, *A* is always better than *B*. Because it has the same SD and a larger $E(R)$, *C* is always better than *A*. Given that *C* is always better than *A* and *B*, these two opportunities can be discarded. Preference between *C* and *D* depends upon the shape of the indifference curves of the investor.

CHAPTER 4: THE BENEFITS OF DIVERSIFICATION

1. (a) True, (b) False, (c) True.

2. When the correlation between every pair of assets is $+1$.

3. If the correlation between the two assets is -1.

4. The share could be borrowed with a view to returning it at the end of a certain time period. Once it is in possession it could be sold, thus obtaining a positive cash flow (in the beginning). At the end of the time period the share would be bought from the stock market and given back to its owner, thus obtaining a negative cash flow.

5. Yes.

6. (a) True, (b) True, (c) False.

7. (a) False, (b) True.

CHAPTER 5: PERSONAL INVESTMENTS

1. By avoiding concentration in a few assets and setting ceilings on positions susceptible to shocks.

2. No.

3. Historical information is probably the most objective. Nevertheless, it must be used with caution because the resulting parameters might not yield consistent risk–return relationships, the future will not necessarily be similar to the past, returns are frequently affected by shocks (especially in emerging markets), and historical series do not give enough weight to the most recent information.

4. (a)

Portfolio	μ (%)	σ (%)	x (%)	$\mu - x$ (%)	Value ($)
A	10.00	5	1.75	8.25	−16,500
B	14.00	15	−10.75	24.75	−49,500
C	20.00	19	−11.35	31.35	−62,700

(b) Portfolios B and $C,$ which yield a negative return for a 5% probability.

(c) Portfolios B and $C.$

5. The improvement of the efficient frontier due to the inclusion of the real investment depends on its assumed parameters (return, standard deviation and correlations). The main issues are as follows: (a) How trustworthy are the assumed parameters and what would happen if they yielded a less favorable frontier? (b) Is the improvement in the efficient frontier large enough to compensate for the investor's risk aversion and (50%) exposure to a unique investment that is susceptible to a negative shock? (c) How significant are the transaction costs associated with total or partial liquidation?

6. If the investor's horizon is shorter than the real investment horizon, the expected return of the investment must be adjusted to allow for any possible loss due to early liquidation. If the investor's horizon is longer than the investment horizon, some kind of assumption must be made about the types of asset in which the money coming from the real investment will be reinvested after its maturity.

CHAPTER 6: THE CLASSICAL MODEL

1. As firms grow, operations become more complex and investment opportunities increase. At this point it is impractical to consult with shareholders on every investment decision, particularly when such investments do not involve large financial outlays. On the other hand, the eventual participation of a shareholder in an investment decision is directly related to the proportion of the individual's stake in the company, and the more fragmented the shareholder structure, the smaller will be the number of shareholders to consult.

2. To assure that investment decisions only affect investor's wealth guaranteeing the validity of the *NPV* rule.

3. No. The investment horizon must be six months as well.

4. This can happen in the case of securities in foreign exchange, because default risk for government securities can be significant when the government does not have the ability to issue currency.

5. Yes. In this instance, the capital market line is equivalent both to the minimum variance frontier and to the efficient frontier.

6. That all investors observe the same investment opportunities, that it is feasible to invest in any possible combination of risky assets, and that there is just one risk-free rate.

7. Because the capital market line gives the risk–return relationship only for portfolios produced by combining the risk-free asset with the market portfolio, whereas the CAPM yield returns as a function of beta, which is a measure of risk applicable to individual assets.

8. Yes.

9. Because it is assumed that investors are well diversified. Therefore, the part of risk that is unrelated to the market portfolio is compensated among the different assets and tends to be insignificant.

10. $$0.2A + 1.8B = 1$$

$$A + 9B = 5$$

CHAPTER 7: A MODIFIED CAPM FOR EMERGING COUNTRIES

1. Not necessarily. Country risk has less to do with the quality of economic policies than with their stability and consistency.

2. No. The bond's yield represents expectations over the whole period. In other words, the financial community's expectations of country risk during that time span are already built into the price. We can think of the bond's yield as reflecting an "average" of the country risk for the full life of the bond.

3. All five statements are true.

4. When the beta is zero, the weight given to country risk is zero as well. As beta grows larger, the weight given to country risk also increases. Therefore, according to this procedure, a low-beta firm will have lower country risk than another with a higher beta.

5. $$\beta_P = \beta_{tM}[(\alpha_{USA}\beta_{MM}) + (\alpha_X\beta_{NM})]$$

$$0.5 = (1 - \alpha_X)1 + \alpha_X 0.3$$

$$\alpha_X = \frac{5}{7} = 71\%$$

6. Emerging country volatility is taken into consideration not in the discount rate but in the cash flow projections. The systematic component of country risk is (partially) factored in through the beta of the local stock market with respect to the reference market (e.g., the United States).

7. Generally not. This is true only if the local stock market is a good proxy of the local economy.

CHAPTER 8: VALUATION IN EMERGING MARKETS

1.

$$\frac{1000 \times 1.10}{1000} = \$1100 \qquad \text{year 1}$$

$$\frac{1000 \times 1.10 \times 1.15}{1050} = \$1.21 \times 10^3 \qquad \text{year 2}$$

$$\frac{1000 \times 1.10 \times 1.15 \times 1.20}{1100} = \$1.38 \times 10^3 \qquad \text{year 3}$$

2. Increase.

3. This approach is valid only when the exchange rate varies in step with inflation.

4. That such risks are diversifiable.

5. The *NPV* of this cash flow discounted at the 15% market rate equals +$83,090. This is the value of the subsidy.

6. (a) The horizon must be long enough for the project's cash flows to achieve stability.
   (b) The investment horizon must be long enough for the *PV* of the terminal value not to be a very significant percentage of the *PV* of the projected cash flows (excluding the initial investment).

7. As the growth rate increases, the perpetuity's *PV* increases exponentially. Thus, relatively small increases in the growth rate can substantially impact the terminal value, pushing the project's *E(NPV)* to unrealistically high levels.

8. Because liquidation value is the minimum we can obtain from a project. If the liquidation value is larger than the present value of projected cash flows, the investment's *E(PV)* will be the liquidation value. If the liquidation value is smaller than the present value of projected cash flows, *E(PV)* will be the present value of the cash flow projection.

9. Because in developing countries real asset markets tend to be less liquid than in developed countries. Hence, it is frequently necessary to cut liquidation prices considerably.

CHAPTER 9: THE VALUE OF FLEXIBILITY

1. Referring to Figure P9.1a, $E(NPV)$ without the option is:

$$E(NPV_{\text{no opt}}) = \frac{1}{1.10}[0.8(100 + 500) + 0.2(-200 - 500)] = +\$309.1 \text{ million}$$

Refering to Figure P9.1b, $E(NPV)$ with the option is:

$$E(NPV_{\text{opt}}) = \frac{1}{1.10}[08(100 + 500) + 0.2(-200 + 0)] = +\$400 \text{ million}$$

The value of the option to abandon will be:

$$+400 - 309.1 = +\$90.9 \text{ million}$$

Therefore, we would be willing to pay \$50 million for this option.

2. As time goes by, uncertainty decreases and we are able to take the most convenient decisions given new information that becomes available. This reduction in uncertainty means that the discount rate should be revised. The flaw is that decision trees do not allow for a way to adjust the discount rate.

3. (a)
$$C_u = (580 \times 1.2) - 600 = 96$$

$$C_d = 0$$

$$m = \frac{S_0(u - d)}{C_u - C_d} = \frac{580(1.20 - 0.8333)}{96 - 0} = 2.2155$$

(b)
$$p = \frac{(1 + r) - d}{u - d} = \frac{1.02 - 0.8333}{0.3667} = 0.5091$$

$$C = \frac{pC_u + (1 - p)C_d}{1 + r} = \frac{(0.5091 \times 96) + 0}{1.02} = \$47.92$$

4. An increase in variance leads to an increase in the value of the option. Thus, a project's real options will be more valuable if the uncertainty of its cash flows is high. Projects in emerging countries are characterized by high cash flow volatility; thus real options associated with these projects might represent a significant portion of project value.

5. (a)
$$p = \frac{(1 + r) - d}{u - d} = \frac{1.06 - 0.7692}{0.5308} = 0.5479$$

$$C = \frac{pC_u + (1 - p)C_d}{1 + r} = \frac{0.5479[(500 \times 1.3) - 600] + 0}{1.06} = \$25.84 \text{ million}$$

The value of the option to defer is:

$$25.84 - (-100) = \$125.84 \text{ million}$$

(b) It must be deferred.

6. Competitors, too, have flexibility. The value of the option to defer could be negatively affected if competitors invest first.

CHAPTER 10: FINANCING IN THEORY

1. An ever larger proportion of operating cash flow is tied to interest payments as leverage rises. Since operating cash flows tend to be risky, this implies a lower probability of compliance with interest payments, hence a higher probability of bankruptcy. Thus equity risk increases with leverage. Shareholders will be willing to accept higher risks only in exchange for higher returns on their investment.

2. Since the cost of capital is a weighted average of debt and equity returns, it is just an indirect way of computing the return on assets, which is constant.

3. We start by computing the figures for equity in Table P10.3 as follows:

	Assets	Liabilities	Equity
Amount ($ million)	100	50	100 − 50 = 50
Return (%)	30	20	20/50 = 40
Return ($ million)	30	10	30 − 10 = 20

If leverage were 20% the return on equity would be:

$$\frac{\text{CF from assets} - (\text{CF to debt})}{\text{Equity}} = \frac{30 - (20 \times 0.20)}{80} = 32.5\%$$

This supposes a return of $32,500 for a $100,000 investment. Therefore, if the investment in shares is X and the investment in debt is $1 - X$, we have

$$0.40X + (1 - X)0.20 = \$32,500$$

$$X = \$62,500$$

The investment in debt will be $32,500.

4.
$$\beta_A = \beta_D \frac{D}{V} + \beta_E \frac{E}{V}$$

If the beta of the debt is zero, we have

$$\beta_A = \beta_E \frac{E}{V}$$

$$\beta_E = \beta_A \frac{V}{E} = 0.8 \frac{1}{1 - 0.3} = 1.14$$

5. As the leverage rises, taxes decrease. This benefit accrues to shareholders and, therefore, the return they demand increases in smaller amounts as the debt rises. This translates into a reduction of the cost of capital as leverage increases.

6.
$$\beta_A = \frac{\beta_E E}{E + D(1 - T_C)}$$

$$\beta_E = \frac{\beta_A[E + D(1 - T_C)]}{E} = \frac{\beta_A[E/V + D(1 - T_C)/V]}{E/V}$$

$$\beta_E = \frac{0.8\,[0.7 + (0.3 \times 0.8)]}{0.7} = 1.07$$

7. When there are corporate taxes, the return on equity rises with debt but at a smaller rate than when there are no taxes. A smaller return means a smaller beta.

8. When leverage increases, on the one hand, the tax shield reduces the cost of capital and, on the other hand, the costs of financial distress increase. Therefore, there must exist a level at which the cost of capital is minimized and leverage is optimal.

CHAPTER 11: FINANCING IN PRACTICE

1. For a given debt ratio, the more unstable the cash flows, the larger the probability of default. Therefore, firms with high cash flow volatility should have low levels of leverage.

2. Companies with high fixed to total assets ratios (i.e., with high operating leverage) are more vulnerable to a fall in income, and more so if sales are volatile. Thus, high operating leverage and instability in income recommend low levels of leverage.

3. Usually, a significant proportion of management compensation depends on company profits, closely tying their wealth to the welfare of the company. Being highly dependent on compensation, upper management income tends to be undiversified and highly correlated to the firm's risk. As an outcome of this situation, occasionally managers avoid leveraging the firm because this would increase the firm's risk, hence the risk of their relatively undiversified personal portfolios.

4. Rapidly growing companies generally find it difficult to finance their (abundant) business opportunities from internally generated revenues. Thus, they have no choice but to issue debt or equity. In this case, the inability to raise funds is particularly costly because many attractive projects must be abandoned. But there are not many financiers eager to lend money (even less so to heavily indebted firms). Therefore, external financing must come primarily from shareholders. In sum, high

barriers to external financing and significant growth opportunities recommend a conservative debt ratio.

5. Because of the issuing costs associated with debt and equity. These costs imply a preference order in the type of financing. Being the least costly (from an issuing costs point of view), retained earnings is the first source, followed by debt and new stock.

6. Because they are costly. These strategies are convenient only if the benefits they produce, either through higher firm leverage or a lower risk of the investors' portfolios, are greater than their cost.

7. (a) Capital rationing and unanticipated investment opportunities require untapped debt capacity for the firm to have access to the necessary funding. The outcome is lower leverage.

   (b) Capital rationing in an oligopolistic market makes leverage a function of the levels of debt of the competitors. This is necessary to avoid being at a financial disadvantage.

8. (a)

$$\sigma = 42.2$$

$$I = \$21.21 \times 10^3$$

$$D = \frac{\$21.21}{0.06} = \$353.5 \times 10^3$$

   (b) The quarterly and present values of the tax shield are:

$$TS = 21.21 \times 20\% = \$4.24 \times 10^3$$

$$PV(TS) = 4.24 \sum_{n=1}^{4} \frac{1}{1.06^n} = \$14.69 \times 10^3$$

   The value of the firm is:

$$V = 5500 + 14.69 = \$5514.69 \times 10^3$$

   (c) $E[PV(CFD)] = 0.01 PV(CFD) \geq PV(TS) = \$14.69 \times 10^3$

   Therefore, the debt will start being inconvenient when the PV of the costs of financial distress reaches $1,469,000.

9. They must be discounted at the market cost of debt. But this rate is not always the same as the actual cost of debt, either because the market cost of debt has changed or because the actual cost of debt may be subsidized.

10. The formula for the cost of capital assumes a constant leverage ratio, but this is generally untrue when cash flows are unstable. Adjusted present value is the right

approach when we face this kind of situation. Once the firm has achieved a stable debt ratio, debt levels stem from the value of the assets, which are determined by the operating cash flows. Hence, part of the future interest expense and the tax shield are a function of and will be as risky as the operating cash flows. It can be shown that the cost of capital formula is the right approach in this instance.

CHAPTER 12: FINANCING AND VALUE

1. The values at the end of year 2 will be as shown in Table A12.1.

TABLE A12.1*

Value of the Project		Debt	Shareholder Value	
V_{uu}	400	60.5	E_{uu}	339.5
V_{ud}	100	60.5	E_{ud}	39.5
V_{du}	100	36.3	E_{du}	63.7
V_{dd}	25	36.3	E_{dd}	0

* Amounts are in thousands of dollars.

The values for the shareholders are as follows:

$$E_u = \frac{(0.4 \times 339.5) + (0.6 \times 39.5)}{1.1} = \$145 \times 10^3$$

$$E_d = \frac{(0.4 \times 63.7) + (0.6 \times 0)}{1.1} = \$23.16 \times 10^3$$

$$Aj(E_u) = \text{Max}[(145 - 22), 0] = \$123 \times 10^3$$

$$Aj(E_d) = \text{Max}[(23.16 - 22), 0] = \$1.16 \times 10^3$$

$$E_0 = \frac{(0.4 \times 123) + (0.6 \times 1.16)}{1.1} = \$45.36 \times 10^3$$

Subtracting the $20,000 initial investment, $E(NPV)$ for the stockholders will be $25,360.

The values for the debt holders are:

$$D_u = \frac{60.5}{1.1} = \$55 \times 10^3$$

$$Aj(D_u) = 55 - 22 = \$33 \times 10^3$$

$$D_d = \frac{36.3}{1.1} = \$33 \times 10^3$$

$$Aj(D_d) = \$33 \times 10^3$$

$$D_0 = \frac{33}{1.1} = \$30 \times 10^3$$

Subtracting the original \$30,000 loan, $E(NPV)$ for the debtholders is nil.
Then, the value of the project is \$25,360.

2. From the debt side, the lending capacity of local banks. From the equity side, the cash demands from shareholders.

3. The asymmetrical information between the firm and potential investors.

4. The implications of a loss of managerial control of the firm.

5. Because emerging countries are so sensitive to local economic and political affairs and to the vagaries of international capital flows that the pool of financial resources could either explode or drain in a short period of time. Thus as long as a firm is focused locally, it is exposed to high uncertainty with respect to its financing sources.

6. The main advantage is a decrease of the asymmetrical information between the firm and its investors. The main disadvantage is that these financial instruments tend to be less liquid.

References

Aivaizian V., & Berkowitz M. 1998. "Ex-Post Production Flexibility, Asset Specificity and Financial Structure," *Journal of Accounting, Auditing and Finance,* Winter.

Amram M., Kulatilaka N. 1999. "Uncertainty: The New Rules for Strategy" *Journal of Business Strategy,* March.

Barnea A., Haugen R., & Senbet L. 1980. "A Rationale for Debt Maturity Structure and Call Provisions in the Agency Theory Framework," *Journal of Finance,* December.

Bekaert G. 1995. "Market Integration and Investment Barriers in Emerging Equity Markets," *World Bank Economic Review,* vol. 9.

Black F. 1972. "Capital Market Equilibrium with Restricted Borrowing," *Journal of Business,* July.

———. 1973. "The Pricing of Options and Corporate Liabilities," *Journal of Political Economy,* May.

———. 1986. "Noise," *Journal of Finance,* July.

Brealey R., & Myers S. 1996. *Principles of Corporate Finance,* 5th ed. McGraw-Hill, New York.

Breeden D. 1979. "An Intertemporal Asset Pricing Model with Stochastic Consumption and Investment Opportunities," *Journal of Financial Economics,* vol. 7.

Chang C. 1997. "Does Hedging Aggravate or Alleviate Agency Problems? A Managerial Theory of Risk Management," University of Minnesota, Working Paper, July.

Cheng N. F., Roll R., & Ross S. 1983. "Economic Forces and the Stock Market: Testing the APT and Alternative Asset Pricing Theories," UCLA Working Paper 20-83, December.

Cochrane J. H. 1999. "New Facts in Finance," National Bureau of Economic Research, Working Paper Series, June.

Copeland T., & Weston J. 1988. *Financial Theory and Corporate Policy,* 3rd ed. Addison-Wesley, Reading, MA.

Copeland T., Koller T., & Murrin J. 2000. *Valuation.* Wiley, New York.

Cox J., & Rubinstein M. 1979. "Option Pricing: A Simplified Approach," *Journal of Financial Economics,* September.

D'Aveni R. A. 1989. "Dependability and Organizational Bankruptcy: An Application of Agency and Prospect Theory," *Management Science,* September.

Damodaran A. 1996. *Investment Valuation.* Wiley, New York.

———. 1999a. *Applied Corporate Finance.* Wiley, New York.

———. 1999b. "Estimating Risk Free Rates," New York University, Leonard N. Stern School of Business Working Paper, January.
http://www.stern.nyu.edu/~adamodar/

———. 1999c. "Estimating Equity Risk Premiums," New York University, Leonard N. Stern School of Business Working Paper, January.
http://www.stern.nyu.edu/~adamodar/

———. 1999d. "Estimating Risk Parameters," New York University, Leonard N. Stern School of Business Working Paper, January.
http://www.stern.nyu.edu/~adamodar/

De Angelo H. C. 1981. "Competition and Unanimity," *American Economic Review,* March.

Diebold F. X. 1998. *Elements of Forecasting.* South-Western College Publishing, Cincinnati, OH.

Dixit A. K., & Pyndick R. S. 1994. "Investments Under Uncertainty." Princeton University Press, Princeton, NJ.

Elton E., & Gruber M. 1995. *Modern Portfolio Theory and Investment Analysis,* 5th ed. Wiley, New York.

Erb C., Harvey C., & Viskanta T. 1995. "Inflation and World Equity Selection," *Financial Analysts Journal,* November–December.

———. 1996. "Political Risk, Economic Risk and Financial Risk," *Financial Analysts Journal,* November–December.

Estrada J. 1999. "The Cost of Equity in Emerging Markets," IESE Working Paper, Barcelona, Spain, September.

Fama E. F. 1965. "The Behavior of Stock Market Prices," *Journal of Business,* January.

Fama E. F., & French K. 1996. "Multifactor Explanations of Asset Pricing Anomalies," *Journal of Finance,* 47.

Fisher I. 1930. *The Theory of Interest.* Macmillan, New York.

Fisher K., & Statman M. 1997. The Mean–Variance Optimization Puzzle: Security Portfolios and Food Portfolios," *Financial Analysts Journal,* July–August.

Froot K., O'Connell P., & Seasholes M. 1999. "The Portfolio Flows of International Investors," Harvard Business School Working Paper, August.

Godfrey S., & Espinosa R. 1996. "A Practical Approach to Calculating Costs of Equity for Investment in Emerging Markets," *Journal of Applied Corporate Finance,* Fall.

Grinblatt M., & Titman S. 1998. *Financial Markets and Corporate Strategy.* Irwin/McGraw-Hill, New York.

Harvey C. 1995. "Predictable Risk and Returns in Emerging Markets," *Review of Financial Studies,* Fall.

Hull J. 1997. *Options, Futures and Other Derivatives,* 3rd ed. Prentice Hall, Englewood Cliffs, NJ.

Inselbag I., & Kaufold H. 1997. "Two DCF Approaches for Valuing Companies Under Alternative Financing Strategies," *Journal of Applied Corporate Finance,* Spring.

Instituto Venezolano de Ejecutivos de Finanzas 1994a. "¿Qué Determina la Inversión en Venezuela?" July.

———. 1994b. "El Costo de Capital para las Inversiones en Venezuela," November.

———. 1998. "Opciones Reales en la Valoración de Proyectos," May.

Intellipro, Inc. 1998. "The Investment Portfolio" (software).

Jagannathan R., & Wang Z. 1996. "The Conditional CAPM and the Cross-Section of Expected Stock Returns," *Journal of Finance,* March.

Khanna T., & Palepu K. 1997. "Corporate Strategy for Business Groups in Emerging Markets," Harvard Business School Working Paper.

Kay J. A. 1995. *Why Firms Succeed.* Oxford University Press, New York.

Kothari S., Shanken J., & Sloan R. 1995. "Another Look at the Cross-Section of Expected Stock Returns," *Journal of Finance,* March.

Kulatilaka N., & Venkatraman N. 1999. "Are You Preparing to Compete in the New Economy? Use a Real Options Navigator," Systems Research Center, Boston University School of Management, February.

Landes D.S. 1998. *The Wealth and Poverty of Nations.* Norton, New York.

Lederman J., & Klein R., eds. 1994. *Global Asset Allocation.* Wiley, New York.

Lessard D. 1996. "Incorporating Country Risk in the Valuation of Offshore Projects," *Journal of Applied Corporate Finance,* Fall.

Levi H. 1984. *Portfolio and Investment Selection.* Prentice-Hall, Englewood Cliffs, NJ.

Lintner J. 1969. "The Aggregation of Investor's Diverse Judgments and Preferences in Purely Competitive Security Markets," *Journal of Financial and Quantitative Analysis,* December.

Mahoney J.T., & Pandian J.R. 1992. "The Resource-Based View Within the Conversation of Strategic Management," *Strategic Management Journal,* June.

Malkiel B. G., & Mei J. P. 1998. *Global Bargain Hunting.* Simon & Schuster, New York.

Mallampally P., & Sauvant K. P. 1999. "Foreign Direct Investment in Developing Countries," *Finance and Development,* March.

Markowitz H. 1952. "Portfolio Selection," *Journal of Finance,* March.

Mayers D. 1972. "Non-Marketable Assets and the Capital Market Equilibrium Under Uncertainty," in Jensen, ed, *Studies in the Theory of Capital Markets.* Praeger, New York.

Mendenhall W., Scheaffer R., & Wackerly D. 1981. *Mathematical Statistics with Applications,* 2nd ed. Duxbury Press, Boston, MA.

Miller M. H. 1977. "Debt and Taxes," *Journal of Finance,* May.

———. 1991. "Leverage," *Journal of Applied Corporate Finance,* Summer.

Miller M. H., & Modigliani F. 1961. "Dividend Policy, Growth and the Valuation of Shares," *Journal of Business,* October.

Modigliani F., & Miller M. H. 1958. "The Cost of Capital, Corporation Finance and the Theory of Investment," *American Economic Review,* June.

———. 1963. "Corporate Income Taxes and the Cost of Capital," *American Economic Review,* June.

Myers S. C. 1993. "Still Searching for Optimal Capital Structure," *Journal of Applied Corporate Finance,* Spring.

———. 1998. "Capital Structure Roundtable," *Journal of Applied Corporate Finance,* Spring.

Myers S. C., & Majluf N. 1984. "Corporate Financing and Investment Decisions When Firms Have Information That Investors Do Not Have," *Journal of Financial Economics,* June.

Nelson R.R., & Winter S.G. 1982. *An Evolutionary Theory of Economic Change.* Harvard University Press, Cambridge, MA.

Olsen R. 1998. "Behavioral Finance and Its Implications for Stock-Price Volatility," *Financial Analysts Journal,* March–April.

Opler T. C., Saron M., & Titman S. 1997. "Designing Capital Structure to Create Shareholder Value," *Journal of Applied Corporate Finance,* Spring.

Osuna E. 1997. "Debates IESA," Caracas, Venezuela, March.

Patrick S. C. 1998. "The Balanced Capital Structure," *Journal of Applied Corporate Finance,* Spring.

Pindyck R. 1988. "Irreversible Investment, Capacity Choice and the Value of the Firm," *American Economic Review,* December.

Porter M. 1980. *Competitive Strategy.* Free Press, New York.

Prahalad C.K., & Hamel G. 1990. "The Core Competence of the Corporation," *Harvard Business Review,* May–June.

Pratt J. W. 1964. "Risk Aversion in the Small and in the Large," *Econometrica,* January–April.

Roll R. 1977. "A Critique of the Asset Pricing Theory's Tests," *Journal of Financial Economics,* March.

Roll R., & Ross S. 1994. "On the Cross-Sectional Relation Between Expected Returns and Betas," *Journal of Finance,* 49.

Ross S. A. 1976. "The Arbitrage Theory of Capital Asset Pricing," *Journal of Economic Theory,* December.

———. 1978. "Mutual Fund Separation in Financial Theory: The Separating Distributions," *Journal of Economic Theory,* December.

Ross S., Westerfield R., & Jaffe J. 1999. *Corporate Finance,* 5th ed. Irwin/McGraw-Hill, New York.

Santomero A., & Babbel D. 1997. *Financial Markets, Instruments and Institutions.* Irwin, New York.

Sercu P., & Uppal R. 1995. *International Financial Markets and the Firm.* South-Western College Publishing.

Shapiro A. C. 1992. "Guidelines for Corporate Financing Strategy," in J. M. Stern & D. H. Chew, eds. *The Revolution in Corporate Finance,* 2nd ed. Basil Blackwell Ltd., Oxford, UK.

———. 1996. *Multinational Financial Management,* 5th ed. Prentice-Hall, Englewood Cliffs, NJ.

Sharpe W. F. 1963. "Capital Asset Prices: A Theory of Market Equilibrium Under Conditions of Risk," *Journal of Finance,* September.

Silber W. L. 1991. "Discounts on Restricted Stock: The Impact of Illiquidity on Stock Prices," *Financial Analysts Journal,* vol. 47.

Simon H. 1959. "Theories of Decision Making on Economics," *American Economic Review,* June.

Smit H. T. J., & Ankum L. A. 1993. "A Real Options and Game Theoretic Approach," *Financial Management,* August.

Solnik B. 1996. *International Investments,* 3rd ed. Addison-Wesley, Reading, MA.

Statman M. 1987. "How Many Stocks Make a Diversified Portfolio?" *Journal of Financial and Quantitative Analysis,* September.

———. 1999. "Foreign Stocks in Behavioral Portfolios," *Financial Analysts Journal,* March–April.

The Economist 1999a. "Safety in Numbers?" February 27.

———. 1999b. "A Better Beta," March 27.

———. 1999c. "Executive Relief," April 3.

The International Bank for Reconstruction and Development (The World Bank) 1997. *Private Capital Flows to Developing Countries.* Oxford University Press, New York.

Triantis A., & Hodder J. 1990. "Valuing Flexibility as a Complex Option," *Journal of Finance,* June.

Trigeorgis L. 1993. "Real Options and Interactions with Financial Flexibility," *Financial Management,* Fall.

———. 1997. *Real Options.* The MIT Press, Cambridge, MA.

Tversky A., & Kahneman D. 1986. "Rational Choice and the Framing of Decisions," *Journal of Business,* October.

Wilmott P., Howison S., & Dewynne J. 1998. *The Mathematics of Financial Derivatives.* Cambridge University Press, Cambridge, U.K.

Index